W9-BLY-009

"I read large swaths of *Poor Your Soul*, breathless, tears held (mostly) at bay, that feeling like someone was standing on my throat . . . because it was telling me something true about being human, something that might have otherwise remained secret. This is a beautiful, contradictory book: big-hearted and hard-hearted, angry and introspective, drowning and triumphant, and suffused with humor both dark and light."

—**Diane Cook, author of *Man V. Nature***

"Vivacity of spirit, pungency and accuracy of observation, and a sharp, disabused, but nevertheless empathetic consciousness permeate her pages. Mira Ptacin soothes us, but she also, always, surprises."

—**Vijay Seshadri, winner of the 2014 Pulitzer Prize in poetry**

"*Poor Your Soul* paints a conflicted, coming-of-age story, one of perseverance through the bonds of family in the face of grief."—*Battle Creek Enquirer*

"Warm, honest, thoughtful, and funny."   —*Michigan Quarterly Review*

"An unblinking and moving literary memoir of grief and love by a talented young writer . . . [and] a beautifully written celebration of the love of family, the bonds between mothers and daughters, and the healing that comes after loss."   —**Shelf Awareness**

"Heartwrenching and radically honest."   —*Dispatch Magazine*

"Compelling and immersive storytelling . . . An emotional and engrossing memoir."   —*Harvard Review*

"In the tradition of Cheryl Strayed, Elizabeth Gilbert, and Melissa Coleman, Mira Ptacin has written a funny and deeply moving memoir of loss, love, and redemption . . . Elegiac and wise, *Poor Your Soul* is, ultimately, about the strength of the human spirit."

—**Kate Manning, author of *My Notorious Life***

"Reading [Ptacin] find her way through her most trying times left me feeling I'd found my own way through my own. There's no greater compliment I can pay. To read *Poor Your Soul* is to come to know its writer very well. Only the best writing does that."—**Cate Marvin, Co-founder of VIDA: Women in Literary Arts and author of *Oracle: Poems***

poor

your

soul

poor your soul

MIRA PTACIN

Published by
Soho Press, Inc.
853 Broadway
New York, NY 10003

Library of Congress Cataloging-in-Publication Data

Ptacin, Mira.
Poor your soul / Mira Ptacin.

ISBN 978-1-61695-766-7
eISBN 978-1-61695-635-6

1. Ptacin, Mira. 2. Women authors, American—Biography. 3. First pregnancy.
4. Loss (Psychology) 5. Children—Death—Psychological aspects.
6. Ptacin, Mira—Family. I. Title.
PS3616.T33Z46 2016
818'.603--dc23 2015028123

Interior design by Janine Agro, Soho Press, Inc.

Printed in the United States of America

10 9 8 7 6 5 4 3 2 1

FOR JULES

Disclaimer

This is a story of my truth. In some instances, I have changed names of individuals and places in order to maintain anonymity, and I have recreated events, locales, and conversations based on my memory of them.

one

Every few Sundays, Segundo, the very short superintendent who lives in the basement at 223 East 32nd Street, opens the back pages of *The Village Voice* and orders two very tall call girls. He doesn't know we know. Segundo avoids all interactions with us. At most, Andrew and I might get a muffled response to the "hello" we pitch him when one of us is coming and the other is going, but most of the time Segundo just stays in the shadows. Sometimes we'll see him taking out the garbage or hosing down the sidewalk. Once in a while, I'll spot him sitting on the stoop, alone, vacantly staring straight ahead.

I find Segundo quite remarkable and often speculate about his place in the universe: What does he eat? And does he cook it, or order takeout? Is he Catholic? Has he ever been in agonizing, consuming, can't-live-without-the-other-person love? His recent haircut (buzzed—I imagine he sheared off his raven-black hair by himself in a dimly lit bathroom of his subterranean apartment) is growing out. Both Andrew and Segundo shaved their heads within the same week; Segundo's grows faster.

One recent evening, after arriving home from a walk around the block, five of us—me, my husband, Andrew, our little dog, Maybe, and two leggy women—clogged the narrow hallway of our apartment building. As the ladies slithered past us, I got a close enough look to notice that they weren't dressed appropriately for the cool October weather. Their skirts were short and sequined. They wore stilettos. They were giggling. To me, they looked like panthers. I nudged Andrew, who was unlocking the door to our bite-sized apartment. As he pushed it open, the two women exited the building and, without even a glance, Andrew said, "Look out front. There'll be a man waiting in a minivan."

There was indeed. I was stunned.

"They're prostitutes," he declared.

"Two of them?!"

"*Two* of them. Segundo's been getting busy."

"No. I don't believe it."

"Right next to *our room*."

Only a thin wall separates one life from another, but unless we are in the right place at the right time, the truths of others remain unknown. Some choose not to think about it, but I can't help it. The world inside of New York City is just a terribly interesting place.

❦ ❦ ❦

"Assistant?" Andrew asks from the kitchen.

"Yes, assistant?"

"The cabbage."

"You got it."

Andrew stirs the tomato soup as I step out of the shower and open the door a crack. Then, leaning out of the bathroom, stretching my arm into the kitchen, I take the frozen cabbage from him. As I grab it, I see Maybe hovering on the floor by Andrew's feet. She's waiting for fallen scraps. She's one year old, and a rescue. Andrew adopted her before he met me.

"Thank you, assistant," I say and quickly slide back into the bathroom. I'm trying to be polite. I'm trying to be a good wife, but I'm not sure how.

The bathroom is less steamy than the kitchen. I set the cabbage down next to the faucet, wipe off the mirror and look at my face. To me, it looks worn. I blame it on Manhattan: too frenetic, too cruel. Also, I'm not smiling. I once heard or read somewhere that if you force yourself to smile, the muscles activate something in your brain, trigger synapses, or massage a gland; something that makes you feel good, like a switch to a lever moving a pulley that tilts a bucket and produces a feeling of contentment. All I have to do is turn my frown upside down.

Dr. Reich explained that if I stuck frozen cabbage in my bra, things would improve. She said that the common green cabbage has some chemical or enzyme that is used for "engorgement therapy." In other words, something in the cabbage stops breasts from producing milk, and if I consistently wear these leaves, production will cease. I don't need the milk because there is no baby. All that's left is the milk.

Dr. Reich used the word "engorged." No one has ever used the word "engorged" in the same sentence as my breasts—typically, they're the size of small plums. But not now. This body is not mine. I used to think I had some say in how it conducted itself. I am twenty-eight years old.

The bathroom door is closed, so I am alone. With this hollow rectangle of white-painted wood, I've created isolation, solitude. This is all I want. Lately, I don't want to be seen, especially not like this. I don't want my husband to see my skin. Skin provokes primal urges in humans, urges that, unlike my newlywed husband, I am not having. Naked invites sex, and I don't want to initiate anything. Whenever I start to entertain the notion of sex, I just get tired. I just want to sleep. So it's out of the question. He should realize this. How can he not realize this? I shouldn't have to spell it out. I'm tired. I'm angry.

I take the cabbage off the counter of the sink and slip it into my bra. It's not something I'd describe as pleasant—the cold, frosty leaves piercing my nipples on contact. In several minutes they begin to warm, and I will smell like my mother's *gołąbki*. At night in bed I sleep on my back because every time I turn onto my side, my arms squeeze my breasts together like an accordion and they leak milk. It's embarrassing. The stuff goes right through my athletic bra, which I've also been instructed to wear. I don't want Andrew to see any of this. We're to believe big breasts are lovable and playful, little breasts are cute and sweet, breastfeeding is beautiful and natural, but what about swollen, leaking breasts with no baby to feed? Would you put this in the same category as burping and passing gas—functions that sexy women do not do? Do I keep this a secret since it's not sexy? What good is a sad, broken machine?

Andrew told me, in some sort of attempt to make me laugh again, that he would make use of my milk. That he would churn butter or make cheese out of it (what, Parmesan? Brie?) and we would save some money. I did laugh at this. Manhattan is expensive.

"Maybe! Roll over! Maybe, roll over!"

"You've got to pitch your voice higher," I tell him. Dogs prefer higher-pitched voices. Andrew says okay and repeats his command, this time in the voice of a man imitating a little girl.

The dog. She's what we talk about now. Maybe is the safest topic, the most neutral, the least baffling thing to discuss. You might say we're avoiding more challenging topics, that we're walking on eggshells, but there's nothing left to break. Really, we're just tired. And we've only just begun. We're trying to wrap our heads around the idea of wrapping our heads around something, quietly trying to accept what *is*. And when you don't quite know how to do that with someone you've only just met, you talk about the dog.

"Yes, Maybe," Andrew says. "Good girl."

This month marks the third year since I uprooted from Portland, Maine, the tranquil oceanfront city where I'd moved after graduating college in Kalamazoo, Michigan. In Maine, I had a steady editing job, saved up a good sum of money, and experienced nothing that would qualify as either anxiety or ambition.

But I was making my parents proud and, I believe, lowering the collective low blood pressure of my family. In Portland, my days were pleasantly unsurprising. The people focused little on work and a lot on leisure, farmer's markets, and things like parades. Winters weren't bad or ugly—you could snowshoe to work—and in the fat of summer, the Atlantic sea breeze would seep through my open window and augment my slumber with a parental embrace. In the mornings, the sun would move across my bedroom floor and bake it like bread before my bare feet touched it. I never felt rushed. In my mud-colored kitchen with uneven shelves, I would brew coffee and polka-dot my cereal with blueberries. And yes, they were local and organic and they were affordable. Life felt flawless. I was at peace. But it wasn't enough.

In Maine, all the pine-tree license plates and rest-stop billboards said things like THE WAY LIFE SHOULD BE, and VACATIONLAND, which Maine is. The state motto is *Dirigo*, which means "I direct"—which I did not. In Vacationland, I didn't live with direction. I didn't live with force or drive or intensity. In Maine, my life wasn't so much about *dirigo*—it was about acquiescence. It was about settling into an uncomplicated life, watching days glide by like little clouds. And even though that's what I'd been aiming for, even though that's what I thought I wanted, or was supposed to want, something in me refused to settle. So I left. I came to New York to be a writer.

"Dinner's almost ready," Andrew calls.

"One more minute! I'm just brushing my hair," I answer, then put my head in my hands for one more moment of solitude. But right as Andrew is pulling the bread out of the oven, the fire alarm goes off. It happens nearly every time we cook, so we developed a system: knock on our Hungarian roommate Attila's bedroom door, grab his giant fan, turn it on high, open the front door of the apartment (for air flow), lift the giant fan over our heads, blow air onto the fire alarm, be nonchalant. The situation is taking place inches away from where I am in the bathroom. It seems as if there is no silence in this city.

In retrospect, I wish I had transitioned into a metropolitan life a little more gradually. My mother had warned me, "Why be small fish in big pond?" My father wasn't a fan of my sudden upheaval either. He knows how sensitive I am. And my friends all wanted to know what I was going to find in New York that was so important, why it was so much better than our town. I thought I'd figure it out, that I'd show them. In retrospect, I wish I'd understood that one must ease into these things, these giant life changes. I simply thought this was my chance to make something of myself. But I didn't think much about all the things that it would involve, about what had to happen between the introduction and the conclusion: the body. There was no set path to follow, no guidebook or road map. Back then I thought that in life you either had to comply or act out. Prove something. So I packed up my car and put it on I-95 and just drove. It hurt a little, because tearing yourself out of a nap always hurts, always just a little. New York City. Three years ago this month.

"Be careful. It's hot," Andrew says.

"Thank you for cooking dinner, assistant," I say.

He blows on the soup. "Mmm-hmm. You're welcome. What's the plan for tomorrow? Will you get a chance to write?"

"Doctor's appointment at eight-thirty in the morning. Will you come?"

"Sure."

"It's going to be our very last one."

"Weird."

"I know. Weird."

With nothing else for us to say, Andrew and I sip our soup as NPR fills the apartment with talk of bailouts, meltdowns, audacity, hope. Change.

We are leaving the apartment the next morning, and I am trying to remember if my doctor's appointment is on 13th or 16th Street. We're running late, but so are they—they always are—so it doesn't matter. We'll take the subway. Yellow cabs speed down 32nd Street. The garbage trucks are swift and brutal. The sidewalks work as highways. And soon, the streets will marinate in cigarette butts and urine—dog, bird, human. Soon, middle-aged Mexican men will deliver Indian takeout to young bankers from Connecticut. What is this? I find the word "misanthropy" resurfacing again and again in my mind. The people of New York generally coexist peacefully, which is impressive, considering there are 27,352 people per square mile. But it is a class-divided society. The city has a rich cultural environment, full of galleries and restaurants and museums and shows, but unless you're incredibly wealthy, it requires sacrifice to enjoy those things. Unless you are rich, you struggle every day. You grind away. You ride the subway for two hours just to work at Starbucks. We go to New York to make our careers, and we end up stepping over homeless people lying flat on the sidewalk as we walk to work.

I just hate what we are allowing ourselves to do in this city, just to survive. For instance: my classmate Grace. Grace has decided to sell her eggs so she can pay her bills. The fact that Grace has gobbled down hormones to pay off her student loans really pisses me off. I hate how she is harvesting her goods just to make a dent in her educational debts. And no one will know, and no one will care. But she is my friend and needs my care, so I'll be picking her up from the fertility clinic and taking her home today after my doctor's appointment.

I recall how Grace once theorized that Manhattan was an alien spaceship that hadn't taken off yet. "You see," she explained, "it's still chained to the ground and keeps filling up with systems upon systems, people on top of people, all with a giant conveyor belt rolling food in and garbage out. Someday we'll feel beneath our feet a great rumble: the giant New Yuck spaceship taking off."

Since moving here, I'd like to think I've become a proficient bullshit detective: I can spot a professional dogwalker who hates dogs, a nanny who wants children of her own, and people maniacally texting because they're afraid of silence, afraid of themselves. "I've felt the ground rumble a million times since I moved here," I told Grace. "It's called the subway."

It was a couple of Thursdays ago, the night of the big 2008 vice-presidential debate, when Grace revealed her plan. We were scrunched into a packed bar in DUMBO to watch a girl and a boy, all grown up in stiffly pressed suits, race for God knows what. "Going through with it" was what Grace had said. "Men sell sperm all the time," she told me. "All they have to do is fist their mister into a plastic cup and their rent is paid."

Governor Palin royally botched the image she'd recently branded herself with: representative of Americana uteri. I sipped my drink while Grace finished hers off heartily. We ordered another, then another, and watched as Palin's ticket shifted into one backed by moose hunters and white people scared of black people. "*Nucular*," she said. "*Nucular* weapons."

Moments before, Grace had gotten us into an uncomfortable situation with a gaggle of French people who had strewn their coats and legs across the seats of one of the booths of the packed bar.

"You can't save seats here," Grace told them.

"Grace, just let it go," I said.

"They're not even American. I'm sitting down," Grace said, looking at their faces. Hers was pale and round, and her mascara had settled as it always did—right under her eyes—making Grace look like a rabid kitten. Or a scary babysitter. Or the moon. I didn't know at the time that this was due to the hormones she was taking.

"I'm sorry," Grace persisted. "But your feet can't just claim territory that's not yours."

"Come on, Grace, let me buy you a drink," I said and peeled her away.

From the balcony, we watched the crowd below. The lighting washed the room in a soft, scarlet haze and made the people below look like red devils. Everyone faced a huge projector screen set to PBS. Their faces flickered, as if they were looking into a fire pit. We stared at it, too.

This was when Grace told me about the harvest. "I guess I fit the bill," she said. She explained to me that she'd been on hormones, and they made her moody and act weird. Before all this happened, someone from school had forwarded a Craigslist ad to Grace and me and a bunch of the other girls from the Sarah Lawrence MFA writing program. The subject line said, *Give the Gift of Family. Think of it this way,* the ad read. *You are not selling your eggs or your body; you are being compensated for your time and commitment.*

I prodded the Internet to find out more. One site explained that in the United States it's illegal to "sell" eggs, so the handover is labeled a "donation" followed by monetary compensation for "time and energy." One site had a picture of a chicken laying an egg. With egg donation, another site read, women who are past their reproductive years or menopause can become pregnant. Thus, the oldest woman in the world to give birth was sixty-six.

I read more about the procedure. It begins with up to ten self-injections of a drug called Lupron, which stifles a woman's natural menstrual cycle. After the Lupron, she starts taking hormones to put her egg production into overdrive and produce not one egg per month like they're supposed to, but up to nearly twenty, just like a chicken. After the harvest, she'll be listed in a catalog that includes her photo, SAT scores, and academic degrees for the potential buyers.

"The procedure is two Fridays from now," Grace said, "and

I was wondering if you could pick me up." I had told her of course, anything she needed. "Thanks, dude," Grace sighed. Then she put her head on my shoulder and fell asleep.

New York. We step over homeless people. Does that make me a misanthrope? Maybe I'm just depressed. I find both terms too scientific sounding to be the root of the problem. I can't just be a misanthrope. I can't just be depressed. There are too many variances for it all to fall under one word; too many pedestrians outside to be dodged, too many isolated faces staring at smartphones to find God in the details. I have been introduced to an unfamiliar feeling. Misanthropy. Depression. It sounds so very academic.

This new feeling must be temporary. It must come from somewhere, from something. There are all kinds of anger.

It's 9:45 A.M. now and we've been sitting in the exam room for over an hour. It's to be expected. During these appointments to Phillips Family Practice, Andrew always manages to keep himself occupied. During all the hours we've accumulated in waiting rooms, he's managed to distract me from the boredom and frustration of this run-down, sliding-scale, open-access medical clinic. He's figured out how to access the Internet on the computers that have replaced paper patient charts with electronic ones. He reads *The Times*, checks his email, and browses cuteoverload.com and hotchickswithdouchebags.com. He puts the sphygmomanometer cuff around his neck, and, with his hand on the pump, turns to me as I roll my eyes and says, "I'll do it. Don't make me do it. I'll do it!" He fills the rubber examining gloves with water from the sink. Later, when the doctor finally knocks on the door, intern at her side, he will extend this glove to shake the intern's hand.

I sit on the exam table and bang my feet against its metal base, then finally lean back, rest my head on a paper pillowcase and close my eyes, wishing I had picked up a cup of coffee on the way here. I didn't sleep much last night. I thought the hot soup and drinking no coffee after 3 P.M. would put me down and keep me down, but it didn't. Before we got into bed, I stuffed earplugs into my ears, took a valerian root tablet, and made Andrew inhale some anti-snoring vapor from Rite Aid. I used to find his snores soothing, soft and endearing, but last night his breath was like water torture. I nudged him with my elbow and he mumbled an apology, then rolled onto his side. Within seconds, he was sawing logs again. I sat up, livid, listening and waiting for the next snore to push me even closer to the edge. He snored again. I kicked my feet from under the comforter like a child. Andrew's peacefulness was driving me crazy, filling me with something that felt like hatred. And even though I was exhausted, I kept myself up, thinking, wondering, *Why does he get to fall asleep and not me?* Which really meant: *Why does he get to feel better and not me?*

Last night I started to accept the idea that I'd feel this way forever: afraid and alone. That the person sleeping next to me had already started to move on. We were only newlyweds and I was beginning to resent the person I was going to be spending the rest of my life with. Andrew snored again and I kicked him hard on his shin, then cried.

Segundo was up, too, drinking. When he listens to the Eagles late at night, he's getting himself drunk. *He was a hard-headed man, he was brutally handsome.*

"Life in the Fast Lane." He turned it up, loud; even with earplugs I could hear the lyrics through the wall. I thought he might be homesick. I pictured him drinking to Ecuador.

"Congratulations."

"Sorry?"

"Congratulations on your wedding, you two," says Dr. Reich, slipping off the powdered, pale rubber gloves and dropping them into a trash can.

"Thanks, Danya," I say and sit up.

"Do you guys have anything planned for the honeymoon?"

"We're going to Puerto Rico for a weekend in February," Andrew says. "For Valentine's Day."

"But we're saving up for a real honeymoon," I tell her. It's part of our plan. "A long one. Like three months or longer. Outside of the States—maybe someplace like Spain or Greece or New Zealand." It's unrealistic but a nice fantasy.

Danya looks into my eyes and nods. "I think that is a good decision," she says. "I think you guys should try to live a normal life from now on. And I'm gonna plan on not seeing you around here for a very long time. At least six months, which is when you should have your women's wellness exam. Six months. Got that?"

I almost don't believe her when she tells me this. She promises that it's over, that we are finished, there's no more, that this is the end of it. I don't believe her because it can't possibly ever just end.

"Thank you for taking care of us, Danya," I say. "I hope we've prepared you for when you become a real doctor."

"Most memorable residency ever," she tells us, and I think about how we just gave her the experience she might have only read in textbooks. Or heard about in a lecture. But Danya experienced it in real time. Helped navigate us through life and death in just a few short months. And now those months are over.

"Oh, it was my pleasure," she says.

Andrew and I leave the room, and Danya leads us down the long, familiar corridor of the health clinic toward the exit. She turns to extend her hand, but the three of us hug instead. "Send me a postcard," she instructs.

Promise, we say.

Good luck, she says.

Thanks, we say.

Goodbye. Goodbye, Phillips Family Practice.

two

In Battle Creek, Michigan, if you smell Froot Loops in the morning, it means rain in the afternoon. Pretty much most of the sixty thousand residents of my hometown, a city in southwestern Michigan, engage in their own surefire practice of predicting the weather, and they're usually right—something about the humidity and the air pressure and the exhaust pipes from the cereal factories and our deep embedded instincts. In the city where I was born and bred, cereal is not just a breakfast staple or a harbinger of the weather. It's an after-school snack. And a midnight snack. Kids find mini-boxes of cereal (sugary, sweet ones, of course) in their Halloween bags when they go trick-or-treating. During the summer, life-size Tony the Tigers and Snap, Crackle, and Pops wander among the picnic tables at the carnivals, giving away autographs and hugs to little ones. Cereal—artificially flavored toasted corn floating in cow's milk—is the theme of the city museums, festivals, and fairs. The production, distribution, and marketing of cereal is what once employed more than half the population. It is the town's foundation and livelihood.

Besides the exports of cereal, Battle Creek's exports include: Carlos Gutierrez, our nation's 35th secretary of commerce (and father of the boy with whom I had my first kiss); the ardent abolitionist Sojourner Truth; Ellen White, cofounder of the Seventh-day Adventist Church; Del Shannon, the guy who wrote "Runaway"; and Jason Newsted, the former bassist for Metallica. Still, Battle Creek is best known for being Cereal City USA, the world headquarters of the Kellogg Company, established by Dr. John Harvey Kellogg and Will Keith Kellogg. They're the brothers who invented cornflakes.

At Kellogg's Cereal City USA museum, you could get your photo on a box of cornflakes. During the summer, Battle Creek's residents put together "The World's Longest Breakfast Table" at the Cereal Festival—a weekend community gathering of local food, blues bands, face-painting booths, Harley-Davidson displays, and dance recitals put on by local dance studios. The highlight of the whole event is an eat-off, annually pitted against "The World's Longest Pancake Breakfast" of Springfield, Massachusetts.

Battle Creek is the city my parents migrated to after falling in love, getting married, and conceiving my sister, Sabina, in Chicago. It's the place where, in 1979 at Leila Hospital, I was born. It's the town where my family attended Catholic Church. It's the town where my dad opened his own private medical practice and my mom started her own gourmet restaurant. And it's the city where my mom decided to adopt a child from her homeland, Poland. It's the city where, in August of 1983, I met my brother Julian.

"Where are da keys? Where are da keys?"

From behind the passenger seat, I watch my mother press her face against the second-floor window's rusty screen as she calls out, in her sharp Polish accent, to no one in particular.

"Who took da damn keys?"

Her lips are cranberry colored and wet looking, and she's wearing pearl clip-on earrings. She is trying to remember everything from her mental checklist: car seat, bag of Apple Jacks, wet wipes, *We Sing Silly Songs* cassette tapes, grape juice, car keys.

For months she's known he is hers. She would never say he belongs to her; it's more as if they were meant to be; this was meant to happen. She's been holding onto the one small picture of him as proof, carrying it around as a reminder, as encouragement to keep pushing, as hope. In the photo, she thinks her little guy looks like a concentration camp baby—round, dark eyes, weak limbs, pale skin, and a rather large head.

"Did you check on the dresser, behind my stethoscope?" Dad calls from the garage.

"Dey not dere! We have to go!"

Below her, my father is in the cluttered garage, searching and scavenging through boxes of our neglected Smurfs, Trolls, and

Strawberry Shortcake dolls, which have all been replaced by our trendier Cabbage Patch Kids—blue-eyed, top-heavy, bald-headed dolls that smell like baby powder and plastic. He searches among the hammers, the jam jars full of nails, the Dutch bike, the wheelbarrow, and the storage bins. He is looking for the infant car seat.

"I set the keys there last night," he calls up to her, "right before we went to bed."

Dad is a tall, lanky man with sympathetic blue eyes and curly brown hair. His personality is a blend of Jesus (patient, self-sacrificing, wise) and Steve Martin. My sister inherited our father's long, giraffe-like legs and optimism, but I've got his metabolism as well as his penchant for absurdity.

"Now where the heck is that baby booster?"

Dad finally discovers the cushiony egg buried behind the old doghouse, dusts it off, and brings it over to the car—a boxy, beige Buick—in the driveway where my sister, Sabina, and I await. We're being very good girls, buckled into the hot leather seats, not fighting, which is rare. We're dressed up very nice and pretty and we're being good. We understand the importance of today. Special occasions require our maturest behavior.

I am four and a half years old, and wearing a huge, yellow satin dress. It's from Jacobson's Department Store in Lakeview Square, the brand new mall that developers destroyed the most beautiful wheat field in the whole world to build. After the golden meadow was killed, confused and homeless herds of deer spewed into our yard and our neighbors' yards, and soon after that, dead ones started to appear on the side of the highway more and more. We got used to it.

Beanie is six, and bouncy. Her hair is blonde, her lips are rosy, and her cheeks are pink. Whereas I'm a brunette and always pale, which worries my parents, so I get blood tests once a month at Dad's office just to be on the safe side. The dress I'm wearing belonged to my sister until just recently, when she outgrew it. It's still too big for me, but I've always loved it, so Mom let me wear it today, even though I look like I've just been swallowed up by a tulip. Also, my bangs are too short and crooked because earlier in the week I found some scissors and gave myself a haircut. The car is parked in the driveway and is running, which is why Mom can't find da damn keys.

As this scene goes down, it doesn't occur to my sister or me that our mother was once a little girl, too, just like us. That she had small kitten feet and ran without shoes along the foothills of mountains. Once, she picked wild strawberries, collected sticks, and played games like "housekeeping station" and "survive in the wilderness" and didn't have two real little children of her own to look after. Once, Mom's life was understandable. Her momma was warm, and her father was a big, silly bear who did not yet seem cold or difficult or corrupt. There was once a time when my mother's life was as simple as it is for Beanie and me at this very moment.

Before I was born, before my brother or my sister or even my father or my mother were born, this Midwestern American city was a bit of a phenomenon—a miraculous, magical destination renowned for its special brand of lifesaving. Before the cereal and the cornflakes, a doctor came to Battle Creek from New York City, raised forty children and adopted seven. He opened a holistic sanitarium, a place where rich folks and prominent Americans like Warren G. Harding and Mary Todd Lincoln and Henry Ford traveled to address their dietetic concerns and indulge their gastronomic curiosities.

The Battle Creek Sanitarium, first opened on September 5, 1866, was a combination hotel, spa, and luxury hospital and the only regional bastion of self-improvement at the time. Patients participated in breathing exercises and postprandial marches to promote the proper digestion of food. They took classes in meal preparation for homemakers and embraced the sanitarium's vegetarian, low-fat, low-protein, fiber-rich diets. The founder of the sanitarium also considered enemas to be very important, so patients participated in frequent cleansings, ones in which the doctor irrigated their bowels with several gallons of water. This was followed by a pint of yogurt—half of which was eaten, half of which was administered by enema, "thus planting the protective germs where they are most needed and may render most effective service."

The doctor also insisted that sex drained the body of life. He encouraged the application of pure carbolic acid to the clitoris, claiming it was "an excellent means of allaying the abnormal excitement." He believed that masturbation was the cause of cancer of the womb, nocturnal emissions, urinary diseases, impotence, epilepsy, insanity, mental and physical debility, and that circumcision could remedy the "solitary vice." He believed the procedure should be done without administering an anesthetic, "as the brief pain attending the operation would have a salutary effect upon the mind, especially if it be connected with the idea of punishment." He believed he had the answers to what we should do with our bodies, and people believed him. This man, Dr. John Harvey Kellogg, went on to invent Toasted Corn Flakes cereal, and put our hometown of Battle Creek, Michigan, on the map.

Mom slams the passenger-side door shut just as Dad begins to back the Buick out of the driveway. In a tubercular wheeze, our old four-door putters past Kellogg Community College and the sleeping jungle gyms of Meyer's Toy World, past Kellogg Auditorium, past Farley-Estes Funeral Home, past Community Hospital and Dad's office, and past St. Philip Catholic Church. It's very early in the morning. The sidewalks are rolled up and the sun has barely shown its face. We climb the ramp of The Penetrator, which merges onto I-94 towards Kalamazoo, and Dad pops a cassette tape into the deck. *Inchworm, inchworm, measuring the marigolds . . .*

My parents have been waiting a long time to take this drive. The gears of the adoption machine started nearly ten months ago, maybe longer. At the very least, it all began sometime after Mom had settled into Battle Creek and after Sabina and I were born. When her dust storm settled; when she just felt right. Maybe she felt loved, and finally loved America. Or maybe she was restless. Her stocked Frigidaire made her feel awkward. Maybe my father's love reminded her of her mother's unhappiness, and maybe that struck her with grief. Maybe she felt guilty. Maybe she was inspired. Maybe she wanted to save a life. Maybe she wanted to save a child that someone else considered an accident.

It started with the women: Lucia, Ducia, Vita, Jeanette, Vera. One by one, they came to us. Poland was in terrible economic condition, so Mom invited the women to live in our home in Michigan, and stay until they could afford to set out on their own. She could get them here and help them find work, but after that, they were on their own. Mom wanted to do more. Save a life more fully. Save someone completely helpless.

There was a woman in Warsaw, an impoverished, unwed girl pregnant with her second child, and she was giving the baby up for adoption.

We are in the car on the highway heading to pick up this little baby boy from the airport.

It has taken months to get to this point. In Poland, a birth mother has a month to change her mind about following through with her decision. Have baby, give baby, keep baby. During the first month, the baby stays at the hospital. Mom and Dad paid the nurses in Poland to take extra-special care of the baby during its holding period. We didn't know if he would come to us or not, but Mom kept sending money anyway because she said he just wanted to be loved. So the nurses named him Christopher and loved him until the baby's mother never returned. That's when Mom hired a lawyer, petitioned a congressman to speed up the adoption process, and paid Vera to take over loving the baby until she could put him on a plane to Michigan and deliver him to her, to us. So now, here we are, over five months later, driving to Chicago's O'Hare Airport to get this little guy. The drive will take about three hours.

We'll wait, and Mom's brother Matteo, his wife Mary, and their first child, a newborn named Marek, will greet us at the terminal. With our faces smeared against the windows, we will watch the plane touch down, and Uncle Matteo will capture the baby boy's arrival on his brand-new Zenith video camera. My new baby brother will arrive at the same international airport where both my mother and Uncle Matteo landed when they started to become Americans.

The little boy will be sick, and will need someone to take care of him. He will have the flu and a crusty nose, and a big head, too, just like he did in the photo. Beanie and I will take turns kissing him on his dimpled dumpling forehead and argue about whose turn it is to hold him, how the other got to hold him longer. My father will cry, overwhelmed with joy, and all at the same time everyone will be touched and amazed and exultant. During the drive back home, the new boy will sit in the front seat of the Buick, nestled in between my parents, and he'll stare at Dad the whole time, wide-eyed, in a trance, like Dad had come from another planet. Sabina and I will sleep.

Eventually, the little boy will get better—Dad will fix him, make his flu go away. Mom will feed him, and he'll gain weight, gain color, and soon we'll all be there when he's christened at St. Philip Catholic Church. There will be a reception in our backyard under a little white tent, and Sabina and I will take off our clothes and run around naked, pushing balloons into the air. Dad will hang a tire swing. Mom will make deviled eggs. And the newspaper will write up a front-page story about Julian, the adopted baby boy from Poland and his foreign mother, Maria.

But for now, Dad will pull our car onto the highway and drive us home. Through the back window, I will stare behind me at the airport as the bustling runway steadily diminishes into a thin, sharp, quiet line.

three

I wasn't planning on having children, or at least I hadn't given it much thought. Even though I'd been taking birth control pills and never missed a single dose, I still got pregnant. (I'm that 1 percent.)

I was a graduate student in Sarah Lawrence College's creative writing program. It's fair to say that the hefty tuition influenced me to work that much harder, but that's not what caused me to walk the thin line between ambition and obsession about my success. It was my neurotic tendency to avoid anything that would cause my parents to worry. They didn't want me to go to graduate school for art, and so I felt compelled to work that much harder so they wouldn't worry. They'd had enough anxiety in their lifetime. Plus, my mother had recently had a stent placed in her heart. I didn't want to do anything that would bring her stress.

Even so, age twenty-seven, September 2007, I bought a Metro North ticket from Grand Central Station to Bronxville, New York, and, twenty-seven minutes later, arrived at Sarah Lawrence College—the institution that, weeks later, was to be voted, once again, the most expensive college in the United States. Four months after that, I'd meet the man I was going to marry, despite the fact that on the train ride to my first day of class, I promised myself this: I would go, I would fight, and I would win. This meant no dating and no codependencies while I earned my MFA. No intimacies other than literary ones with my new classmates. Outside of graduate school, when the girls of Sarah Lawrence did hang out socially, we spent our time doing nerdily fruitful things like attending poetry readings or going to book launches where the most harm done was too many glasses of red wine remunerated by our Grad PLUS loans. No distractions until I'd earned my MFA, sold a book, and come up with a brilliant way to quickly pay off my loans. No relationships, at least not until the choice between purchasing a MetroCard and buying groceries was an old memory, fuzzy as mold. Which, back then, and on bread, I'd probably have eaten.

It meant having to leave my desk and interrupt my work. I wanted success and there was urgency about it. My mother always told my siblings and me, "First you work hard, then you play hard." This mantra worked for her quite well, so I reckoned the stricter I was about my labor, the quicker the payoff would arrive. When I wasn't in class, I was sharpening my sword. I read and studied during the day and I wrote at night. Sometimes, I'd forget to eat. I would get annoyed when I had to go to the bathroom. I isolated myself. There was an imaginary hourglass sitting on my shoulder: the sooner I could soothe my parents' discomfort, the sooner they'd be at peace with my decision to pursue my own path. I wouldn't be causing any heart attacks. I didn't know exactly how to achieve the sort of success I was after, but until it came, all I had to do was placate them. This is what I was thinking at the time.

"You should go online."

I was home for winter break after finishing my first semester, and we were hiking—Dad, me, and our family dogs, Yolanda and Gonzo—in the Kellogg Forest the day after Christmas. Despite being bundled up in layers of mismatched wool, flannel, and polyester, I couldn't cover up the fact that I was pale and slightly underweight and possibly in the beginning stages of becoming a recluse.

"It's important for you to meet other people, Mira," my dad told me. "Get yourself out there and connect with others. No man is an island."

"But I don't want to meet anyone. I'm too busy with school," I said. "Plus, I'm not going to shop for a boyfriend the same way I shop for my shoes."

"The older you get, the harder it's going to be to meet people. Several of my patients at the office have done it. You should give it a shot."

I wanted to suggest that those patients were probably divorced and over fifty, or that even if I were looking for companionship, it wouldn't be some mail-order mate, but I said nothing.

"Just a thought, Mira. Just a thought."

The next day, my mother found him. The minute I had given them permission to create an account for me, which, really, was so that my mom and sister could "window-shop for boys," the two of them were glued to the computer screen, browsing men and reading their online profiles aloud to me as I ignored them from the other room. I was making guacamole.

Big sister yells: "This one has a dog!"

Mother declares: "Yes. Yes. This one. He is it, Mira. Good-looking. Good job. Nice boy. He is the one!"

The photograph is of a dark-eyed, dark-haired guy on a couch with a dog on his lap. *Cute dog,* I think, and study the picture closer. White T-shirt, blue jeans, round head but not too big. Athletic build, sort of looks like a G.I. Joe figurine. Scar on left eyebrow. Pretty lips and a quizzical smirk. Quite handsome. Looks like he must have liked digging for worms as a boy. Looks like he'd be the kind of kid that tried to sell them for profit, too.

I'd like it if you enjoyed words, alcohol, science, smooching, live music, art, and buildings. Or if you could teach me to like things that I don't like right now. (I don't really trust picky eaters.) But you shouldn't be ugly either. Or male. Or an alien zombie, powerful in life, unstoppable in death. I ride a bicycle whenever I can. I have a puppy that loves the dog run and licking my face. I eat everything (except cilantro). I'm comfortable speaking in front of a crowd. I enjoy parenthetical asides, not abbreviating in text messages, and semicolons.

Hooked and curious, I slide between my big sister and mother, tap the keyboard, and respond:

My favorite place to be is outside. My idea of a comfortable relationship is not ordering Applebee's takeout, renting I, Robot, and raising pit bulls. I have no tolerance for womanizers, aspiring Don Juans, Casanovas, wandering eyes, men on missions, etc. etc. etc. Who I'd like to meet: You. Or Abe Lincoln. Or Mark Twain. Or Sir-Mix-a-Lot. Or world peace.

I remember what I was wearing the night I first met Andrew: a long black dress, brown boots, and a rose-colored wool coat—a gift from my mother. She said it made me look French. The ends of my hair tickled the tops of my shoulders, and I wore red lipstick, just as my mother had instructed me to do. It was January 4th, 2008. A Friday night. I did not shave my legs.

Ten minutes before we were supposed to meet in Union Square, I slipped away into a bookstore. I wasn't sure if I planned on ever leaving it, either; I was just being a coward. I wasn't sure if I was brave enough to go meet this stranger, so a voice in my head suggested that I buy a book instead. I needed a book. I *had* to get a book, and I would stay in the bookstore until I found the perfect book for that moment. He could wait.

The idea of Internet dating—digital window-shopping for a

mate—struck me as extremely bizarre. The guileless logic of it, of paying money to proclaim your vulnerability and your need for care, was difficult for me to take seriously. *I am looking for love.* I was embarrassed. *I am in need of love.* I just wasn't sure if I was willing to let someone else, some complete stranger from the Internet, know this about me. *I am in need of love.* I was. But who isn't?

Then I spotted the book: *Pigeons: The Fascinating Saga of the World's Most Revered and Reviled Bird.*

At 8:00 P.M., precisely when my blind date was leaning up against a brick wall outside a noodle joint on 17th Street north of Union Square, perhaps rubbing his hands to stay warm or checking his phone and trying to look like Mr. Cool in case I saw him first, I was inside a warm, crowded bookstore on Union Square and East 17th Street, reading about pigeons, trying not to think about what was going to happen next.

Pigeons have a fixed, profound, and nearly incontrovertible sense of home. Pigeons have been worshipped as fertility goddesses and revered as symbols of peace. It was a pigeon that delivered the results of the first Olympics in 776 B.C. and a pigeon that first brought the news of Napoleon's defeat at Waterloo.

At 8:10 P.M., using my graduate school loan money, I purchased the book, slipped it into my bag, and walked out of the bookstore and into a gusty winter night. Two minutes later, I stepped onto one specific square of sidewalk in New York City where I met my match, Andrew Michael Jackson, my first and last blind date. I still have the receipt for that pigeon book, which I bought and never read.

Three months later, I am cautiously aiming the stream of my urine. Knees bent, back hunched, panties shackled around my ankles. My hazel eyes are frozen in a look of punctilious concern.

It is April and raining outside. To my left, a bathtub. To my right, a brown wicker basket of magazines—*Cook's Illustrated, Runner's World, The New Yorker*—all marked with a small white label revealing the address of the man who lives inside this apartment: 223 East 32nd Street, Apartment 1D. Across from me, a smudged window with a pigeon roosting on its ledge, and behind the bird, the superintendent of the building, tossing garbage into a bin. And then there's me, a brown-haired, elk-faced, slender-bodied woman, straddling a toilet, peeing onto a plastic pregnancy test. My eyes, my face, my entire body—all numb. I am petrified, and targeting the stream of my urine as scrupulously as I possibly can, because I feel as if the fate of my life were being carried within it. My urine, like a crystal ball, will reveal my future.

A one-knuckled tap on the bathroom door. "You okay in there?" Andrew asks.

My knees lock together. *Please don't let him come in and see me like this. God, please don't. What could be worse than a beautiful man walking in on me crouched over like this, trying not to pee all over myself?*

"I'm Fine! Fine in here. Just finishing up!" I sing. *Frog-legged with your pants down, squatting like an old granny. Nothing much less flattering than that.*

I pull my underpants up, zip up my jeans. I am one of four million women living in New York at this very moment. What is the likelihood that one of those other four million women in New York is doing and thinking and feeling the same exact thing that I am right now? Who else is squatting over a toilet taking a pregnancy test? Who hadn't planned on it? Who will be pleased with the results? And what will happen to those who aren't?

This is how it happened: It was wild and universal and complex. We were charged and unaware of what was going on underneath the surface. We let go, and I let him take me in. We fell in love. Exposed kneecaps and collarbones, and entire evenings spent devouring one another; we were like wild forces. I knew it was a bit much—we were just so drawn to one another; we were so brand new. Then suddenly, three months later, I was pregnant. I thought we were safe. I never missed a pill. We *were* safe. And then, pregnant. It was as if my body had been wanting and waiting for this and I hadn't even realized it. *Pregnancy*. I didn't find it beautiful. I found it disturbing. But can't something be both disturbing and beautiful at the same time? Can't things be tremendous and lonesome at the same time? Simultaneously heartbreaking and glorious? Wasn't that New York?

At first, I believe the plus sign is a negative sign, and a perpendicular line has floated out of its boundary. It has migrated out of its home base. At first, and deludedly, I am calmed by this. Not pregnant. But after I take two more tests, it finally sinks in.

Next, we are sitting on his couch and I am crying. "I don't

even have health insurance," I say between huffs. Plus signs. Sniff, sniff. Positive. Andrew is leaning on the windowsill, waving two pregnancy test sticks in front of him as if they are Polaroid photos. He is calm, and appears almost glad. This offers a tiny bit of relief, because I'm not yet thinking about my parents and what this might do to them. I'm not thinking about disappointment versus approval, or my mother's heart. I'm just trying to formulate some kind of game plan, to treat this like a math problem. We look at all the other options and possibilities with barely a glance and say "no." *Abortion?* We don't consider this a mistake; we don't want to wipe anything out. *Adoption?* Neither one of us can fathom having our creation disappear into the same world we live in. It would be like having our very own ghost.

"I love you," Andrew says.

"I love you, too."

Behind us, the sound of children shrieking on a playground is making me want to smoke a cigarette, or maybe three hundred, all at once. It is spring, and I am not ready to be a mom. I don't want to be a parent. But now I am. There is a baby growing inside my uterus and there is nothing I can do about that right now, so I will not smoke cigarettes and I will not drink alcohol and I will not do anything that may cause the least bit of harm to this tiny speckle of a human I'm nurturing. Is that what they call motherly instinct? Maybe jumps onto my lap and licks my face. I will do my best here. It is my responsibility.

"Your dad is a doctor. Can't he help?"

I can't think about my father, or my mother right now. Dad

used to be in the seminary. He's from a large Catholic family. And my mom is Eastern European, and intimidating.

"My dad practices in Michigan," I say. "And I'm not asking my parents for help. Or money."

"What about your school's health insurance?" Andrew asks. He sits down next to me on the couch. "Doesn't health insurance just come in the student package?"

I explain: I have no health insurance because I opted out of Sarah Lawrence's plan so I could save an extra two thousand bucks. I was willing to risk it. I have an excellent immune system. I wear a bike helmet. I hadn't planned on getting pregnant.

"Medicaid," I decide. "That's the only option I can think of. Tomorrow I will go to the Medicaid office and fill out an application." It's government assistance or no health care. They can't turn us away. Medicaid. Just until we figure out what to do next.

"I'm not going anywhere," Andrew says.

"Don't say that. You don't know that," I tell him. You can't go back from here, but you can always go away. Things will never be like what they were five minutes ago, two hours ago, two weeks ago, one month ago. Nothing will be the same from here on out. We're not just dating anymore. The simple stuff is over. We won't be fresh anymore—we'll be raw.

"I love you. We'll get through this together," Andrew says.

"I love you, too." And I do.

It's only been three months since we met, but we are in love, and we can't really comprehend much more than that, so love is what we agree on. Love, and just letting the rest unfold on its own, seems to be the right choice for now.

four

Eight days or so later, Andrew asks me to be his wife. When he proposes, we are at the edge of a pond at the Brooklyn Botanical Garden. It's afternoon in early April, right in the prime of the cherry blossom season.

Everything about the day feels like an impressionist painting—vibrant, floral, blurry, blue. I am feeling hopeful, confident. No one knows the secret that Andrew and I are sharing. We saunter through the gardens without motives, or so it seems. Every time we see a baby or a family, we softly elbow one another and smile, even though I'm not exactly sure what I mean by it. But I feel strong.

We walk through the Japanese gardens and stop to look into a pond. The carp are thick and surreal. Scattered families

of Hasidic Jews are regrouping, and groundsmen impatiently
shuffle loners toward the exit gates. It is closing time. Andrew
and I finish a loop around the water.

"We should go," I say.

"Just a second." He has stopped, and is staring at a bird on
the shore. I watch him for several seconds, and then he turns to
look at me. He put his hands on my shoulders, steadies me, then
kneels down. "Will you marry me?" he asks, and I give a short,
breathy laugh.

"Get up," I say, feeling embarrassed. "Get up." I don't like
seeing him on his knee, proposing. It's almost like we are acting
out a script. He looks so vulnerable down there, almost naïve;
it makes me feel sorry for him, love him more. At the same
time, this act—the act of getting engaged—is being performed
in such a generic, old-fashioned, archaic way that it makes me
feel uncomfortable. It is not ours.

"I love you," I say, pulling him up and telling him that of
course I will marry him. We kiss, hug, and ask a stranger to
take our picture. The photo still sits on my parents' mantel in
Michigan.

In the weeks that follow, we tell our parents the news of the
engagement, but tell very few people—only my sister, my best
friend in Michigan, and our new doctor—that I'm pregnant. It's
my request.

I cry, and often. During the day, alone and in hiding, I cry
because I feel like I failed. I worry that when they find out about
my pregnancy, I will be perceived as lazy, reckless, irresponsible,
selfish. By whom? No one in particular. I feel defeated because I

don't want a baby, but know I must keep the baby. Andrew and I loved one another and we had sex and the pill didn't work and we made a baby. The question of whether I wanted one is moot. It doesn't matter because somehow I know that my whole life has led me to this place; this is what has happened and I will have to take responsibility for my actions. The time has come for me to step up. Grow up.

At night, and quietly, I cry because I am in mourning. I am suddenly pregnant. This makes me feel suddenly apart. Isolated. In an instant, I am separated from my life as I knew it. Separated from my classmates at Sarah Lawrence. I am no longer a writer to be critiqued so much as the subject of their popcorn gossip. Separated from my role as a sibling, I am no longer the spirited younger sister but the knocked-up one. Suddenly separated from the layover I'd been enjoying between youth and adulthood. And, even though they don't know it yet, I am suddenly separated from my parents. I am no longer their daughter so much as I am now one of them—a parent, with her own child. I will have to learn, and quickly. Learn how to support the head. Learn how to breastfeed. Audition for daycare. Make budgets. Meal plans. I am *pregnant*. And defeated. Andrew already has an established career as an engineer; I am a struggling writer with impending student loan payments. How on earth will we make this work? What kind of mother will I be?

As if having no control over these sudden shifts and new roles weren't baffling enough, I have no control over my body, which is now a real adult body. Goodbye, Forever 21 clothing. I won't be able to get away with your cheap, cute, disposable tops anymore. My body is a primal, mature one. It is an animal's body, shifting and growing and doing things I never knew it could do. I'm swelling, and my body isn't under my control, and it's leaving me more isolated and unfamiliar with this new self and it's terrifying. And this fear produces, on top of everything else, an overwhelming guilt.

Andrew, on the other hand, is optimistic. He embraces the first weeks of the pregnancy with his own brand of humor. For instance, during our transvaginal ultrasound, the one where the delivery date is predicted, he asks my doctor if he himself could perform the ultrasound on me. Patiently, our doctor tells him no. Then Andrew requests that the ultrasound be performed on him. Again, Danya denies him, but Andrew keeps on pushing. Finally, he asks if the machine is advanced enough to predict if the baby is gay, and if not gay, will it be able to tell us if the baby is going to be a Republican. The room falls silent. I am sprawled on my back in a paper gown, legs locked in stirrups as Andrew wheels his stool close and whisper-yells into my ear, "Don't worry, darling. I'll love our child just as much if it is gay. But not if it's Republican."

Weeks pass, and I go mean on Andrew like a snapping turtle. I continue to remind him that I didn't want any of this, that none of it was a part of my plan, that this will destroy my parents, that my life is over. I'm not sure if I mean it or not, but it doesn't really matter. The only thing that matters is that we both just shut up and start taking good care of this new part of us.

"Calm down, just calm down. Everything is going to be fine," Andrew tells me, lovingly, again and again, but I can't just calm down. I am overcome. I don't want to be the one who ruins things, ruins lives, the fuckup. I just want some control over something.

"I'm not going anywhere," he says, over and over again for weeks, but I keep fighting him on it because he doesn't understand. No matter what happens, whether he stays or goes, whether we get married or not, whatever happens from here on out, we'll be living in separate worlds with separate feelings and understandings and interpretations and memories of this pregnancy. It's as if being pregnant is a reminder that we are all born alone and die alone.

I am about two months along in my pregnancy when we break the news to the first set of parents: Andrew's. Andrew is confident that his mom and dad will be happy about it. They are old enough to be grandparents and Andrew is thirty-one. I interpret this as a hint that they are much less emotional than my parents. It is Memorial Day weekend. We are sitting around the breakfast table at a family restaurant in southern Illinois. It's the day after his sister Kerri's wedding reception and it's only the second time I have ever met Andrew's kin. We drink our orange juices, our tomato juices, and coffees and read the menus. Everyone is happy. We make a nice bunch. The waitress takes our orders, then Andrew taps a silver spoon on a small water glass and says cheerily, "I have an announcement to make!"

Now? I didn't know he was going to do it right now. I don't even know what he's going to say, or how he's going to say it, and I regret trusting him to be sensitive about this. I'm worried about what this will ignite. Andrew said not to worry—"They'll be excited. They love you."—but I am worrying.

"I have an announcement, everyone," he repeats, and my stomach twists. *Goddamnit, Andrew. Why are you so fucking confident?* And before I can tell him to stop with the grand announcement, Andrew halfway stands up and says, "I have asked Mira to marry me."

"Already?" someone says. I cower.

"And," he continues quickly, like it's a punch line, "she's pregnant."

And-she's-pregnant. Just like that. Her. Right there. That girl, right over there. Every speechless face at the table turns to me, including Andrew's, in pewter silence. Then my face starts to burn. Andrew's mother gasps and his father begins to cry.

"How—?" someone starts to ask, then stops.

More silence.

"Congratulations," Kerri tells us, nobly, and I thank her with my eyes. *Jesus Christ.*

"Thanks," I say. *Thank you, Kerri, for your understanding on how I might feel at this very moment. Thank you for breathing some air into my lungs as I drown in this torrential awkwardness.*

"Yes, congratulations," the chorus repeats. And then, like turning the channel on the television set, the flow of the conversation is switched to sports. And that is that.

Occasionally, during the next several weeks, we communicate with Andrew's parents over the phone. Andrew and I have a strategy, and we have a request for his folks to please, please remain tight-lipped about the news of our pregnancy until we tell mine. Our plan: In a couple of weeks, Andrew and I will deliver the first news flash (we are engaged!) to them. We'll give them time to celebrate and let it settle. Let them rejoice and be glad. I don't want them to think we're getting married only because I'm pregnant. I want them to be happy. To see that we really do love one another, and that our love is solid. I want them to feel proud. I've heard enough stories about young patients of my dad's that were fifteen, sixteen, seventeen years old, single, and pregnant. I don't want my parents to think about my pregnancy in the same way. But the concealment makes it worse. I dwell on how they will respond, what they'll think, what everyone will think. For weeks I lie about who I am, what is happening in New York. I talk to my mother every day, and every day I paint a picture that things are good and ordinary.

We decide to call them on Father's Day. It is my sister's idea. I am already living with Andrew. They don't know that. Or that I have already heard the baby's heartbeat. We are sitting on the stoop outside his apartment on 32nd Street when we make the call. My parents are at home in the kitchen. It is Father's Day, a humid Sunday evening.

It is Andrew's idea to have them put us on speakerphone, but the speakerphone makes things worse. There are taxis honking and sirens wailing in the background. Strangers are walking by on the sidewalk.

"I have some good news for you," is what I first say, but it doesn't feel like good news. And it doesn't feel good to say it.

"What? Say it again, we can't hear you."

"You're going to be grandparents," I declare, but my parents can't understand anything I am saying, so I have to repeat it again and again. "I said, YOU'RE GOING TO BE GRAND-PARENTS." I have to shout.

"You're kidding," is what my dad says when he finally hears it, but I'm not. We're not kidding. We're not terminating; we're not putting it up for adoption. You are going to be grandparents.

After a long pause, my mom finally speaks. "Okay! Here we go!" she sings. "Let's get to work! How can I help?"

But I have no response. I am crouched on the stairs of our apartment, barefoot and pregnant in New York City, trying to play it cool with everyone, but at the moment, everyone feels like an opponent.

five

A memory: I am nine years old. My sister, Sabina, my brother, Julian, and I are chickens with our heads cut off, running around our backyard in retaliation against the assigned chore of cleaning soggy dog crap out of the spring grass.

"I spend two years wiping *esses*," Mom shouts from the front porch, "just so I could afford to eat!" She continues. "Before I meet you Daddy, I supported myself and lived off one chicken for ze whole week. Chicken soup, chicken salad, chicken pot pie . . . " I've heard this one before. Mom saved every penny, shopped at Goodwill stores in the rich neighborhoods, ironed all her clothes and always looked good. ". . . and I saved up twelve thousand dollars cleaning poop, so I don't want to hear you complain," she says in a frustrated huff, and, as usual,

Mom's frightening testimonial wears me down. Next thing I know, I'm reaching out to accept the blue broomstick-handled pooper scooper, the one with the aluminum claws. She steps off the porch and back into the kitchen when all of a sudden a wad of dog feces shoots toward me. It's lavender colored.

"Look out," Sabina warns in a desultory kind of way, a bit belatedly, after the shit has already dropped to the base of my feet and covered the toes of my brand-new, white LA Gear high-tops.

"Frig!" I yell and catch a fleeting glimpse of my little brother's backside: a stonewashed, multi-pocketed Teenage Mutant Ninja Turtles jean jacket as he gallops down the hill, snickering.

"Poop cemetery," he hollers. "Poop cemetery!"

Five years later, Jules and our cousin Marek are crouching among the bushes behind Mom's restaurant, picking at dry soil and olive-colored vegetation. Their chore: pull out all of the weeds, don't touch Mom's tiger lilies, leave the corn flowers and the feathered reed grass. The sun-drunk cousins are hunched over like two old men, but instead of sipping warm beer and gnawing on tobacco, they've got Big League Chew cherry-flavored bubblegum and cans of Mountain Dew strewn about their island of shrubs and Midwestern flora.

They are cousins but not by blood. The younger one is adopted, which means that if I or my sister, Sabina, or cousin Maya want to, we could end up marrying Julian and it wouldn't be gross, but we don't. We'd rather battle. Uncle Matteo's two children, Marek and Maya, are visiting us for the summer from Chicago. We've formed our alliances and must try to keep our lines of separation clear; strictly girls versus boys even though us girls secretly enjoy getting chased by Jules and Marek. We secretly enjoy fleeing from their spit wads and their wedgie threats. Why? Because it's funny. And we really are laughing with them when Jules makes that juicy noise as he hand-pumps the air under his armpit, but we will never tell them that. And even more than we enjoy the armpit farts that we pretend to believe are disgusting and soooo immature, we enjoy sniping insults at the boys about their hair (greasy and nappy), their lack of social life (losers, numb nuts, monkey fuckers), and all the other things Sabina, Maya, and I have a penchant for comparing them to. We are adolescent girls with blooming insecurities about our own blossoming bodies, which we are projecting onto the boys. Regardless, there is a distinctive air of Polish in all of us that can't be denied: our far-set, almond eyes, our chipmunk cheeks, our workers' hands, and our heavenly foreheads. None of us are very tall, except for Julian.

"Boooooooyyyyys!" Mom shouts from the top steps of the back terrace of her restaurant. Her outdoor voice is shrill, high-pitched. "If those weeds are not cleaned up in two minutes, then poor your soul. Poor your soul!" What she means by this is, "If those weeds are not cleaned up in two minutes, then I feel sorry for your poor soul because it is going straight to hell." My mother's warning glides through the balmy summer air and, although she is shouting just three short, low words, you can still detect her sharp, high accent. Slavic.

It's a muggy one out here today in Battle Creek—sultry, over-cast, and as pallid as a bowl of leftover milk. The year is 1994. And even though it's mostly cloudy, the boys' shoulders and round faces have gotten tanned, freckled, and burnt. Julian looks just like Leonardo diCaprio in *What's Eating Gilbert Grape*. He's skinny and lanky in jeans and sneakers and his cheeks are as bright as a hot-pink Easter egg, and it's not even three o'clock yet.

"We go. Now." Mom calls again, this time reminding them from behind the screened-in porch door, then strides back into the industrial-sized kitchen without waiting for their response. She's looking for her keys. Her keys are in the car.

I am standing behind a sink at my mother's restaurant. My fingers are soggy and my forearms are covered in greasy suds. I'm looking down, scrubbing dried sauces off the rims of last night's china. It is my summer vacation. I have small boobs and I really would like a padded bra before August ends and school starts up. A little while ago, I stole a bikini top from Sabina's dresser drawer. It is red with white polka dots and a foamy push-up insert, though I don't have much for it to boost. The makeshift bra adds two petite mounds to the center of my level chest, about two inches higher than where real breasts should be. I am a dishwasher.

Some of my friends from W. K. Kellogg Junior High work at Cereal City USA for their summer jobs. They snap photos of out-of-towners, then print their pictures on Corn Flakes boxes. Some of my friends are employed at Marywood Golf Club. They drive golf carts around the greens, selling the beer in their coolers to men in khakis and pine-green polo shirts. They steal Pabst Blue Ribbons and make good tips. Some of my friends work as lifeguards at Full Blast Water Park. They get to scold little kids for running by the pool, stuff them in plastic tubes, and then shoot them down curlicue water slides. This summer, I'm stuck at Mom's restaurant washing dishes, which I do pretty much year-round anyway, remaining pasty with soggy fingers. I wash plates, dry plates, put them away. I sweep floors, take out the garbage, scrub the sinks and the toilets, and it is impossible to call in sick unless I really am. I have no choice. I can't argue with the woman who drives me to the mall, buys my clothing, feeds me, birthed me, shelters me. You work hard, you play hard.

My mother named her restaurant RSVP. When she opened the place a few years ago, she explained that RSVP is a French phrase that translates into "Respond if you please." That to RSVP is to employ the polite and customary etiquette when confirming or declining an invitation. I told my mother she should've named her restaurant Momma Maria's, but Mom said what our town didn't need was another burger joint.

It hadn't been her plan to be a professional chef. Before having us kids, my mom had been a physicist. She said she didn't immigrate to the US to cook for people, that she is a scientist, not a server, and that the reason she left Poland in the first place was to stop *pumpering* people. She meant pampering. But after Jules started the first grade, Mom was suddenly alone in an empty house and didn't know what to do with herself.

She was a good cook. In Poland, my grandmother taught her the art of concocting delectable meals for any occasion out of whatever food was around, even when all they had to choose from were a few potatoes, bread, and an onion. When she brings a dish to a funeral, the mourners momentarily shake their postures of bereavement and ask her to please give them the recipe.

At his wake, Vernon Butler's wife Dody told Mom that, sure as shit, if Vernon'd had the privilege of sampling Mom's butternut squash and creamed-spinach gratin, he'd return from his grave for a second helping. What Mom didn't tell Dody was that she just grabbed the leftovers from our fridge and the vegetables on their way to our compost, added lots of cream and butter, then baked it. Anyone who tasted her food insisted that Mom should cook for a living.

Often, Mom would warn me that life could bring all sorts of surprises when I least expected them, and that it's best to be prepared for the worst. In a raw voice, she'd remind me to always cover my ass and always have something to fall back on. "Just in case. I work for myself. Just in case. What if you Daddy die? What if we divorce?" Mom said she always wanted to be in charge of something, and since she was from a Communist country, the possibility of being her own boss seemed like a dream come true. So after we kids were old enough to hold our own, Mom shifted gears. She rented out the commercial kitchen at St. Philip Elementary School, and once the lunch ladies had left for the day, she started cooking. But this time, it was strictly business. Spinach squares, raspberry tortes, stuffed mushroom caps. Baby showers, funerals, anniversary dinners. Soon enough, Mom's rinky-dink catering company was the best food in the city, and when Mom's business took off, so did the competition for storage space in the shared refrigerator. Following a confrontation about the cafeteria lunch ladies' meatloaves and her truffle pâtés, Mom told Dad *they* were interfering with *her* work, and that she needed her own space to create. That's around the time our family purchased and renovated an elaborate Queen Anne-style building on Capitol Avenue Northeast. It's where my family spent an entire summer painting, weeding, moving, and paving, until it looked like it did in the nineteenth century—presentable—and then my mother erected a big wooden sign that read *RSVP Fine Dining: European Elegance with American Flair* in fetching teal- and rose-colored letters. This is where I'd been working ever since.

The building that housed RSVP Fine Dining is a nationally registered historical home with a flat, jade-colored face and huge, forward-facing windows. To me, the house looks like a fabulous owl. The bright purple door has a beak-like appearance and perched above it are conspicuous ornamentations—tremendous turrets, metallic wreaths, a pink-sash upper trim, and a chimney shaft. And on the very, very top of the bird is a widow's walk, and circling the perimeter below, like a sautoir necklace, is a baby-blue wooden veranda.

The house was built in the 1850s, right around the time a Michigan Quaker by the name of Erastus Hussey became a conductor on the Underground Railroad and began leading slaves through Battle Creek to Marshall, Albion, Grass Lake, Ann Arbor, Plymouth, then on to Detroit and freedom. This was right around the time Sojourner Truth made her famous "Ain't I a Woman?" speech in Ohio, then moved to Battle Creek to lead the abolitionist movement until she died in her home on College Street, just down the road from Mom's restaurant. "Look at me! Look at my arm! I have ploughed and planted, and gathered into barns, and no man could head me! And ain't I a woman?" Mom told me that once, during one of her speeches in Silver Lake, Indiana, someone accused Sojourner of being a man in disguise, so Ms. Truth ripped open her blouse and bared her breasts to the audience to refute the preposterous claim. I've given this story a lot of thought because I doubt I'll ever be brave enough to do something even a third as courageous. I don't even have the guts to ask my mother for a padded bra.

Residential homes line both sides of RSVP's block, and across the street is the Emily Andrus House, where, in all the seasons except winter, a large lawn is dotted with old ladies in metal walkers moving like three-toed sloths. It was Leila Post Montgomery— widow of the breakfast cereal magnate C. W. Post (Grape-Nuts, Fruity Pebbles)—and her mother, Emily Andrus, who opened the Andrus Residence about sixty years ago, after visiting some friends at a nursing home. The mother-daughter breakfast cereal heirs returned home devastated and in tears, shocked by the poor caregiving, so Leila and her mom started the project "to provide and maintain a secure, attractive, independent residential environment for self-sufficient senior ladies of our community." The place opened in 1924. One winter, Mom made Sabina volunteer there, so my sister decided to start up a Jazzercise class at Emily Andrus. Every summer, Mom had me deliver strawberry shortcakes to the elderly ladies once the berries were in season, and I'd catch my sister in her brightly colored leotard, leading the women on a slow walk around the building. Sabina called it the "finale" of their workout.

I've been working here since mom opened RSVP, and this is the first year I am getting compensated in cold, hard cash. This year, I'm no longer considered a volunteer. I get $6.50 an hour, while the boys still get paid in 3 Musketeers candy bars and Beef Jerky from the C-Store down on Emmett Street.

"Your keys are in the van, Mom," I say as she grabs her colossal purse off the wooden peninsula covered with a batch of crème brûlées waiting to get their sugary little tops scorched. "Where are you guys going?"

"Subway," she says, rushed. "Or McDonald's or Arby's or whatever indecent place the boys choose." It's lunchtime now, time for Jules and Marek to get paid for half a day's work of lawn care with the sort of junk food that Mom detests.

"How come Sabina isn't taking them?" I ask, but I already know. It's because when Mom found Sabina's birth control pills last week, she went bananas and grounded Bean for the rest of her life. No car, no phone, no social outings, and definitely no boyfriend as long as Bean is living under our parents' roof. After the contraceptive incident, the only liberty Beanie was allowed was when she ran errands for Mom, like taking us to and from violin lessons or the math tutor or work. But then last night Bean got banned from even doing that. She was driving Jules and Marek home after a long day at the restaurant. The boys were slaphappy and making toilet noises in the backseat, and my sister told them that unless they learned to shut their pie holes, they'd be walking the rest of the way home. But that only got them more excited, and they made more noises, even real farts this time, thanks to the Cheetos and Beef Jerky, so she pulled the car over to the side of the road and made Jules and Marek get out, which they did. Later, Bean told Mom and Dad that she had honestly just planned on making just one loop around the block, but somehow she reached Morgan Road and forgot. It wasn't until two hours later, after Mom drove past Jules and Marek on 6 Mile Road, covered in sweat and mosquito bites and flagging down cars, that she brought the boys home and reminded Sabina that she'd forgotten something.

"I drive," Mom says.

"I can take them for you! Can I drive?" I suggest, and hold my breath.

"You don't even have a certification," she says. "If you got caught by police, poor your soul."

"But Dad lets me drive all the time!"

"In the driveway, Dad does," she says. "And I am not your daddy."

"Fine," I sigh. "Then do you think you can pretty pretty please pick me up a Charleston Chew on your way back?"

"Seventy cents," she says in a grave and precise manner and extends her flattened palm.

I watch Mom as she leaves the kitchen and gets in her Chrysler minivan. She turns on the engine, shifts gears, then reverses halfway around the shrubbed island in the middle of the asphalt driveway where Jules and Marek are weeding. The two cousins emerge from the bushes like teenage lions, yawning, and I push open the squeaky porch door that leads out back, pull out an empty plastic cassette tape holder from my back pocket, and sit down on the moist concrete porch steps. As my brother and cousin slide open the side door of the van, I roll a single cigarette out of the case and into my hand. As the van door slams shut,

I pinch the tube of tobacco between my thumb and forefinger and place it on my lips, and away they go.

Now it is late September and I am almost seventeen years old. I am peeling off shrimp husks and then gliding the pointed tip of a bamboo skewer down their backs and scooping out their intestines. One shitty blue thread after another and my heart just isn't in it.

After I finish the rest of this batch that Mom's assigned me, the shrimp will be rinsed under a faucet and dried, brushed with extra-virgin olive oil and specks of garlic and dill, pierced with kabobs, and assembled on a large barbecue grill, then eaten before the wedding cake and after Uncle Matteo's second sacrament of marriage.

Jules walks into the kitchen and over to my station. "Hey, Bubba Gump," he says. He reaches into the sink, pulls shrimp shell out from the basin drain, and holds it in front of his eyes. "Holy Crap, did this guy have one huge last meal," he says. Jules is fourteen years old, and soon I'll be teaching him how to peel and devein these little bastards.

"Can I help you with something, Turd Ferguson?" I ask.

"Mom told me to tell you that after you finish the shrimps, you need to get cleaned up."

"What time is everyone getting here?"

"We have to be ready at four o'clock, so hurry up, scrub," Jules says, dropping the shell back in the sink. "And by the way," he says, turning before leaving the room, "Mom's not in a good mood."

This morning, when Dad dropped me off at the restaurant, I found Mom on her hands and knees, washing the floor and muttering.

"What's going on, Mom?" I asked.

"US of Shit!" she said. "That is what is going on." Mom told me that her bid for a liquor license had been rejected yet again, and that tonight's server had checked himself into an alcohol rehab clinic and she had no one on her wait staff to cover tonight. "All this before ten in the morning. I guess I'll be serving dinner myself?"

I knew she was overwhelmed. I had recently been diagnosed with attention deficit disorder, which Mom suggested was an excuse for people with low self-discipline, and she had already missed two of Julian's football scrimmages because of having to work overtime. "I don't have enough hands for tonight," she cried. But in her own secret language, I knew she was telling me more than the obvious. It wasn't her staff. It wasn't the liquor license or the football or my lack of focus and declining math grade. It was her brother.

A month ago, Uncle Matteo phoned to tell Mom he was getting married. His girlfriend, Vladka, was pregnant, and they'd set the date of the wedding for September. In his phone call, Uncle Matteo had requested that the wedding be at RSVP, and that Mom do him the honor of catering the reception.

This was a month ago and the wedding is tonight, and I don't understand why she is doing it for him.

"He just doesn't get it," Mom said. "You have a duty and you do it. I don't know why I hire him in the first place."

"Mom, it's not a big deal. I can be your server tonight," I said.

"No, no. I just do it myself. I do all dis on my own," she sighed. "I pull myself up by my boots and I make my own living and I still get stuck pulling up slacks of everyone else. People here just abandon ship whenever they feel like it. Americans just do not get it," she cried.

"I'm American, Mom. Do I get it?" I asked.

"This country is a McDonald's culture," she continued, talking past me, "and this country is just eating me out!" She dipped her rag back into the bucket of soapy water, and I didn't correct her.

I toss the bowl of shrimp shells into the garbage disposal, and flip the switch. The blade pulverizes the skeletal remains, making a noise like boots crunching dried leaves, then I turn off the machine and go get cleaned up for the ceremony.

In this particular memory, my mother is forty-seven years old, with perfectly straight teeth, tomato-red nails, and short-trimmed hair. She looks like a pixie with curves. She has a voluptuous bottom that rounds like a McIntosh apple and squishy, munificent breasts that give all her necklaces the appearance of being impeccably placed. My mother is not tall; she wears sleek dresses with high-heeled shoes and an apron when she's working. Whenever she laughs, it is a long-lasting, satisfying explosion, but lately she hasn't seemed so happy. She's been racing, and her words are prickly and staccato. She is often hurried and tense; ever since she started cooking professionally, she has seemed that way, as if there is a tightness in her that will not break.

The story always begins outside of the story:

My mother's childhood home was a small house in Maków, something that looked like it belonged to the set of *The Sound of Music*. In photographs, the house looks edible—a rustic, graham-cracker brown A-frame built of rough-cut lumber with a red-shingled roof, and sugar-white trim.

My mother's father, Karol, was a protective, defensive and an oversexed grump. The man was embittered, but he had his reasons. He had left his family to set off on his own when he was only fourteen; and when Communism engulfed Poland, the man just gave up. He excused himself from the principles of public decency and civic responsibility, and in time, my grandfather got to be as crooked as a do-it-yourself haircut. In time, this bled into his home life. When he wasn't lying on the sofa or yelling at his transistor radio (a radio that he'd clandestinely tuned to Radio Free Europe each night), Karol was with another woman.

As a little girl, it's not something my mother could even talk about. It wasn't so much forbidden, just simply outside the realm of her comprehension. It wouldn't be until the road rolled out behind her that she would be able to look back and understand the peculiar habits of her father in his little kingdom, and the family's curious acquiescence. Not until she was a grown woman and her parents had taken their reasons to their own cold graves could she begin to make sense of it all. Nowadays, and with an air of sad resignation, my mother diagnoses her father as bipolar or manic-depressive. Other times, she pins him as a male chauvinist or an alcoholic. The labels take turns.

I can see my young mother trying to make things right, helping her mother gather the empty glasses sucked dry of mulled wine and the *babka*-smeared plates that were left scattered about their home. I can imagine the look of calm on my grandmother's face change to pity, then pity to anger, then anger to sadness. Mom whispers, "It's not your fault." She's old enough to understand the reasons of her father's behavior but too young to grasp the consequences.

She called her daddy's mistress the "Unofficial Official." He dragged my young mother to the Unofficial Official's home during their daylight trysts, whereupon he explained to her that they were conducting political discussions. On the days when my grandmother Henrika was at church, Karol brought the Unofficial Official home with him, where the two of them toasted from the glasses my grandmother herself had washed earlier in the week. They ate the cakes my grandmother had baked for their three children. Behind closed but unlocked doors, the Unofficial Official unlatched the buttons on the shirts that Henrika, despite her rheumatoid arthritis, had starched and ironed earlier in the week.

The dissolution of their cursed marriage was slow and excruciating. First it was Karol's frustration, then his anger that led to the couple's estrangement. Then it was separate beds, separate bedrooms, separate worlds. Finally, when Karol brought the Unofficial Official to little Maria's First Holy Communion mass, Henrika packed her bags and moved permanently into the family's cottage up in the Tatra Mountains, where she retreated to her own private world to obscure all her husband's darkness and deception.

My young mother also avoided her father and brothers, who sided with Karol. Maria was devoted to her mother. But by the time Maria was grown and left for college in Kraków, Henrika's fingers and toes were as twisted as ginger roots. In sync with the breakdown of her marriage, my grandmother's rheumatoid arthritis took control over the rest of her body like a painful invasive species. She could barely walk. She was crippled. Unemployed. And just like the government he despised, Karol withheld and controlled their money. Henrika was helpless. And then suddenly, while my mother was away at school, her mother died.

I can see my mother arriving at the damp Maków station: her brown hair springs loose and free as she tumbles down the steps and leaps onto the platform before the train comes to a complete stop. In her mind she's rewinding and replaying the transcription of the morning's telephone call: *Come home immediately. She is dying. Go straight to the hospital.*

It's not supposed to happen this way. They have a plan. "Mother," she had promised, "when I am awarded my master's, I will take you far away from here." They'd already set things in motion, begun executing the plan. A tedious one, but still, it was as simple as a glass of water on a hot day: physics degree, then Kraków. Steeples. Autos. Libraries. Poets. Cobblestone. Freedom. She would make her mother happy again.

March 3, 1968. With the Communist government limiting

the number of people who could live in the larger cities like Kraków, the spiritual heart of Poland, she'd need to earn a government-sponsored position to earn her mother and herself a place in the coveted city. She'd need to make herself employable.

There has been a lot of saving and working and waiting. She is so close to their ticket out: the final exam for her master's degree is tomorrow, the last procedure before she will be given the liberties she yearns for. Once this is done, her mother will be waiting on the front porch, bags packed, and the two will finally be able to break free . . . to the cathedrals! St. Peter's, St. Andrew's, Church of the Virgin Mary's Annunciation. The people in Maków sulk to church as if they were on their way to a funeral, but in Kraków the people bring life to the cathedrals.

But now my mother is running. The distance is about a mile. The sun has gone down; it is cold and dark and raining. Run. She might be racing across a field of edelweiss or forget-me-nots to get to the hospital. Just run. She's not thinking of the mathematical equations in the schoolbooks sprawled open on her dormitory desk, books as lifeless as the nerves in her mother's arthritic limbs. She's not thinking of the past, nor of the future. Nothing. Just the wind and the rain blowing in her face and the sixth-sense knot in her stomach telling her that if she runs fast enough, soon enough she will get an answer. And then, sopping wet, she arrives at the gates of the Mazowiecki Hospital.

At first, my mother doesn't notice the expression on the hospital guard as he looks her up and down from the gate. The sight of wet stockings and muddy, heeled leather shoes; a wild, drenched woman standing in the center of a puddle like a soggy, stray cat—that might have done something to him. As she bangs on the window of his booth, the man says nothing, only watches.

Then something. He speaks. She's arrived too late. It's three minutes past hospital visiting hours. This presents an opportunity for him: solicit a bribe. "If you pay me, I'll let you see your mother," he spits. But the only thing my mother can gather from her pocket is a soggy handkerchief, her return ticket, and collected rain.

"Please let me pass," she begs. "My mother is dying in there."

He asks for a better reason.

With a smeared look of exasperation, my mother pleads. The rain catches her tears and the more she cries, the more satisfied the little man, insulated in apathy, seems to become. Then finally, the last of her energy gone, she turns around and walks home in the frozen lines of rain and the lifeless night, defeated.

Early the next morning, after staring at the ceiling all night with spring-loaded eyes, the sting of the doorbell gets my mother out of bed. A telegram from the hospital: Henrika is getting worse, she should come back and be prepared to say goodbye. Upon arriving at Mazowiecki Hospital for the second time, she finds her mother already dead on a gurney, wrapped in a white sheet in the hospital hallway. And not just dead, but parked in the middle of a lane like a broken-down automobile.

She will watch the body being lowered into the stiff soil. Her brothers, Matteo and Lolek, will be speechless; Karol will be brooding. The physics department at Jagiellonian University will have already conducted their master's degree final evaluations without her.

The next day, my mother will wear black, and again the day after that, and she'll continue to wear black for another year. After the funeral, my mother will learn she cannot resume her studies until the next year, so she will return to Maków to her mother's cottage. She will work as its new caretaker, because the men there will not.

After her mother's death, after crying herself nearly to the point of dehydration, my mother inherits what's left: the cottage, the domesticity, and the men.

She is alone. And without the complex mathematical equations and academic pressure clogging her attention, my mother quietly fills her time with soft, uncomplicated musings: Food. Laundry. Nature.

With Karol, Matteo, and Lolek off following their own bearings, Maria mashes, marinates, and pours. Inside the cottage, she mixes and spreads, creating a new landscape, an understandable, controlled environment. She builds mountains of sweet potato and pumpkin kale pie, pierogies and sauerkraut, and fields yielding harvests of *gołąbki* and hunter's stew.

She is content enough. Home is mild, benign, and, at times, pleasant. Yet, as clever as this kind of escape is, it doesn't work for long. The same activity that comforts her also lures her brothers. With their new housekeeper around, the brothers' infrequent visits to the cottage become more regular. They eat the food my mother cooks, and when they eat they drink. And when they get drunk, their excitement leads to sudden eruptions and outbursts; and when the outbursts get angry, Maria becomes the object of her drunken brothers' fury. With each visit, they vociferously berate their sister with words so unsweet and insolent they have no English translation. She does nothing. There is no one to defend her.

This is how my mother came to be what I call a Polican-American: A new school year begins and Maria returns to Jagiellonian. She gets her master's degree; she makes it to Kraków. The Communist government gives her everything she's been working toward: the teaching career, the apartment where she will hang her framed degree, a salary. Months pass; Maria settles in, but there is something missing from her Dream Come True. As she politely threads her way through the morning masses and evening trolleys, her routine feels hollow and her agenda feels like an egg-white omelet—buoyant and flavorless. To her, Kraków feels like some kind of skeleton city, as if dreariness has been spread throughout the city by osmosis.

And then, along comes 1974. The exchange rate of the American dollar is so favorable that Poles—any Pole, Poles with and without advanced degrees—immigrate to the States in hordes, taking on any and every kind of menial job (as housekeepers, house cleaners, manual laborers, nannies) to make some money. Mom's brother Matteo has moved away, married, and immigrated to Chicago. Matteo invites their brother Lolek to come to the States, but his visa application gets denied. So Matteo's wife quietly notifies my mother of the open spot, and she takes advantage of the opportunity. With the laurels of her degree and her good looks, Maria snatches the visa her brother couldn't.

My mother leaves Poland with the intention of staying only long enough to pocket a couple of thousand dollars, thinking she'll return by the year's end. She puts one foot in front of the other, and steps away from what's familiar and toward what she believes will be a brief stint abroad. What she doesn't know is that she will stay forever. And that even after she leaves Poland and arrives in the United States, she will continue to be haunted by the past.

My mother learns English by watching American soap operas. This is how I picture her: sitting in a dark and musty attic that is her first apartment in Chicago. My mother is beautiful and shy, like a deer. I can see her scooting to the edge of a crooked, quilted bed, strong legs dangling over it, Greta Garbo-face lit up from the tiny television screen. The lesson begins. *Like sands through the hourglass,* she repeats after the narrator, *so are the days of our lives.*

Shortly after arriving in the United States, Maria Magdalena Piergies lands a job as the housekeeper of a very old and very rich, pasty-faced widow in a big museum of a home on Chicago's Lake Shore Drive. During breaks, when her employer is having her nap, my mother studies English. As if her life depends on it (quite probably it does), she scribbles and struggles to keep abreast of the new language, labeling everything she's got with pieces of paper containing the vocabulary words gathered from the week's daytime television dramas.

What the hell are we going to do when we get to the executive offices, Stephano, take everybody hostage? My mother's mind is looping and stringing together new vocabulary and new phrases.

In the quiet moments, she'll recite them to herself, whispering: *Meet me at Pier 14 and come alone. That little boy will know that his mother fought hard to hold on to him. I'll distract Adam; you go to Barbara's office and seduce her.*

Shortly after leaving Kraków and landing on the tarmac of O'Hare airport, my mother had been taken in by something of a Polish welcoming committee. They looked out for my mother and helped her by putting some starter money in her pocket, by giving her directions to the necessary places, and by translating for her—because they, too, were immigrants. Suffice it to say, they'd *been there*. My uncle Matteo, who was already living in Chicago, introduced Maria to his mother-in-law, Stella, the clan's matriarch. Stella the Matriarch found my mother a place to live. Stella the Matriarch found her a job cooking and cleaning and wiping ass (if need be) and drove my mom to this new gig in a long, white Cadillac, an albino alligator. As Stella opened the alligator door and dropped Maria off at her very first day of work, she made a demand: twenty words a day. "If you want to survive in this country," Stella told her, "you must learn twenty English words a day."

It is a while before Mom can trust herself to speak the new language in front of others, particularly Americans, partly out of fear, and partly because of her stubborn determination to master a vast and impressive range of vocabulary skills before she puts them to use. The new words will come slowly, starting with a timid conversation at the corner grocery store about the sponges and paper towels she purchases; then she will work her way to a full-blown interview at Presbyterian/St. Luke's—the hospital where she will research pulmonary medicine in the radiology department—put her physics degree to good use, and meet my father, who will be in his final months as a medical resident.

On the weekends, all the immigrants gather at Stella's apartment to cook and eat and talk up a flurry about Polish politics and this strange new land. My mother will join them, and one day, she'll even bring my father, who will quickly realize that Mom's life—and the life of the immigrant—is difficult. That people judge her, and treat her poorly because she is different. She has a shy disposition, which is often interpreted as being stuck-up. But my mother is tough, cautious, thrifty, and she fends for herself. She explains to my father what the workplace is like for a female immigrant. She shows him how a woman deals with it, how she endures. Because starting from scratch in a big city isn't easy. Because even a master's degree in physics from Jagiellonian University ("the Harvard of Poland," as my mom still calls it) won't guarantee you a decent living in the land of the free, home of the brave.

But now it is twenty years later and Maria's youngest daughter is in the kitchen of her restaurant, peeling shrimp that will be served at her Uncle Matteo's wedding dinner tonight. Uncle Matteo and his fiancée are nowhere to be found, and the wedding was supposed to start an hour ago. Somehow, and miraculously, the minister doesn't bail. We wait and wait, picking almond pebbles off the Roquefort grapes until finally, nearly two hours tardy, Uncle Matteo and Vladka burst through the back door to the restaurant, sharply dressed, eager to wed, and awkwardly late to their own wedding without even a phone call or a made-up excuse. The rest of us look at one another for a leaden moment until Dad clears the air, suggesting we get the show on the road before the food gets stale.

I stand next to an old grandfather clock and when I'm given the cue, I slip my violin under my chin and start churning out "Jesu, Joy of Man's Desiring" all by myself, even though it's a piece for four or more instruments that requires at least two to sound halfway decent, and I still don't know how to make vibrato. Also, my fingers smell like shrimp. Through an oval mirror, I see the faces of my cousins Marek and Maya. They're expressionless as they watch their father tie the knot for the second time to a woman who isn't their mother. Throughout the brief ceremony, Mom sports an unnatural smile, sad as the blues.

I'm dispatched into the kitchen where my mother is cloaked in an apron and plating Beef Wellington. In assembly-line fashion, she hands the plate to my sister, Sabina, who plates sautéed peppers, then hands the plate to me, and I carry the hot dish very carefully into the dining room and slide it onto the table in front of each member of the wedding: ladies first, serve from the left, remove from the right. After the meal is eaten, we clear the plates and cut the cake (flourless orange chocolate rum); and after the cake, it's business as usual: Jules and I clear the dishes, Dad washes, Sabina dries.

Mom is standing on the back porch, sipping on a glass of wine when Marek enters the kitchen looking for her. "Aunt Maria, my dad wants you," Marek says. Mom tips back the glass, polishing off her wine, and mutters, "Dat man will push me to my grave." Mom pushes through the kitchen door and I trail her into the dining room. As I pick off the used napkins from the dinner table plates, I watch my new aunt tip her head back, laughing as my uncle turns to my mom. "Marisha," he says. "*Proszę*, sister, do me one more thing? Go get me some more—" And before he can finish his sentence, and with eyes looking mad and vulnerable, Mom answers, "Yes?" and goes back into the kitchen to bring out more wine.

My mother has always had a habit of giving too much of herself, so often and to such an extent that she harms herself in pleasing others. She puts herself last. She makes sacrifices, sometimes too many. She strains and works so hard to make people happy. Then she'll renounce her compassion, and declare that she's going to stop putting others first, that she'll take care of herself and herself only. She always relapses. This peculiarity is sort of a trait running in our family—the stubborn vices of guilt and pride. I see it in her. She doesn't see this about herself and I have yet to recognize it in myself.

Years later, I will wonder what difference it would have made if she had learned English from something other than a soap opera. What if she had simply set her TV to another channel, like *The Price Is Right*, or an infomercial, or *Mister Rogers' Neighborhood*? Could a different program have altered the way she spoke, influenced her way of seeing the world, the way of seeing her place in it? Could a different channel have changed the kind of woman she became and, in turn, raised me to be? Would turning the dial on the tube have set us all in a different motion?

Maybe these traits would have been passed on to me regardless, maybe not. But one thing is clear: anyone, any Pole, Kenyan, Korean, anyone who learns English through the dialogue of soap operas develops very potent diction, and an intense way of looking at the universe. And the fact that my mother's sharp-accented English comes out of her mouth slightly butchered only adds a more dramatic flair to it all. Soap opera plots are beyond realistic; their storylines generally circumnavigate amnesiacs, resurrections from the dead, cheating lovers, and switched paternity tests. An episode can switch between several themes at a time and intersect with other narratives by chance meetings, coincidences, missed meetings, and last-minute rescues. They're like tapestries that never end. When one thread ends, there is always another that slithers in, before you've even fully made sense of the one that came before it.

six

June. New York City.

I'm next in line to see Dr. Reich for a checkup. I'm hopeful that she can get me out of here in time to meet Andrew during his lunch break. We're going to ride our bikes to Chinatown, and if we're lucky, we'll return with two white-gold wedding bands that are within our budget. Then he'll be back at work before his lunch hour is over. I've never sat in Phillips Family Practice's waiting room for less than an hour before making it into the examination room. And once you make it to the exam room, you wait again. Dr. Reich told me that a patient of hers once drew a giant mural covering the entire exam room wall while he waited to be seen. When Danya finally knocked on the door, the guy was nowhere to be seen but left in his place a

colossal pencil sketch of a human skeleton sitting on an examination table with his skull in his phalanges and a handwritten
caption: *You will die before you are ever seen at Phillips Family
Practice.*

Twelve weeks pregnant. Things are blossoming so quickly, life
is moving along so steadily, so seamlessly that I almost can't recognize I am any different than I was before. But I know things
have changed: the size of my torso, the volume of my uterus,
my feelings toward being pregnant. There is a flicker of joy in
me somewhere, slowly growing more intense by the day. Underneath all the anxiety, I know somewhere there is joy and love
ahead. But it's hard to be joyful when you're still just getting
used to the idea of the cost of daycare or when you know you've
shocked the hell out of your parents, and there are probably
points throughout the day when they think about you and your
situation and cry alone, secretly, then quickly move on to other
things.

I like my doctor but I hate where she works. Andrew and I
picked this place because it was one of the few Medicaid options,
and because they have sliding-scale fees. It's what we can afford.
It's what everyone can afford. You don't need health insurance or
loads of money to see someone here. Well, maybe some money,
and those bills will come later. Andrew originally found Phillips
because it was close to his office and easy to get a last-minute
appointment, because most of the appointments here are walk-
ins. The place doesn't have much of a system or order. Even if
you did make an appointment, there is no guarantee you will
be seen. Rather, there's a slim chance you'll be seen by a medical

specialist and a strong likelihood that both the clinic and your place of employment—if you're employed—will close up shop before you even make it into an examination room. Andrew and I briefly considered going elsewhere but haven't done much research, mostly because we're planning on going in another direction: skip the medical facilities all together.

A few weeks ago, we watched a documentary about the business of being born, and it asked us, *Should most births be viewed as a natural life process, or should every delivery be treated as a potentially catastrophic medical emergency?* The film made me realize that I'd like to do things the natural way—no painkillers, no C-section, no epidural. Maybe a home birth, maybe in the bathtub. Maybe a midwife or a doula. But we haven't gotten to that stage yet. I'm still in the first trimester. I am waiting to pass into the safety zone of the pregnancy before I make better plans. I imagine after the ultrasound will be a good time to start looking for doulas. So we'll keep going here for now, or maybe we'll stay here until the end—who knows? I like Dr. Reich. I don't want to insult her.

Like most of the doctors at this office, Danya is doing her residency, and she tells me that, like me, she's getting tired of the place, too. It's wearing her out. "Don't I look haggard?" she asks me each time I see her, but she doesn't. Even though she's almost over the hill, Dr. Reich is as youthful and spirited as a college basketball player. She's alert, and her mouth is always open and slightly turned up in a smirk. "This place sucks," she whispers during our appointments. She says it's lessening her desire to be a doctor, making her feel less compassionate.

I've been here since 10:15 this morning. My appointment was scheduled for 10:30. It's almost 11:20. I am pregnant. I am hormonal. I'm trying very hard to be Zen, to do that thing where you step out of your body and take a look at the thoughts running through your mind and consider them as objects just passing by—labeling them as "thoughts and thoughts only" and not getting attached to them—but right now it's very difficult to step out of my body because I just cannot get over my body. Right now, my body is a completely foreign terrain of which I'm both terrified and in awe. It is in constant flux, and although Andrew is amazed by my breast size, I still feel like it's a joke, or a fluke. I don't have control of anything. It's like I'm trying to catch the wind. The morning sickness has subsided a little, but mostly because it's been trumped by heartburn. I'm hungry, but can never decide what I want to eat because I know it's something specific, but there are too many things that it's *not*, and only one thing that I do desire. I don't know who to talk to about this—I still feel embarrassed to talk about it with my mother, and I have no pregnant friends. They are all aspiring academics, and they are all on summer vacation. I'm just figuring this out on my own. I don't want anyone to see me come off as unsure, I don't want to complain, and I don't want to draw attention to myself. Here's what I did recently: I added new items to the list of foods and smells that make me nauseous: broccoli, Andrew's breath, oranges, Greek food. And what I want to eat: tacos, peanut butter ice cream, potatoes.

Andrew and I are also in the process of putting our lives together. We're still getting to know each other while we're buying baby books. We are students, coworkers, teammates. We're having sex a little, but in the back of my mind I can sense that I am not comfortable. Part of me feels that there isn't much of a point to it now, and part of me feels that we have a third party that is too young to be exposed to it. Part of me imagines that he might poke the baby inside me. It's a bizarre notion that makes just as much sense as my desire for taffy, but still. Part of me doesn't recognize what sex is anymore, what it *means*. It has taken on a completely different meaning.

My wardrobe has started shrinking. I'm having trouble fitting into my clothes and this upsets me. It's like my pants have a vendetta. Luckily school is out of session; I have no reason to dress up for anything or impress anyone. Summer in New York and all one really needs is a thin dress and plenty of water to remain cool and calm. I have my water and I'm trying to remain cool and calm, but right now everyone is pushing my buttons. Like this guy next to me in the waiting room. He's talking loudly on his cell phone. I get angry, I get mean. I ask myself, how can someone pay for a cell phone when he can't even afford medical bills? He is talking as if we're in the middle of a construction site. This is what I have learned about him: he recently passed a kidney stone ("the most painful fucking thing in the world, man"). I know and the rest of the waiting room knows what his urine looked like when he passed it. We know the last time he pooped, and we know what that looked like as well. I want to tell him to shut his mouth, have some respect, and that he has no idea what giving birth feels like, so suck it up. But then again, neither do I.

"Mr. Ross?" A nurse appears and calls the name. I look around the waiting room, wishing Andrew were sitting here with me, but I remind myself that I don't want to be a bother, a nag, weak, too dependent. We're not even married yet. "Is there a Mr. Ross next in line?" the nurse asks but gets no response. I'm hoping Mr. Ross just gave up and left. "Mr. Ross?" she repeats. And then, from behind the bathroom right next to her, a voice calls out, "I'M GOING TO THE BATHROOM!" It's the kidney stone guy. *"Jeeeeezus,"* Mr. Ross says, "just hold your horses, lady." The toilet flushes.

11:40 A.M. Twenty minutes before I am supposed to meet Andrew in Union Square and I've just now made it into the exam room. Soon, I'll be meeting Andrew in the same spot where we first met six months ago. Since then, we've spent most of our "courtship" in the waiting room of a doctor's office. We discuss the delivery more than our pending marriage. We have an obstetrician but no wedding planner, and I'm wondering if I've spent more times in this office than I have on dates with my fiancé, getting to know the father of this baby. I don't even know what he thinks about God, or Christmas, or nursing homes, or rodeos. It's during these life minutes I spend waiting in this doctor's office that I loathe the fairy-tale ideal of marriage the most. It's in this waiting room that I often feel sorry for myself, realize what I'm doing, then immediately make myself stop. We are talking about a baby here.

At 11:55 A.M. Danya is finally able to see me. She explains that around this time, the fingernails and toenails begin to appear. The eyelids, arms, and legs are formed. The larynx is beginning to form in the trachea.

"The voice box?" I ask Danya, wondering what the baby's voice might sound like someday. Wondering if we'll have a boy or a girl. Wondering if she'll be a scatterbrained artist like me, or an organized engineer like her father.

"Exactly," she says. "The trachea is the voice box."

She explains more: All of the major organs and body systems are forming. They can be damaged if your baby is exposed to drugs, radiation, tobacco, and chemical and toxic substances.

"I'm not doing much of anything other than eating a lot of ice cream," I say.

I remember my mother telling me once that during her pregnancy with my sister, she ate a banana split every single day. Sabina turned out fine. "An abundance of ice cream is okay, right?"

"Ice cream is perfectly fine. You're pretty much all set to leave now, but before you make like a fetus and head out," Dr. Reich says, "I need you to take a urinalysis for me."

I sigh. Another step to complete before I can get out of here. Another task to cram in. I'm going to be late to meet Andrew; purchasing the wedding rings will have to be even more rushed.

"We just have to test for infection, sugar, and protein. Even though the organs and body systems are fully formed by the end of twelve weeks," Danya says, "the fetus cannot survive independently," and hands me the cup.

If Chinatown were an amusement park (which it could be: bright banners, plastic toys, and fried foods), Canal Street would be the bumper-car ride. The tunnel-bound traffic on Canal clogs the road and dumps smog into the air. Like it's a game, drivers honk and threaten one another as they inch forward toward the entrance of the Holland Tunnel.

"Do you know the engineer of that tunnel died in Battle Creek?" I shout to Andrew. He's several feet ahead of me and I'm not sure if he can hear me or not. I pedal faster and continue: "Clifford Milburn Holland. They renamed the tunnel after him after he had a heart attack on the operating table. He was getting a tonsillectomy."

I follow Andrew's fearless lead as he dodges aggressive trucks and whips past taxis until they, too, get trapped in the traffic jam like the rest of the gas-guzzlers. "Hey! Did you know the baby's voice box is forming, right now, right as we speak?" I yell ahead. I pedal faster but I can't keep up with him. He's going too fast, zipping through lights seconds before they turn red.

"Andrew!" I yell as I tighten the brakes on my bike. "You're running through all the red lights."

"I don't want to be late to work," he answers.

"I'm not you, okay? I'm pregnant. I'm not you."

"Sorry. I forgot, okay?" he says, pedaling ahead again.

This bike trip to Chinatown will be our second attempt at finding wedding bands, and at this point we are impatient. Our enthusiasm is gone and we are not even picky. It feels like we have trekked all around the world just to find something we can afford. Last week, we traveled to Little India in Jackson Heights, Queens, looking for rings. It was a Sunday. The air was hot as hell, humid and thick with incense and bus exhaust. On one particular drag in Jackson Heights,

almost every other storefront is a 22-karat gold jewelry shop.
They sell golden molds of nearly everything. As Andrew and
I walked up and down the strip looking for *white* gold, not
yellow gold, I saw golden statues of deities—Shiva, Ganesh,
Durga, and other Hindu figures. "Good deal for you," store
owners beckoned from their doorways. "Cheap price on deities. Cheap price for you."

My name is a deity. One time I went to get my eyebrows
threaded by an Indian woman at a salon on Fulton and Flat-
bush Avenue in Brooklyn. The woman's name was Rita, and
when I told her mine, she asked how I got it. I didn't know.
Whenever I ask my mother how she chose Mira, she gives me
a different answer. Sometimes she says she chose it because it
means "sweet and sour"—"because dat is what you are." Sometimes my mother says she chose it because it's just a pretty name,
or because it means "prosperous." When I look up my name, I
find different explanations. *Mir* means "peace" in Russian. And
there's Mira, the name given to a red giant star, an estimated
two hundred to four hundred light years away in the constellation Cetus, which is more popularly known as The Whale.
There's also the Spanish verb *mira*, which means "to look." Rita
on Fulton Street told me that I share my name with a famous
Indian mystic.

"Mirabai," she said. "She is the incarnation of Radha."

"Who is Radha?" I asked.

"Radha is the main companion of Krishna."

"And what's Krishna's story?"

"Krishna is the reincarnation of Vishnu," Rita said.

"Who is Vishnu?"

"Vishnu is the preserver of the universe," she explained, "while Brahma is its creator and Shiva is the destroyer."

"Brahma and Shiva?"

"Let me just tell you about Mira," she said.

The story, according to Rita, is this: *There was an Indian mystic, poet, and saint by the name of Mirabai, born many, many years ago in the village Kurkhi, near Merta, a small state in Marwar, Rajasthan. It is said that when Mira was a very young girl, looking out her window, she witnessed a marriage procession passing by in front of her home. There were painted elephants, flowers, music—a beautiful parade carrying a finely dressed bridegroom. And when Mira saw the bridegroom in the wedding procession, she asked her mother very innocently, Mother, who is that?*

That is the bridegroom, Mira's mother replied.

Where is my bridegroom? Mira asked.

Her mother smiled, pointed at a picture of Sri Krishna, and said, jokingly, My dear Mira, this is the image of your bridegroom. Lord Krishna is yours.

Shortly after, Mira's mother died, and as Mira grew up, her desire to be with Krishna grew intensely. Through an arranged marriage, Mira wed Bhoj Raj, a prince, but she refused to commit herself to her husband. Instead, she spent more and more of her time praying to Krishna. This was not considered appropriate behavior for a woman. Mira rebelled and became a bhakti, devoted to Krishna and rejecting traditional customs and material wealth. There were three attempts on her life made by her in-laws, so Mira fled and became a wandering mystic. Legend has it that eventually her in-laws found her and forcefully detained her. But before she was taken back to their home, Mira asked to be allowed to spend one last night in a temple with an image of Krishna. The next morning, when they came to fetch her, the doors had to be broken down, for they were locked from within, and Mirabai had disappeared, nowhere to be found.

"How's this one, Mira?" Andrew asks, extending his ring finger.

We are in the first jewelry shop that we saw in Chinatown. It's 12:45, Andrew is late to work, glancing at the ring, then at the clock. It makes me feel rushed, and makes me feel wrong for not rushing, not wanting to hurry. "Sure, they're just rings," I say for him. We are the only two customers here and the women behind the counter are very excited, either for us or for themselves.

"Or this one?"

"Sure. Looks good to me," I answer. "Go for it," I tell him, but I still haven't found the right one yet: something simple, unassuming, and real. The size, the metal, the maker—none of that is really important to me.

"Try this on," the store clerk says to me, handing me a dime-colored circle. I slip it around my ring finger. A little loose but a good enough fit. Lately, my hands have been swelling up.

"This is good for you," she decides and I agree. The ring doesn't have to be anything spectacular; it's just a ring. No big deal. The hardest stuff is past us: we're not a secret anymore. I love this man, and I'm pretty sure that's all I need. That, and an affordable band. From here on out, this is what I am looking for: simple, unassuming, solid, and real. This will do just fine.

"Check this one out," I say to Andrew, showing him my hand. It's not what I'd imagined, but I'll take it. "Look at this one," I say. "Look."

seven

We are in a cab headed straight to Phillips Family Practice from LaGuardia after spending Fourth of July weekend with my parents in Michigan. Andrew and I left New York with the hope of starting and then knocking out our list of wedding tasks in just two days in Battle Creek. We accomplished our tasks and I felt good about it. But right before we left Michigan, while I was in my bedroom packing up my suitcase for our trip back, Dr. Reich called to tell me she found a blip in my blood test—something about abnormal hormone levels. "Really, nothing to be worried about," Danya had said; she just wanted to let me know. But still, I was worried.

"It's a common thing," my dad said when he and my mom dropped us off at the Kalamazoo Airport. "The results of these tests are never perfect. This happens to my pregnant patients often."

My father is a caring man and a respectable man. He's a man who kisses his patients on their foreheads, a man who makes frequent stops when we are out on a jog to pick up trash on the side of the road. Out of guilt, I'll follow his lead, and by the time we're back home, we'll have accumulated armfuls of discarded soda cans, baby diapers, and empty Doritos bags.

My father told me not to fret about the abnormal results. But even he couldn't calm me. I was frantic. I began to cry. I thought maybe it was my fault—maybe I forgot to take my folic acid one morning, maybe I was too stressed and cantankerous and it was poisonous to the baby. Maybe I wasn't being sweet and motherly enough. "If it's nothing then why am I crying?" I'd asked as we got out of the car and said goodbye to my parents.

"Welcome to the worried world of being a parent," my dad said before they drove away. "Believe me, it gets worse."

The days before we left Michigan, Andrew and I had been triumphant: first, a successful pursuit of the Reverend Al Schipper, the chaplain from the hospital where my father works. Even though my parents raised me Catholic and tithed a good portion of their income, neither my parents nor I could find a single priest to officiate our wedding— and not because I was four months pregnant. It was because Andrew and I hoped to be married outside of the Catholic Church. "Outside" as in out of doors, on the earth, on top of grass, under divine trees and a yawning sky. No priest, not even the man who gave me my First Holy Communion and performed funerals of loved ones, would marry us because of this. The outdoors was too wild.

But Reverend Schipper willingly agreed to officiate our wedding. He wanted to talk to us first, to be sure our desire to marry was legitimate. Andrew and I met him in a ketchup-and-mashed-potato-scented cafeteria in the basement of Battle Creek Community Hospital. Reverend Schipper had a white beard and a rosy complexion, and wore a pine-colored fleece. He asked us some questions, questions about ourselves—if we had any favorite Bible verses or poems or lyrics—then outlined the order of the ceremony on the back of a paper tablecloth. He said he could really see that we loved one another, "but I can tell you one thing about marriage: it's not going to be easy. I've been married for thirty-some odd years and believe you me, I know." Then he asked if we ever turn to the Higher Power when we need guidance.

"Do you belong to a church or some kind of spiritual community?"

I sank in my chair a little. I was prepping a shotgun wedding at warp speed, and not counting Christmas Eve service with my parents, I hadn't been to a church service in three years. It had been on my list of things to do, but I hadn't found the right congregation. I knew it would do me some good. I had noticed a change in my ability to center myself and remain calm since I had stopped attending, but the last time I went to church, I just couldn't get into it. Something about the robed white man calling God a "he" felt funny and distracting. I was struck by the image of a pasty Caucasian sitting on a cloud, judging us as we judged each other, and how strange it was that I had accepted that for so long.

Andrew responded to Reverend Schipper's question by talking about his volunteer work every Monday night chopping vegetables at a place in SoHo called God's Love We Deliver. But it wasn't a religious affiliation, just a charity. Then the reverend replied that being a Boy Scout wasn't going to do much good when the shit really hit the fan, and before the boys could take it any further, I squashed it.

"We're currently looking for the right spiritual community," I said, smiling firmly and squeezing the top of Andrew's knee, "and we go hiking in the woods a lot."

We had just about two months to plan our wedding. We didn't have a wedding planner, so my mother and I teamed up. The two of us booked a string quartet from Kalamazoo made up of former college classmates of mine, got a caterer from the nearby town of Climax, and then my childhood best friend, Amanda, picked me up from my parents' house and drove me to the Crossroads Mall in Kalamazoo, where I chose the least expensive bridesmaid dresses and a matron of honor gown for her that didn't make her feel uncomfortable and "fat." "Fat?" I retaliated as I buckled myself into her Toyota. "Try pushing down vomit while browsing the Internet with your Catholic mother to find a maternity wedding dress," I said.

Every detail I worked through for my wedding felt terribly awkward, like I had done something wrong but there was no way to apologize. My mother had me type a dozen or so word combinations into a search engine on her computer to relocate a dress she'd found on her own for me a week or so after I told her I was pregnant. I typed in the words "maternity wedding gown," "pregnant bridal dress," and "alternative wedding dresses," and, eventually, the one Mom had scouted out popped up on a website from a maternity boutique in Australia.

If you knew my mother, even superficially, you'd know that she is Polish, that she is thrifty, and that she is direct. Maria Ptacin is a woman who puts sour cream on sunburns and makes you leave it on after it begins to stink. She is a woman who will return french fries at the McDonald's drive-through if they do not meet her standards. A woman who, despite the humiliated pleas of her children in the backseat to just *let it go*, will circle her minivan around the restaurant again (most likely hopping up and over a curb), lean into the drive-through speaker, and explain in a shrill Eastern European accent that she asked for her fries to be piping hot, paid for her fries to be piping hot, but was given fries that were not piping hot. Those fries may have only cost her forty-nine cents, but those were forty-nine cents my mother had worked hard to earn. If she was going to hand her money over to someone—in this case, an oily-faced sixteen-year-old with gray dirt under his fingernails—she would make damn well sure she got the very best french fries Battle Creek, Michigan, had to offer. Meanwhile, my siblings and I ate our tepid fries in the backseat, flavored with embarrassment and muted admiration.

When I was ten years old, my family took a two-week trip to Europe. We started in Poland, my mother's motherland, first traveling to Maków, the town where she was born. We picked wild strawberries off the fence surrounding her childhood cottage, and went hunting for morels in a nearby forest. We visited her parents. The cemetery was lush with overgrown shrubs and difficult to navigate, so the five of us pulled dandelions and crabgrass until we found the right grave. It was a small, silver tombstone that popped out like a Chiclet from the grassy, green lawn. It read *Karol Piergies Henrika Piergies* in faded letters and was speckled with moss. We scraped and raked and polished that headstone with our bare hands and the spit from our mouths, and I remember that my mom said very little. I don't even think we prayed.

We drove to Kraków to visit her brother Lolek, a car salesman, and his wife Ala. They served us sausage and Ritz crackers and butter and Fanta, and my mother got to have an actual conversation in her native tongue, which she hadn't been able to do for years. My siblings and I played with my uncle's cats and listened to my cousin Magda's Gloria Estefan tapes on a rug in the next room, but I kept my eyes on my mother. I couldn't understand Polish or what she was saying, but I remember that she spoke in a guarded fashion, and her tone was conservative. My father stood next to her, arms crossed, listening intently to them speaking in their native tongue, chiming in when he thought he understood what was being said. Mom was solemn and less joyful than I was used to. She seemed so vulnerable. It was the first time in my life that I realized that my mother had once been a child.

On that European vacation, we depended on my mom much more than usual. Even my dad did. She spoke the language,

she knew the culture, she was our guide. This was her country.
How badly I hadn't wanted to go on that trip, how I worried
that my friends would forget about me while I was gone. I hated
my mom for making me go, but once we were in Europe, I felt
ashamed. I felt like one of those "stupid Americans" I'd heard
her so often speak about. The McDonald's Culture. That's what
she called it.

After Poland, we went to Italy. One night, our *Fodor's Travel*
guide led us to an Italian restaurant with the most delicious
spaghetti carbonara but the least pleasant waitress. She did not
like Americans. She reeked of contempt, practically throwing
the menus down onto our table. She seated us outside, then
proceeded to ignore us. The weather grew cooler outside, and
then cold, but my mother insisted we ride it out. The longer we
waited for water, for wine, for silverware, the more the tension
grew. But my mom dug in her heels. That European waitress
did not like my European mother's family, but my mother was
not going to let her win. So we waited. And waited. The food
finally arrived and we ate quickly. Mom had us order dessert.
Once we finished and paid for our meal and were leaving to
go back to our hostel, Mom stopped suddenly, remembering
she'd forgotten something back at her seat. We all turned to
look back at her. Her broad back. The small, white lightbulbs
on the wicker awning surrounding her like stars. The dark sky
above. We stood there and watched as she returned to the table,
reached for the unfinished glass of wine she'd been drinking,
and with a silent but palpable anger, lifted and poured its red
contents across the white linen tablecloth. Then she calmly set

the glass back down in its place and returned to us, said nothing, grabbed my hand, and led us away.

My mother takes her money and her food seriously because her money and her food—really, her *sustenance*—have been hard earned. She has labored. She has suffered. She has a rope-thick callus of work ethic. It does not matter if you're in Italy or at the McDonald's drive-through. What matters is *principle*. "How you do sometimes is how you do all the time" is what she likes to say.

My mother is also a sophisticated and complicated woman, practically impossible to decode. For example: Despite having retired over ten years ago from owning and operating a restaurant, and despite there now being only two mouths to feed at home, she still keeps four fully stocked refrigerators in her house. Whatever she can't fit in the refrigerators, she stores on top of the two doghouses in the garage. Whatever doesn't fit on top of the doghouses, she will put out on the deck. And if there still isn't a place to store the food, she might put it on a fancy plate, garnish it with chopped parsley from her garden, cover it in aluminum foil, and deliver it to one of the neighbors as a gift.

And those are just the perishables. The dry goods that don't fit in the kitchen cabinets will hibernate in the downstairs laundry room, the wine cellar, Dad's workbench. At least twice a year, my mother will send identical care packages to my sister and me with a combination of boxed quinoa, oatmeal, wine, a personalized clip-art card that she and my dad made on the computer, a bundle of neon-colored anklet socks, unsweetened baking chocolate, and on occasion, vegetables—like three green peppers, which will have already begun to rot by the time we fetch our care packages from the post office.

The food hoarding bothers me. I'm a minimalist. I hate waste. I need order. Shoes neatly in a row. Squeezing always from the bottom of the toothpaste. Books organized by color. Chairs always tucked into the table. Folded fitted sheets. White holiday lights. I live by deadlines. Expiration dates. Control. Often, the entropy within my mother's four refrigerators paralyzes me. Like when I come home to visit and just want a quick bite to eat, I'll open one of the refrigerators, stare at nothing in particular, then close the door. I'll repeat this several times: open, stare, close. Unless you enjoy snacking on mango chutney or raw Brussels sprouts, there are no ready-to-eat things in my mother's kitchen. "Snacks" are an American concept. You want a meal? You go make yourself a meal, a *real* meal. It's all in there. Just dig around. But I am overcome by choice, so I just eat stale water crackers dipped in chutney.

However, if it's Christmastime and I'm preparing my Dad's birthday cake—my father shares a birthday with Jesus—I never have to run to the grocery store. Thanks to my mother, we have all the ingredients for anything. Molasses, pistachios, dried cherries, buttermilk? Check. Spumoni *bûche de Noël*? Done. My mother's kitchen, which has tentacles extending through the entire house, is fully stocked. She has prepared us for blizzards, tornadoes, heat waves, post-funeral potlucks, forgotten anniversaries, unexpected dinner guests. Yes, 40 percent of the "pieces" in the fridge are spoiling and blanketed by velvety green mold, but how is that any different than having a garden? My mother, as usual, has everything covered.

Depending on how you look at it, one of us is being logical and one of us is being neurotic, but it doesn't really matter who's what. After years of arguments about those damn refrigerators, I've finally let the issue go. I've come to terms with the fact that I cannot persuade my mother to get rid of at least two of the refrigerators and donate them to a homeless shelter or soup kitchen, just as I can't convince her—I mean, *my mother* (she will not let us address her as "her")—to join my father and my sister and my husband and me in our vegetarianism. Sure, my mother loves to cook. Sure, she is not a terribly neat person. Sure, her excuses are plausible ("Why drive fifteen miles to the grocery store and waste gas and an hour to pick up a few things when everything can already be here?"), just as mine are ("What's the point of all that wasted electricity and those watery bags of decomposing baby carrots?"). We have debated it more times than I can count, each time the dispute ending with my mother's reminder that this is her house, and if I don't like it, then I can leave. End of story. But at the end of the day, what we both comprehend is this: the four refrigerators are not about avoiding a trip to the store or saving gas or time. They have to do with the Poland of her youth. They have to do with standing in line once a week for over an hour to *possibly* get a chicken. They have to do with fear: of not having enough, of losing what you have, of things falling apart. With those damn four refrigerators, in her own way, my mother is defending and protecting us.

The wedding dress she picked out for me was a beautiful

white gown that looked like it belonged to a Greek goddess or an angel, regardless of the fact it was a maternity dress. I was surprisingly pleased with my mother's choice. Before, when I'd typed in the key words that described my current situation—"maternity wedding gown"—the experience of hunting for a wedding dress with my mother felt less cathartic than I imagined something like this would. It felt more like confronting the cold, hard, frightening fact that this wasn't the type of wedding we had planned, or had much time to plan. "And it's only three hundred dollars!" we later cheered to my father as he handed us the credit card. "Only?" he'd responded. "How much do those things usually cost? Like, the normal ones?"

More than feeling pregnant, I couldn't shake feeling guilty. No one in particular was making me feel this way—my mother called me all the time with her favorite baby names (Louisa, Camilla, Will, Brogan) and rejected the ones I suggested (Harper, Harry, Oscar, Theo); we narrowed it down and agreed on Lilly or Henry.

My parents also arranged a weekend trip to meet Andrew's parents, and the four of them made a baby tote bag with their handprints on it. They picked out their grandparent names and gave us a framed picture of the four of them. Our families finally seemed excited about the new addition and were finally showing us. The night of July 4th, my mother pulled me aside and told me that this was a good thing: "Finally!" she said. "Finally, something good is coming into our lives. Not a funeral, but a baby! No more news of death or dying for once!"

My parents' support made me feel somewhat better, maybe

even proud, but something still felt dissonant. I didn't feel the pregnant-mother glow I had heard about from others, and I still hadn't felt the baby move. I hadn't seen any images of the baby, either. It didn't feel real, and I was waiting for this feeling so I could believe it and start getting excited.

Right on time, straight from LaGuardia, the cab drops us off in Union Square, at the steps in front of Phillips Family Practice. Even though Dr. Reich said that I didn't have to come in for this and that it's probably really nothing to worry about, I just want to hear her tell us that in person. I need to read her face when she explains exactly what she found.

"Are you worried? I'm not worried. Are you worried?" I ask as I close the door to the exam room and slouch into a chair.

"I'm sure it's nothing," Andrew says, standing above me, his chest straight, offering a hearty, masculine reassurance. "Even if there was, what can we do about it right now?" he says, then begins opening up drawers and digging through cabinets and pulling out rubber gloves.

A knock on the door and in comes Dr. Reich. "Well, well, well," she says. "If it isn't Mr. and Mrs. America."

"Hey, Danya." Andrew snaps a rubber glove around his wrist. "I asked the nurse who took Mira's blood pressure who her favorite doctor at the clinic was."

"Oh yeah? What'd she say?" Dr. Reich and I look at each other and roll our eyes.

"Well, it wasn't you," Andrew continues. "But do you want to know who it is anyway?"

Dr. Reich explains her findings: "Just a little bit of elevated alpha-fetoprotein levels, nothing too unusual, nothing you've done wrong." But this alarms me.

I'd been seeing the world through a haze of guilt and regret and extreme superstition. Since becoming pregnant, I'd been interpreting things in a new way—not quite from the perspective of a parent. Not quite that. But from the perspective of my parents. Or *any* parent. How awful it must be to constantly worry about the safety of your child—even before your child is born, and then be conscious of the fragility of your child's life for the years and years that follow. To wonder whether or not you're being a good parent. If your behavior, your actions, your inactions, your thoughts, the karma of your past was shaping your child's life.

I was a rude daughter; I knew I'd been that to my parents. I'd been a terrible teenager. I ran away all the time. How terrible it must've felt for them to lose control. To have a child take the independence they so yearned for. What it would feel like to essentially lose your child. This realization, and the realization of the part I played in their particularly painful parenthood, nearly paralyzed me with fear. What a fool I'd been.

As Danya talks to us, fragments of my youth begin to bubble to the surface of my brain: I am fifteen years old and in the car with Mom, Sabina, and Jules. We're puttering down Raymond Road, a shabby, gray stretch of potholed pavement that runs past Cornwell's Turkeyville & Dinner Theatre and an old cornflakes cereal factory. To the left, there's the Optimist Club, a senior picture photography studio, a Beanie Babies outlet, and Mount Ever Rest Cemetery. To the right we have a train depot, a trailer park, Hots Gentlemen's Club, and litter—lots of litter, like empty McDonald's bags and broken 40-oz. malt liquor bottles. And a few doors down from Hots, perched atop a hump of dead grass and patches of brown mud is a little yellow house with four tinted windows and a sign out front that reads: HAPPY SPA.

Jules and I rib jab each other and attempt to make risqué jokes; the Happy Spa is the launching pad for our one-dimensional puns.

"They say it rubs people the wrong way," says Jules.

"Hands down, they've got all you *knead*!" I say.

Sabina rolls her eyes. And Mom, gripping the wheel of our Chrysler minivan, furiously threatens to write a letter to the community board. "It is not okay," she says. "What happens to those women is not okay."

Every time we drive past the Happy Spa, Mom's heart seems to sink, as if the massage parlor were a personal insult. Something about the place upsets her, bothers her more than it bothers other people—she sees parts of herself in those women. Women who have fought to move forward, but who were now stuck. But there is little she or anyone can do. The entire stretch of I-94 from Kalamazoo to Detroit has more of these "Oriental massage parlors" than gas stations. The Velvet Touch. The Lion's Den. China Garden. They're like dandelions: when one gets crushed, another pops up. And we all know what's going on in there. The local police, the community board, even my Old World, Catholic mother knows what a "happy ending" is. Any place that claims to be an "exotic massage parlor" is really just a place that gives rub-'n'-tugs, and probably more.

She is driving us to my orchestra rehearsal. My high school is performing *Man of La Mancha*, a musical about the mad knight Don Quixote and I'm the concertmistress. They're expecting me to direct the string section tonight, but that's not gonna happen. Once my mom drops me off at W. K. Auditorium, I'm going to leave. After depositing me, she'll take Jules to football practice, then Sabina to Science Olympiad, then head back to her restaurant to work for a couple of hours, assuming we are all getting rides home like we said we would. Mom will leave RSVP around 9 P.M., drive home, go into the kitchen and reheat dinner—leftovers from the restaurant—because by 9:30, Dad, Bean, Jules, and I are expected to be scooting our chairs closer to the dinner table, taking hold of each other's hands, bowing our heads, and saying grace before we begin another late-night dinner of lobster bisque and whole-wheat rolls. But I won't be there. Nobody knows this yet, not even me, but soon, I will thrust myself forward and keep on running and nothing will ever be the same. I will run away.

Looking in the rearview mirror with eyes both sympathetic and angry, my mother declares, "The Happy Spa is slave quarters." I don't quite get what she means by that—*slave quarters*. Why so dramatic? Why so offended? Why can't she just laugh at these kinds of things like everyone else? I don't understand because I'm still a kid, a girl in her first bloom of adolescence. I am wild and unworldly, inexperienced and addled with hormones. A moist constellation of youth.

My response: "You *knot* like a massage?"

Everything is new. The hair on my armpits. The scent of my armpits. The routine of gliding antiperspirant over the surface of them after I shower. I've started shaving my armpits, my legs, sometimes my crotch. I steal my dad's razor. Now, once a month, I get my period. My parents have purchased metal for my mouth that is now glued to my teeth; each month, Dr. Grubka tightens the strip with a tiny screwdriver, forcing my teeth to shift painfully into obedient rows. My body is chaos, a figure in hideous transition.

Also: my parents have pulled Julian and me out of St. Philip Catholic and enrolled us into the public school systems, saying we needed more culture, something about a "bigger aquarium." Jules goes to Pennfield, the rural school, because they have a good football team, and I'm at Battle Creek Central because they have an orchestra. Sabina is staying at St. Phil; she's almost graduated and she spends half her day at the Math and Science Center, a school for exceptionally bright, young academics. (Jules and I did not make the cut.) What Jules and I do is leave a class of twenty-five students we've known since kindergarten and enter one of up to three hundred. And with our parents working all the time, we hardly see one another. A team that used to be inseparable now behaves more like neighbors: Dad installed locks on our bedroom doors and gave the three of us our own set of keys after we complained about lack of privacy; our bedrooms are now like our very own apartments. We weren't prepared for the sudden shift. This independence: new. This loss of routine: also new. We've been thrust outward. We've been pushed upon ourselves. But I am not afraid.

At my new school, I'm considered "weird" but "hot," a combination that puts me under the microscope. "Did you see what she did after that hall fight? She picked up a piece of weave from the floor! Homegirl holds it up in front of her face and goes, 'THIS IS SOMEONE'S HAIR.'" They look at my last name and can't pronounce it, or catch my mother's voice when she does pick me up from school and assume I'm an alien. "What country you from?" they ask.

At school there are no uniforms. Now we can wear jeans to class, and now we are not reading about Jesus. Now my class doesn't go to church together. Now kids do fight in the hallways, in the bathrooms, in the cafeteria. There are security guards. I've seen a gun on several occasions. It belonged to a student. All the time, the energy is wild, close to bursting. It's like being inside a piñata.

I make some new friends like Amanda, a wholesome girl from a wholesome family. Amanda is nice and smart, very sincere and very short; she leads me around the school like a museum guide, narrating the place with resentment and cynicism. I meet other kids, kids with no rules—"bad kids," Amanda warns me, and tries to steer me away like a voice of reason, but it doesn't work. The Bad Kids are so interesting—independent thinkers, I think—so they become friends, too. They remind me of unpruned gardens.

Some of them have nonexistent parents. Some of them are addicted to drugs. Some of the Bad Kids smoke weed with their families. I get invited to a sleepover at my new friend Molly's house and get stoned for the first time with her mom and dad. We watch *Big Top Pee-wee* and I end up sleeping in a closet because I'm too high and it just feels like I should be surrounded by shoes. My parents have no clue because they're working all the time. Plenty of my classmates know my dad because he delivered their babies. Sometimes, at home around the dinner table, Dad tells me he delivered so-and-so's baby. "I believe she is in your Spanish class." He'll bring it up and I won't know what to think, or how to respond. Often my mom chimes in, giving her two cents or shaking her head disapprovingly. Dad asks me in an emotionally tone-deaf way, the way he might ask his patients, "Are your friends sexually active?" Some are. "Are you?" I am not.

We're at a point where we only catch glimpses of one another. At the start of each new week, before we scatter to our separate schools, my parents write down instructions on a notepad and then they leave for work. *No TV on school nights, get your home-work done before you play, dinner is in the fridge.* Without the buoy of my family's togetherness to keep me afloat, I dive deep into the aquarium. From there, everything becomes improvi-sation. I get a skateboard. I become the girl who isn't afraid to try things. The girl who dyes her hair red with Kool-Aid and pierces her own nose.

My third-hour orchestra conductor, Ms. Phelps, a zany woman with mad love for her students and massive eyes and a giant Tom Selleck poster that hangs over her desk, delegates me to lead first violin sectionals in another building. On our way to sectionals, my first violins ask if we can just leave. "She'll never know," they tell me, so I try it. We sneak off, smoke cigarettes, get away with it; so we try it again. And again, and again. And now each time I lead first violin sectionals, I say, "Just go do whatever, but be back by the time class is over."

I start skipping math class, too, then Spanish, then history. My art teacher tells my mother I am "provocative," so I stop going to *that* class as well; too bad it was one of the only ones I gave a shit about. I'm prickly and nauseating, but I don't see this. My behavior is encouraged by the Bad Kids. "Do what you want," they whisper, and I realize for the first time that I actually can. Amanda urges me to stay away from them, but I'm howling like a wolf on the inside and want to run with the ones who do the same on the outside. We are passion searching for a target. We are uncontrolled energy. We take ourselves seriously and we make a game of it.

We make believe and we believe it hard: that we run the school, that we run the town, that we are the adults. We are gruff and we are wiser than everyone around us, but in reality, it's stupidity by osmosis. We drink rum and coke in the parking lot in the mornings before school. We try acid, cocaine, crack (once); we try crystal meth, and I am still under the influence two days later when I have to go take my PSATs.

The boys are new.

I have a boyfriend named Jeff. He used to be good, smart and studious, but now he's bad. A rebel. Says yes to everything. Will try everything. The boy courted me for months and months, giving me rides to school, bringing me sugar-powder-water cappuccinos from the gas station, letting me drive his car. Persistent as hell until I realized the word "no" didn't make any sense to him. And that, to him, I was a goddess. And that he was brilliant and daring and funny, and that I'd started to fall in love with him. So I said "yes" and now we are together. He's had a hard life. After passing out in his easy chair with a cigarette in his hand, Jeff's dad died in a fire, so now Jeff lives with his stepdad, who works the night shifts and sleeps during the day, so the boy can do whatever he wants. Jeff has a car, and after my mother drops me off at rehearsal for *Man of La Mancha*, he scoops me up outside of the school, just as we'd planned. I've got the booze in my backpack and a bag of weed in my violin case. But Dirt is also in the car, sitting in the front seat. My seat. Not part of the plan.

Dirt is Jeff's friend. To me, Dirt is more like a cobra, but we don't call him that—Cobra. Dirt picked up the name because he's dark skinned, and because he's been with lots of ladies. Either the boys gave him the name, or he took it to them. Either way, he keeps it and introduces himself with it. He is smart and he is sly. Sometimes the boys call him Ol' Dirty Dawg because he's real smooth with the ladies. Because of this, he's had lots of success—I've heard he's fathered some kids—and this makes my hackles go up, so I keep my distance. Sometimes I like Dirt because he smokes me out and can freestyle very smoothly and I think he has a photographic memory, but what I don't like is how he can shift from being lax and tender to being angry and hot. Sometimes when Jeff isn't looking, Dirt turns to me and licks his lips all tender while staring hard and says things like, "Girl, you're so cute, like a little white feather. I'll bet you taste so good." I tell him he's a turd and ask him where his mother is. "She stay in Chicago," says Dirt.

Jeff and Dirt are inseparable, so that means the three of us are always together. I'll wait around while the boys steal rap music from Sam Goody and blast it from Jeff's car stereo while he drives Dirt around to wherever he wants to go, bass on high, and lends Dirt money and lets Dirt live with him. I think it's because Jeff is ashamed to be white. I think he wants to get out of it by association. I think Jeff knows we are privileged, just by being born with this skin color. Sometimes I feel that way, too.

Without saying anything, I get in the back of Jeff's car and shut the door, disappointed. We drive to Irving Park, get out, and go sit on the grass underneath a statue of an American Indian where we drink wine and smoke Marlboro Reds. Jeff drapes his arm over my neck and tries to impress Dirt with some raps he just made up. Across the street is the hospital where my father works. He's probably there now.

The sun has set. We open another bottle, finish all the wine—two bottles total that I've stolen from my mother's wine cellar—and then some Tanqueray that Jeff had in his pocket. I am weightless. It is hilarious. Nothing else matters now but now, and me. This is my park, I own this park, and I fear nothing. I love these guys, and I'm drunk and I've forgotten to watch the time, so when 9:45 rolls around and I'm running so sloppily late, I don't even waste time trying to come up with a valid excuse for my mother. I tell Jeff to drive fast. I tell him to forget about stopping at the C-Store where I should have picked up some gum, and by the time I'm out of Jeff's car and booking it down my driveway toward the garage door, I realize that I've also forgotten to spritz myself with Dirt's Cool Water cologne to cover up the smell you get when you're up to no good.

"How was rehearsal?" my mother asks as I try to sneak through the kitchen.

"It ran late," I tell her. "Sorry."

"I beg your pardon?" asks Dad. He is also in the kitchen. Jules and Sabina are not. "Because Ms. Phelps called to see if you were okay after you didn't show up."

"Let me smell your breath," says my mom. Before I can refuse, she grabs my cheeks and squeezes my lips apart like a conch shell. She takes a short whiff. "You've been drinking."

"No. I haven't," I say. "You're insane."

She turns to face Dad. "Mira is drunk," she tells him.

I am drunk and I wobble back, raise my finger, and point it at my mother. "No," I say, "I think yoooou're the one who's drunk," and she smacks me. A warm bud begins to sprout on my cheek as Dad steps in between us.

Now we are in his car, my father and me. In the kitchen, Dad suggested we head to the hospital to pick up an alcohol detector test—"just to be fair," he proposed. Either we'll prove my guilt or Mom's overreaction. We drive the twelve miles in silence, then pull into the physician parking lot. Dad shifts the gear into park, leaves the car running, and unbuckles his seat belt. "Stay here," he tells me. "You'll take it at home. Mom will want to be a part of this." He gets out of the car, closes the door, and walks with tall posture toward the back of the hospital. His stethoscope is still draped around his neck. It's nearly 10 P.M. on a school night.

On the floor of Dad's Nissan are mini-Snickers wrappers, empty cans of Diet Coke, and a half-eaten bag of Oreos. He drinks and eats this stuff to stay awake. My father says, "I'll sleep when I'm dead." He told us he's planning on giving up caffeine and junk food for Lent, and for good. He said that when Mom isn't around, he turns into a caveman. Sometimes Dad eats ice cream for breakfast. I do that too. I've inherited my father's metabolism and athletic legs, his long fingers and sensitivity.

Like my mom, I'm hot-blooded. Sometimes, Jules and Sabina and I make her so angry that she just explodes. She gives up on us and disappears. We'll come up from swimming down at the lake or playing in the yard and find out that something we did pushed her over the edge. Mom will have left a note on the table saying she needed a break, that she was going to stay at a hotel or just drive somewhere and that she didn't know when she planned on coming back. Dad will come home from work, we'll hand him the note, and in an unruffled tone he'll say, "What did you guys do to your mother this time?" He'll order Little Caesars for dinner and we'll hang around ruefully, waiting for Mom to come home, which she always does, by dusk. She'll pull into the driveway and Dad will meet her at the front door, walk her into their bedroom, and close the door behind them. Like my mother, I have a short temper and am easily moved. Unlike my mother, I have small breasts.

It was my father who bought me my first bra. The event did not go well. We were in the checkout lane at Meijer's Thrifty

Acres, just Dad and me with Mom's shopping list. The conveyor belt cluttered with lots of things we didn't need—stalks of broccoli, a pound of pecans, more grapes, Stove Top Stuffing—had created a traffic jam of grocery carts and impatient shoppers. After asking the cashier about her day, Dad turned to me with an expressionless face and said, "Mira, do you have a bra?" I was simultaneously mortified and thrilled. Mortified, because my father had broadcasted MIRA PTACIN HAS BOOBS, thus planting the image of my naked chest into the minds of everyone nearby with ears, and thrilled because, no, I did not have a bra of my own. The closest thing in my possession was the padded red and white polka-dot bikini top that I'd stolen from my sister. I was going to get a bra.

I didn't walk—I sprinted through those thrifty acres until I reached a rack of Hanes Her Way lady undergarments. My business was urgent. But I didn't know how to pick out a bra. No one had ever shown me how to measure myself, or explained what the letters or numbers meant, so I grabbed a handful of friendly-looking cotton trainers that came in either small, medium, or large and darted back to the aisle where my dad and the checkout woman were waiting. I slid the brassieres onto the conveyor belt and placed a massive box of Cheerios on top of them, then impartially thumbed through a *Reader's Digest* while my bounty worked its way toward the register. Just as the checkout clerk was tallying up our goods, my dad reached into one of the grocery bags and pulled out one of my bras, still on its little plastic hanger. He held it under his nose and studied the price tag.

"Mira, do you really need four bras?" The words came out in slow motion—*fooour braaas?*—as my father turned to face me and the clogged line of customers watched. Then he held out an open hand, folded his thumb into his palm and repeated the question. *FOUR BRAS?* I looked down and shook my head. After I'd returned three of the four to the rack where I'd found them, after that silent, sullen ride car ride home, after we'd finally unpacked the car and put away all the groceries, I rushed downstairs to my room with my one new bra—*my* bra—and closed the door, threw off my t-shirt, tried it on. It didn't even fit.

In my father's tape deck there is a recording of *Con Te Partirò*. Dad has been memorizing the Italian ballad so he can serenade Mom on her birthday, which is in a couple months. May 1st. May Day. On Saturday mornings, Dad's been going to the home of one of his patients, an Italian man, who corrects my father's pronunciations and translates the lyrics so he'll know what he's singing about. *Con Te Partirò*. With You I Will Leave. My father is affectionate, but it's not an inherited trait.

"She was a tyrant." That's what Mom says about my paternal grandmother. That she was a dictator, cold and unsympathetic. When my father was a boy, he pooped the bed once. Mom said that as an adult, Dad confided in her. He told her that after the accident, Grandma got angry, laughed at him about it and rubbed his nose in the soiled sheets, as if she were potty training a puppy. *Good grief.* That's what my dad said a lot as a child. *Good grief.* It's what Dad's parents named their cottage up in the Wisconsin wilderness. After they'd built their vacation home but before they'd christened it, my grandparents asked each of their six kids to come up with a name for the cottage. Dad was maybe eight or ten years old. He proposed "Corn Is High," a saying he'd made up, something he thought sounded cool, something he imagined the Native Americans would tell one another when everything was in harmony. *Corn is high. All is well.* It meant that you could be hopeful. You'd think that the sight of a little boy sharing his secret wishes for peace would be warmly received, that it was precious and poetic and that Corn is High would trend, but when little dad pitched his idea to his family, all that happened was that his siblings teased him for being a big sap and, maybe so they could rub his nose in it even more, his parents named the cabin "Good Grief" instead.

When we'd visit Dad's parents in Chicago, Mom made us do things the way Grandma expected. We had to always be helping and asking what else we could help with. We had to eat everything that was on our plates and when we were finished, we had to say, "I had an elegant sufficiency," even though we didn't even know what that meant. It was a phrase Grandma had us say. After we were excused, we were to clear the table and wash the dishes. Mom hated it. She hated being there, felt unwanted, but still, she made us do it. "Kill 'em with kindness," she'd say. She did it for Dad. Even when she was furious or insulted, if it was for her husband, she exuded dignity. Maybe Grandma was a bully, or maybe she was just strict, but judging by the surface of things, it was hard to notice. The details didn't reveal themselves until after Grandma Ptacin died. I was eleven. During the wake, Mom and I ate peanut M&Ms and she told me that Dad's parents never said *I love you* to one another, rarely said it to Dad, and that it was a mystery and a miracle how Dad turned out the way he did: the most loving man in the entire world. Mom believes she has to protect my father all of the time because he loves everybody and is always giving people credit instead of criticism. *He pulls me up and I pull him down and we reach the right level,* is how she explains their dynamic. *We make the good balance.* I always admired that—how much love Dad would give. How Dad could share his hope for peace and prosperity while putting himself at risk for sounding silly or naïve. One year, out of the blue, my mother bought a personalized license plate for herself and one for Dad. For Mom's minivan: RSVPI. And on the rear of his Nissan, stamped onto a royal blue in long white font is Dad's cheerful reminder, *Corn Is High.* But it's scrunched together in crowded capital letters and looks like this: CORNSHI, which makes everyone scratch their head and wonder why my father has a license plate that reads, "Corn Shit."

The instant the hospital door closes behind my father, I open the passenger door and step out. I'm busted, I've already lost; Mom is at home waiting for me and I can't pass that Breathalyzer test. I scan the parking lot to see if anyone is watching, but I'm the only one here and Dad's is the only car. The amber light of a streetlamp casts my shadow along the asphalt and I tense up to prevent something deep inside from unraveling. *Fuck that,* I tell myself and spit at the ground, half-supposing it will sizzle.

"Bye-bye, Cornshit. I am so out of here," I say, and walk away.

The night is cold and fresh on the streets of Battle Creek. I will walk about two miles, past the dry cleaners and B.C. Burger on Calhoun Street, past the cantaloupe-colored halfway houses lining Fremont. I will reach the Dixie Mart on Emmett Street and hang a right. Bundles of tennis shoes dangle by their laces from telephone wires over Orchard Street, where the gardens are small and gated. These miniature yards make me think of how when we were kids, Jules and Sabina and I invented a game called "Survive in the Wilderness." The purpose was to gather provisions. We'd pile grass and dandelions onto giant ferns then roll them up like tacos. We'd collect water from the lake in pails and sharpen the ends of birch branches, just in case. We were preparing for something, for what I'm not sure, because that thing never came. Growing up, there were no school playgrounds near our home and we didn't call the place where we played a "yard." We called it "land" because that's what it was, *wilderness.*

The trees lining Orchard Street, however, are singular and scrawny. I continue to meander, round a corner or two until somehow, *somehow*, I arrive safely at my friend Luke's house. I pick up a few rocks and throw them until I hit Luke's bedroom window and wake him. He laughs at me, then comes down to the lawn where we smoke Newports. Then, from the phone in Luke's kitchen, I'll call Jeff, who will pick me up, bring me back to his house and I'll fall asleep rather quickly. In the morning, while my parents are at work and my siblings at school, I'll sneak back to my home and gather what I need: some clothes, my stereo, my wallet and violin while Jeff waits in the car. It'll be enough.

One afternoon before my parents were married, my mother

sat in the cafeteria of St. Luke's Presbyterian, the hospital in Chicago where she and my father both worked, and watched my dad search for her in a snowstorm. "Shit or get off the pot," she'd told him a couple of weeks before. They'd been dating long enough and he still hadn't proposed. Shit or get off the pot; my mom had a life to live. So they split. A week or so later, Dad came to his senses and realized Maria was the one woman he wanted to spend the rest of his life with. He raced back to tell her the good news but she wasn't anywhere to be found. Dad searched the hospital cafeteria, table by table, then went outside to search in the snow, hoping she was taking a smoke break despite the snow blowing hard from above and despite Dad being clad only in scrubs. Mom knew he was looking for her, but she let him panic. A little suffering did one a little good. She'd let her phone keep ringing, let Dad keep leaving messages and writing apologies, let him get a little bit scared. The day he came searching for her in the hospital, she watched him from her seat in the cafeteria. As Dad lunged from bench to bench through several feet of snow, desperate for her forgiveness, Mom knew she'd marry him. *The man should always love you a little bit more than you love him.* When she'd seen enough, she stood up, cleared her cafeteria tray and returned to her lab.

This was exactly the same way Mom treated my situation. *Mira will come to her senses. Just let her be.* I'm just a dumb kid. If they step back, I'll calm down, come to my senses, give in and return. My parents find out where I am and they give me space. A week goes by. I stay with Jeff in a two-bedroom house with Dirt and Jeff's stepdad. It's a party house. There are always people swinging by, teenagers, strangers. I eat Hot Pockets from the freezer and Jeff introduces me to Miracle Whip and bologna sandwiches, which I never got to eat at home and I think they're delicious. Jeff starts selling acid. We each take a hit and go see *Jurassic Park* at the movie theater where I work for eight bucks an hour. Jeff has a dog, a boxer named Louie, who keeps me company when Jeff isn't home. I stay up late, sleep in, and skip a lot of school, but I continue to go to orchestra rehearsals. I like my orchestra conductor Ms. Phelps because, despite how horrible our ensemble sounds, she isn't ashamed of us. She still has faith in me and trusts that I will lead the violins, possibly improve them. I try a little. Three weeks pass. All is well.

A month into things and still no word from me. My parents are learning about my progress through others. My mother calls Amanda and pressures her for information, but Amanda doesn't have much to share; we don't talk anymore. My parents get bits of information from Ms. Phelps. My high school principal, Mr. Rasmussen, gives me a copy of *Zen and the Art of Motorcycle Maintenance*. At the movie theater where I work, my manager sits me down and tells me I should talk to my mom and dad. "I can see your point," I tell him. "Sure. I'll give them a call," I say, but I don't.

I receive a letter from my parents. *We're not mad at you. We just want to talk*, it says and they propose a date and place. I dismiss their letter, and the next one that follows. We have started performing *Man of La Mancha* and during each show, the star Don Quixote rides in on a real live horse that belongs to one of my neighbors back home. I think it's ridiculous and a little sad to see this giant beast standing miserably in the middle of a high school auditorium. It makes me want to put down my violin and protest. Or smash my violin to pieces. One night, from behind the horse, I spot my family in the crowd. My parents don't stick around after the show but Julian and Sabina find me. "You're being dumb," Jules says before Sabina peels him away.

For them, things are awful. Nearly two months have passed and the whole household is still holding its breath; the mood is somber, nothing is going as planned. "Mira will be back," Mom assured them. They thought by now I would have come to my senses and returned. At home, Julian is very quiet and says nothing about it. Sabina is spending more time with her boyfriend. When they're not working, my parents are up late in the kitchen, arguing over what they should do, over who is the bigger victim, who is more at fault. *You're a pushover. You're too harsh on them.* The sadness is consuming them; my parents worry about divorce. I refuse to respond when they reach out to talk, and these new friends of mine, the "bad" ones, won't talk to them, either. Neither will their parents. Instead of helping out, these parents are reveling in it, taking pleasure in the fact that Dr. and Mrs. Ptacin's daughter is not such a goody-goody, that the Ptacins are not so holy after all. My mother has found out where Jeff lives and at least once a day, she slowly drives past the house where I stay then circles the block several times. She's panicking. She's crying all the time because there's nothing she can do. I'm alive but I'm a ghost to her. Or maybe she's dead to me. Two months turns into three. *Mira won't be coming back.* Everyone is losing weight.

Most nights, Jeff doesn't come home. He avoids conversation but gets mad at me for putting a dent in his Hot Pocket and bologna supply, so I eat the leftover popcorn from the movie theater. I bring home garbage bags of it. Then Jeff gets expelled for bringing a knife to school so I have even more difficulty finding a ride to class, to work, from work. Rumors are floating around that he's sleeping with another person. And another. And another. I stop talking to him. Jeff's dog Louie growls when Jeff comes near me and this makes him even more resentful. When I go to our room and find that my stereo is missing, Jeff tells me that Dirt took it to a secondhand store and pawned it for fifty dollars. I'm making plans to join the Marines. Otherwise, I'm going to be a nomad. I'm a runner, I'm coming to accept it.

The first time I ran away, I was maybe eight years old and on my red two-wheeler, the very first bike without training wheels. "I'm running away," I declared as I backed my bike out of the garage. Jules said nothing but just looked at me in a completely neutral way. No one seemed to care; our babysitter had even packed me lunch. She was Polish, her name was Lucia, and she didn't get it. "You will never see me again," I threatened, but she handed me a sandwich. Peanut butter and orange marmalade sandwich on rye bread. I hated it. Jules and Lucia walked me to the edge of the driveway and watched me pedal away furiously. I was trying to make a statement. I don't remember my reason. Maybe it was because of a rule I didn't want to follow. Maybe I felt left out of something I wanted to be a part of. Whatever it was, I would remove myself from the situation and prove my point. I was so angry when all I wanted was to feel powerful. I felt unimportant and weak. I wanted Julian to join me. But as I was making my dramatic exit, Jules stood back, held onto his stuffed animal Woofie and watched me saddle up and go. I rode my bike about a hundred yards to the birch wood forest behind Greencrest Manor, climbed a tree, and listened. As I waited, I promised myself that I would stay in that tree forever. They'd find me up there, nothing but an ivory skeleton, and they'd regret it. I would show them. But no one came. No one called. I stayed up in the tree for hours, peeling off the papery birch bark, singing songs and feeling sorry for myself. I got bored and lonely and wanted to climb down that tree and go home but I couldn't. I was so knee deep in shit that it was easier to keep sinking than pull myself out. Surely the police were looking for me, surely major trouble awaited. It started to rain. I was cold and wet and hungry and eventually I just gave up. I walked my bike home and when I walked into the house, it seemed as if nobody noticed I'd left in the first place. They'd eaten dinner, even. That's when I realized I'd done it to myself. Maybe it was my problem. Maybe I was the problem.

The third month is when my parents begin seeing a counselor. They start buying books. My mom reads something about "tough love" and shortly after, attends a Tough Love workshop in Kalamazoo. This is when their sadness turns to anger. It's nearly four months into things when I receive a letter in the mail from my mother. *The* letter. It says: *That's it. I've had it.* In the letter, my mother writes that she cannot do this anymore, that she cannot always be on the edge, that I'm being destructive to the rest of the family. She writes: *You come home, or you never come home again.* She writes: *You can go on, but you won't be part of our family.* Now, or never. She reminds me: *You know that when I make my mind up on anything, I keep my word. You know I will follow through.*

I call home the next day. School has just ended; I have completed my junior year. When I ask their permission to come home, they tell me I can return, and ask if I've got a ride. A friend from the movie theater, a sassy girl named Amber who goes to Julian's school. That afternoon, Amber helps me pack my belongings into her car. We move quickly, and I scribble a note for Jeff. Just as we're finishing up, he pulls into the gravel driveway.

"What the hell do you think you're doing?" Jeff barks and tells me to get back in the house.

"I'm taking her home," Amber says and calls him a cocksucker. She tells him that his penis is going to fall off, then she picks up a rock from the driveway. She tells me to get in the car, but I just stand there frozen with my violin case in my hands. Jeff calls Amber a bitch, tells her to stay out of our business, and she throws the rock at him. I slide my violin into the car and pick up a rock, too.

"Don't," I say. "I love you, but I'm leaving. Get in your house, Jeff. Go home."

Amber and I wait in the driveway, watching with rocks in our hands as he walks all the way to his front porch, backward.

Otherwise, there is no fanfare. When I arrive home, it's Father's Day. My parents are expecting me. We sit down for a meal, the whole family, but no one says much and no one points out the obvious—that this sudden reunion is very strange.

In the weeks that follow, I'm treated fairly but no differently than before. My parents try to be forgiving; they know I am young. A young, stupid kid not conscious of her own delusions. But still, there are no exceptions for me or anyone; we're all equals. The house remains calm but in a strained way, almost as if we're trying not to wake something that is slowly falling asleep.

Summer rolls around. I'm still working at the movie theater. Sabina is serving at Mom's restaurant and Julian heads off to basketball camp in Ann Arbor. The hot weeks pass and then school starts up again. Sabina packs up for college, Jules heads back to Pennfield, and I'm now a senior at Battle Creek Central. During the first semester, there are a few hiccups, but things are improving, things are getting better. Things are getting normal. Four months go by and just as we are becoming our family again, Julian dies.

I slide off the examining room table feeling tense and culpable.

"Are you sure there's nothing I should worry about?" I ask Dr. Reich as I slip on my jacket.

"Don't worry. They can find out more about the test's results when you go in for your ultrasound in a few weeks," she says, her tone upbeat. "I'm sure everything is fine. You've done nothing wrong."

Oh, what a fool I'd been.

eight

October 1997. It's drizzling out and another lot of Canada geese has left the Great Lakes. Above us, they honk and streak the calico sky in a giant V-formation of elegant black necks and little white chinstraps, lifting their wings and lowering them, lifting and lowering.

V-shaped, like an arrowhead. Dad once told us that these birds fly forward with a sense of duty, to themselves and to one another. He explained that each wing flap creates uplift for the bird immediately behind it. That they honk from behind to encourage those up front to keep up their speed, their hope, and their spirit. "Just like we do when we go to Julian's home football games," I replied. Dad said that when the lead goose tires, it peels off from the point position and rotates to the back of the V, then another goose moves up to take its turn fighting the wind. *To one another.* Dad said that always, when a goose weakens or is wounded and falls out of group, one or two geese drop down with it, down to the earth to help and protect it. *Always.*

From behind the chain-link fence of the cemetery, I watch the gaggle as two birds break from the sky, dive, and land next to the soggy spot of upturned Astroturf where our herd is huddled. I watch the two geese, pecking at the synthetic grass, five or six feet to my right, paying us no mind.

Rewind three days and it's Saturday evening. The fall air smells musty, like Halloween, and is syrupy with anticipation. Everyone is waiting for something. In October, at the start of a new season, who isn't?

My girlfriend and I are cruising down the highway in the secondhand car I share with my older sister—a blueberry-colored 1989 Buick Regal. We are smoking sweet Black & Mild cigarillos we bought at the gas station. Ivory-tipped, vanilla-flavored. We glance at one another and nod. We believe we look cool.

The sun is lowering, and the cornfields are shadowy and crackling. Our blue ride steals past front doors behind which farm families are eating dinner. We drive past the bronze Sojourner Truth memorial, the Lakeview Square Mall, the Calhoun County Humane Society, a small brown cabin nestled in a bitter golden valley. My one hand is on the wheel and the other adjusting the volume of the stereo. I turn it up. *Who rocks grooves and make moves with all the mommies?* The

Buick merges onto The Penetrator, passes Climax township, and, like we always do, my friend and I point out the obvious innuendos that dot our forty-mile route from Pennfield township to Kalamazoo, Michigan. And, as usual, we snort with amusement, even though the glory of it all has worn off over the years.

But tonight my laugh feels more counterfeit and stale than it ever has. It's forced, and irritably fake. I mean irritably. I really want tonight to be gratifying. I really want to have the most fun I've ever experienced. I want tonight to be worth it. This desire of mine is mandatory and urgent because I really do not want to be here—"out," "going out" as we call it—in the first place. I would much rather be home.

I want to go home.

I don't spend enough time at home.

I could've worked for Mom at the restaurant tonight. I could've earned some extra bucks as a dishwasher, but I didn't. Or I could've stayed at home. I wanted to stay home because tonight is a rare night when Jules and Dad and Mom will all be there, after work, just hanging out, but I didn't. I want to turn this car back around, call the whole trip off, but every time I get close to doing it, a voice in my head scolds me and says, *You are young. You are young and fun. You are a pretty girl. You are supposed to want this. You are supposed to want to be going out with your wild girlfriends and your boy toys. It's what you young people do.*

My girlfriend blows an impressive smoke ring through her lips: thick, sturdy, a perfect halo fresh from a cartoon. We are driving to Western Michigan University and we are going to flirt with boys who are done with high school. Boys who have left their hometowns. Boys who don't live with their parents anymore. Boys who are in college.

We have straightened our hair. We are wearing transparent lip gloss that tastes like strawberries. We are seniors in high school. I am almost eighteen. I will be eighteen in less than three weeks.

I am almost an adult, and aware and growing increasingly anxious that tonight's night on the town as an almost-adult will prove to be just as insignificant as any other night on the town. My front teeth clutch the plastic filter tip of my cigarillo as I consider what lies ahead: flaring teenagers with planned outfits, wine coolers, sloppy games of playing hard to get, drunken kisses—the sweet muddle of hormones. Tonight's foolish, juvenile games really won't amount to much in the grand scheme of the universe, I'm sure of it. But, still.

Back in Battle Creek, a man turns into one of the three slim, gravel parking spaces at the Dixie Mart on Emmett Street. His name is Gordon. He is nearing forty years old. I don't know how Gordon spent his Saturday. Maybe he was at home doing not much of anything, messing with his broken television set a bit, drinking Diet Rite and rum, maybe Tanqueray. You could say Gordon has a drinking problem. And he's also got a girlfriend. Her name is Deborah. She's fat. I bet they fight a lot.

This evening, Gordon needs more alcohol. He's been busted a couple of times for drinking and driving but that doesn't stop him from doing it again tonight. As long as he doesn't get caught. Just drive slow.

And Deb is close by. She's driving around the block in her car, searching for Gordon, creeping. Deb's just down the road, one stoplight from view.

Gordon gets out of his car, slams shut the door to the running vehicle, and swaggers toward the entrance of the Dixie Mart. He has a thin wad of cash in his pocket and knows exactly what he wants. As he pushes open the door to the party store, the cluster of bells on its handle jingles.

Not even one mile away from the Dixie Mart is my mother, working at RSVP. Even though she's fifty-one years old, she doesn't look a year older than forty. Her cheeks are soft red, like her lips, and her skin is flawless. She's serving up dessert to the last of her customers, sprigging flourless chocolate raspberry tortes with mint leaves, scorching the circular roofs of yellow crème brûlées, switching in and out of her chef's apron to schmooze with her restaurant's patrons. It's been a long day of work for my mother and the end is near. Soon the engorged patrons will roll themselves out of her restaurant; soon Mom will be free to go home and soak her swollen ankles in a hot bucket of water.

Back home, my brother Jules has finished his chores. He's fourteen years old. He's downstairs flipping through the TV, searching for clips of the University of Michigan football game he attended earlier in the day. During the commercial breaks, Jules thrashes around on the floor with his dog, Gonzo, trying out wrestling moves. The dog lives for it; he's a Lab. Earlier in the day, Jules was up in Ann Arbor visiting Sabina, who is now a sophisticated college freshman at University of Michigan. Bean scored two extra tickets and took Jules and his friend Blake—*sooooo immature*—to the game with her and her boyfriend. The boys didn't leave their seats once, so the autumn sun tanned the whole right side of their faces a shade or three redder than their left sides. Then, after the game, on the walk back to Sabina's apartment, the boys trailed behind and wandered into some sex shop where they snagged novelty condoms; and when Mom picked the boys up before heading to work, she found the two of them tossing the rubbers back and forth at one another, prophylactics blown up like balloons. She didn't really mind.

Now, in the basement, Jules wrestles with the dog. The Texas Piledriver. He drops into a sitting position with Gonzo's head falling between his thighs, crashing down into the carpet. "Need a little excitement, ah?" Jules imitates the gruff voice of Macho Man Randy Savage, the famous WWF wrestler and Beef Jerky spokesperson, and Gonzo recognizes the tone and buzzwords as a cue. His tail wags and the dog braces himself, ready to brawl with his master. Julian is toughening up Gonzo, riling him ready for hunting trips. Quail. They've been hunting one time already, just once so far. Jules bought boots and a hat, camouflage pants, and an orange vest. He bought Gonzo a bright orange vest, too, with Velcro straps across the chest, and they waited patiently until Dad finally convinced Mom to let him buy Jules a shotgun. He stores it in his closet, I think.

"Snap into a Slim Jim!" Jules rumbles and demonstrates a Diamond Dust on Gonzo. The black dog slips out from underneath his grip, tail wagging like a machete, and once more, Jules plows into him with a Diving Double Axe Handle. Two leviathans battling over the couch pillows. "Ooooooh yeahhhh!"

Dad is in the kitchen studying for his board exams. He's already consumed an entire tub of spumoni ice cream while reviewing his patients' charts, and he's just about to open a fresh bag of Oreos when the phone rings. It's Mom calling to let him know she's finishing up with work. She asks if he and Jules, "the boys," could come lift all the heavy stuff. "Of course," Dad tells her. "We'll get you out of there faster," he says.

At some point, I untangle from the college boy's arms and look at the clock. 9:20. I tell him I have to go pee, which I don't, but I'm bored with sucking face. I get up from the carpeted floor. I tell him I'll be right back and step out of his dorm room and into the hallway. The neon lights are blinding, and ugly. Little morsels of crumbs and lint from the carpet stick to my jeans and I brush them off as I stroll to the bathroom.

Bobby, the checkout boy working the Dixie Mart register this Saturday night, sells the *Chicago Tribune* in front of St. Philip Church every Sunday morning. He plans on going to bed early tonight, right after he closes at ten o'clock. Bob'll turn in early just like he does every Saturday night, because he's got to be up on the corner of Cherry Street in time for the early church crowd. When he's got another forty-five minutes or so before he closes up shop, Bobby tells two small children from the neighborhood that today their cans of pop are free. He tells them to just go home, quickly now. He wants them to leave because, at this point, Gordon is talking to anyone who'll listen, slurring and swaying at the counter and making a scene. He's getting scary. Thick, shiny bald head. Bulldog face. But then he pleads sweetly, almost singing to him, but Bobby still refuses to sell him any booze.

"Sir, I apologize. I cannot sell you any alcohol." Deadpan, Bobby repeats the line again and again; he's done it so many times to so many customers—the neighborhood winos and underage kids, or regular people drunk as balls, hoping to slip by, drink and drive. Bobby's impersonal denial makes Gordon even more hot, and more desperate, and now Deborah has arrived, is in the store, flailing her arms around, making a racket, crying and fussing, acting all dramatic until Gordon finally caves, gives up and bangs out of the Dixie Mart, clomping back to his car. From behind the counter, framed by plastic cases of cigarettes and the glossy spools of lottery tickets, Bobby's brows furrow while he watches Gordon rev up his engine and exit onto Emmett Street. Deb power walks to her car and does the same, leaving behind a bitter cloud of chalk and exhaust.

The boys arrive at RSVP restaurant; unload some dishes; stack chafers, China plates, and trays in the basement of the restaurant. They break down cardboard boxes next to the dumpster, mop, stack leftover dip and plastic-wrapped broccoli, peppers, carrots, and cherry tomatoes in the cooler, and kiss Mom on the cheek before heading to the video store.

"Do you want some dessert?" she asks her son, motioning at a fat triangle of white frosting.

"No thanks," Julian responds. "I'm not hungry."

"You should take some dessert," she insists as he climbs into the car. "If you don't take the dessert now," Mom says, "you'll regret it later." But Jules leaves the dessert anyway.

I'm looking at myself close up in the mirror of the girls' bathroom. A ring of irritated skin has formed a ruby circle around my mouth from making out with a fervent college boy, a former high school sweetheart who's crazy about me but whom I'm not in love with anymore. My heart is still with Jeff. I find a hickey blossoming on my neck. Great.

I dig through my purse, look for gum. Contents: melted sticks of Doublemint, a tampon, two cigarettes, car keys, eleven dollars, one pager, and three Black & Milds. I calculate that I can smoke for about another year. I'll quit before I turn nineteen. I don't want to be one of those people, I think, those leather ladies with scratchy voices and hide so tanned that they look like a corpse. Those ladies in misery who spend Tuesdays in despondent church basement bingo halls, lonely and still smoking. Women who won't admit they lost a grip on themselves when they turned eighteen, didn't stop smoking, had a bunch of babies and still didn't quit smoking. It's too easy to get like that in this city. It's too easy to get lazy, too easy to crash and burn. I'm going to do something big with myself, I think, stepping back from the sink. Get out of Battle Creek and do something big. I smooth the part on the top of my head, kick open the door to the carpeted hallway, saunter back to the boy's dorm room.

Five blocks away from the Dixie Mart, a first-time expectant mother is sitting at her kitchen table, collecting scraps and bits of evidence for the case she's putting together. She's suing her doctor. She's about four months pregnant and blaming the doctor, his instruments, his nurse, and the hospital for not being able to detect a heart murmur in her fetus. A mild heart murmur in an otherwise healthy baby. "If I'd known the baby would have problems, I would've stopped it," she says. She blames the doctor, even though there was nothing he could've done.

"But the doc couldn't have detected it, honey," her mum tells her and suggests that her daughter consider dropping the whole thing (and she's right, her girl won't win) when the debate is interrupted by a long, high-pitched screech. An abrasive squeal, like a shrieking witch, followed by a sharp crash. Friction, the burning of rubber, and then the collision of metal—the cluster of noises is deafening. The car accident happens right outside their front door. In one of those cars, and half conscious, is the doctor the woman still sues anyway and loses her case against: my father.

Neighbors run outside, chasing the noise like the trails of a comet. This is what they see: Shards of aluminum and dented rims. Chains. Metal scraps. Two shattered windshields, windows broken into a million little pieces of glass, spread across the dark avenue like the swirling Milky Way. A black door, broken right off its hinge. From above, two cars form a T-bone shape in the middle of the East Avenue and Pitman intersection. Smoke rising. Sirens. Ambulance. Paramedics. More and more people gather, and everyone stares at the scene like it's a bonfire.

In my mind's eye, I can see Deborah, pathetic and heaving, crouched on a concrete curb. And just down from her, underneath a willow tree, there's Gordon, pacing back and forth like a caged cheetah. For him, it was an invisible stop sign. He wasn't that drunk, it was invisible, and he will swear this to be the case forever. And even further down, in a black Nissan, my father is trapped inside. He has a broken collarbone, a few broken ribs. He is holding his son, rocking him like a little baby. His son was a boy. Fourteen years old. Just a boy, and suddenly, he's asleep. A lamp overturned in the rain.

Two blocks away, my mother is doing the last of the paperwork and splitting up tips when she hears the sirens. For a second, she reflects on the sound of ambulances and fire trucks in the late night and what their sirens mean—a wailing song like that on a Saturday night is never a happy song, never good news. Just for an instant, she pauses, feels sorry for those people, then goes back to counting tips and paying her employees. Twenty minutes later, her telephone rings.

His dorm room is locked. I knock three times, *ba-bum-bum*, and the bolt clicks. The door opens slowly and the college boy is standing there, all Vincent Price-like, holding the door back open with his shirt on now; he's fully dressed and all grim, just standing there.

"Ha, ha, I say, lemme in," but he doesn't move or step aside, just looks back at me. "What?" I ask. "Do I have something on my face?" In the dark cubby behind him, two more sets of eyes stare at me—stiff, dream-like, iridescent eyes like the opossums in our woods. One set is his roommate's, and the other set is my girlfriend's. She steps forward into the glare of the fluorescent light, reaches out.

"It's for you," she says and passes me a beige cordless phone.

It's not my mother. It's Mom's friend Claire. Claire's voice is like sugar. Sweetie, your mother needs you to come home, she says. And Mom, tired of Claire pussyfooting around the awful truth, takes the phone from her and delivers half of it.

"Come. Home. Now. Someone is dead."

We leave.

We drive back home, not knowing. I chain smoke the remainder of what's left: two cigarettes and three Black & Milds, and try to figure out what the hell my mother was talking about. It's raining very lightly, and with each drag of tobacco, I attempt to realize who is dead, try justifying in my mind which of my three family members it could most sensibly be, in terms of God's way, in terms of fate. Sabina? Dad? Julian? Someone has just died. My senses are numb. I think it might be my father. In the grand pattern of life, would it make more sense to have it happen to Dad? What about Sabina? I try to solve this like it's a mathematical problem, not yet incorporating into the equation what the outcome would've been if I hadn't left home tonight. If I had left five minutes later, three minutes, one minute. If I'd went with my gut and stayed home, rather than listen to that false voice in my head telling me what I *should* be doing, what I'm *supposed* to do. With each drag, the car gets closer to Battle Creek, and with each drag, we move closer to the prolonged answer. I smoke, and my friend drives us through forty minutes of bitter silence. Finally, the Buick pulls into the turnabout of Battle Creek Community Hospital, where my father often works. I get out of the car, float through the sliding glass door of the emergency room entrance, the fluorescent lights lighting my way until I find someone I know.

The two geese have gotten what they came for. I watch as they hobble away from the casket, increasing their speed, flapping their wings and jumping, hoping to get airborne. They want to migrate south; that's where the food and warmth is.

A boy is dead. Fourteen years old, lean and lanky. His face was uncommon and his eyes were blue and set wide apart, just as they are said to be in imaginative people, just like they are in statues of Joan of Arc. This boy's sand-colored hair was always tousled, except today it is combed. Pomaded, combed, and neatly parted, I imagine, but can't say for sure because I haven't looked. I didn't and I won't. He didn't dress himself today, either, in what I've been told is a checkered, brown shirt. He didn't lay out his clothes last night, or tidy up his room the other day. Three days ago, he didn't know he should've been getting rid of the stacks of *Playboy* that he and his buddies hid in a shoe box in the tool shed, or telling us the combination to his gym locker, or saying all his last goodbyes.

Everyone else came here wearing all things black—black pants, black dresses, black coats, black patent-leather shoes, black umbrellas, all things dark except for the football team in their mesh jerseys that match the color of the grass they're standing on; grass as turned up and tumbled as the turf from their football game last week. The boy's last football game. Looking at them, I imagine that the question *How could God let this happen?* has blossomed inside their young minds, will continue to bud and bloom for the next days and weeks and months and on from there. They'll have no idea how to behave, what to do, what kind of expressions to bear. There are different ways. The football team will hold vigils, plant a dogwood tree, pin ribbons to their shirts and dedicate a yearbook page, but the question will remain unanswered. Their eyes are red and soggy—everyone's are—and hopeless looks are exchanged in such a way that it doesn't really seem to do much good standing here waiting to figure out what to do when things fall apart.

The past few days feel as if everyone has been underwater, idly swaying like the slow limbs of a sea anemone. The life that surrounds us has been muffled. We are woozy, and our reaction time is slow. We talk in a strange staccato rhythm like the snapping claws of crabs. Green bean casserole. Green bean casserole. Cheese plate, cheese plate. Spaghetti. Iceberg lettuce. Italian dressing. Brownies.

I will never forget the smells that woke me last Sunday morning. Alone and fully clothed in Mom and Dad's otherwise empty bed, I floated into the kitchen, where I was immediately pounced upon by a flock of women with tepid condolences and baked goods. Comfort foods. Those are the real scent of death to the living. If every single one of those dishes broke into pieces and pierced me like a hundred daggers, I'm not certain I would have even felt any pain. I'm numb and not sure I will feel anything anymore. The only thing that is certain is death. That and the fact that everybody always wants something sweet. We all want something sweet.

The priest clears his throat.

"Benedictus Dominus Deus Israel; quia visitavit et fecit redemptionem plebi suæ."

Ten years ago, this man gave me my First Holy Communion.

I can't remember the last time we were gathered all together on purpose, the whole cast of family, friends, and those from our elementary days: the gym teacher, the violin teacher, the carpool drivers; even the football team's girlfriends are here. We are stitched together, we are gathered here on purpose, standing in a circle declawed of hope, rich with a smell that reminds me of earthworms, and of the first day of school.

"Et erexit cornu salutis nobis, in domo David pueri sui."

Everything is damp and foggy and in the center of our circle there is a boy who is dead and I don't know who he is. I know the name; but the face and the timeless body are not his, and does anybody here even understand Latin?

"Grant this mercy, O Lord, we beseech Thee, to Thy servant departed, that he may not receive in punishment the requital of his deeds who in desire did keep Thy will."

This funeral, this sentimental gesture, one that stands for a last goodbye, is a silly gesture. This is not natural. This is not our last goodbye. We missed our chance for that. Nonetheless, I'm supposed to be doing it. It's what we do, right? And in this conventional gesture, I'm trying to hold onto the moment, freeze time, because it seems less insane than the idea of going backward in time. Trying again. Starting over. A redo. But time keeps moving forward, further away from that night, away from the moment I had that choice, and there's nothing I can do about it except live better. Live for two.

"And as the true faith here united him to the company of the faithful, so may Thy mercy unite him above to the choirs of angels, through Jesus Christ our Lord."

They say we are supposed to cherish these moments, honor these last goodbyes, hold them in our hearts forever, but really. Really, I just cannot get into this. This is not for me. So I have a choice: I can sit quietly with my hands under my seat and watch this robed man toss his prayers over the poor youth.

"Ut sine timore, de manu inimicorum liberati, serviamus illi. In sanctitate et iustitia coram ipso, omnibus diebus nostris."

Or, I can shout, freeze this last time we'll all be together, run over to the boy, and hold on until we are both ready to let go.

"As we forgive those who trespass against us. And lead us not into temptation, but deliver us from evil."

But I don't shout. I can't freeze time. I can't go backward. Instead, I sit quietly. I don't move. I've already done enough. Why did I leave the house? I should've stayed home.

The casket is in its final resting place, and Mom and Dad watch as strangers drop handfuls of dirt and pinches of grass into the open chamber. I see my mother. Mom's lipstick. Always on, always red. She has lost the boy she had saved. She has lost her son, yet she remains composed. She says nothing, she is silent. Sturdy, like a thick tree. I finger the moist Kleenex in my pocket. It tears and rolls into tiny balls that stay in my pocket for years to come.

"May his soul and the souls of all the faithful departed through the mercy of God rest in peace. Amen."

A collective paralysis locks together every spectator. Convention, an unseen agreement that this is okay, that we accept that this will stand for the last goodbye: our black clothes, this concrete vault, these words led by this man. A coffin: polished oak, sealed, smooth, firm, and eternal. A boy is dead, and that is that.

My focus shifts to the back of their heads—Mom, Sabina, Dad. Then my cousin Marek, my brother's best friend. Beyond my arms, I see our aunts and uncles, our other cousins, kids from Julian's class, Bean's class. I see my best friend, Amanda. I see my entire orchestra class, our conductor. I see that relentless newscaster standing behind the chef from Mom's restaurant. I see the receptionists from Dad's office. I see the boy I was kissing Saturday night. I see Ken, Dad's friend from the seminary.

I lean forward and whisper in Bean's hair, "Kenny G. is here." Sabina's head whips around, makes a sharp right turn. "Where?" she mouths, and instructs me to get him, so I turn around, walk toward the rear of the immense group of mourners, through all the bodies toward Ken's. I grip his arm and tug him up toward the front to where my family is, near the casket.

If we asked him to, Ken could lead the whole memorial service. He knows how to perform mass. My dad and Ken were students together at the Saint Mary of the Lake Minor Seminary in Chicago almost all the way to priesthood, but they both dropped out. Ken's a lawyer now, practices in Champaign. Every single Sunday he plays the organ in all three services at his church.

After Dad and Ken quit the seminary, they started losing touch, eventually dropped off each other's radar entirely. Then, maybe twenty years later, Ken found Dad and started visiting him, started visiting our family. Totally out of the blue. Soon he was visiting almost once a month. Soon we started to expect him for the holidays. Mom practically adopted him. He has become part of our family. We love Ken.

Jules loved Ken.

I give Ken my spot, the chair in between Sabina and Dad. It's a green chair, covered in some jade, velvety blanket to protect it from the rain. A blanket probably from the storage room in the funeral home's garage. We are the only people with the velvet chairs, the privileged. As if the velvet chair quietly announces that those who sit in it are the people who loved the dead person the most. Dad's arm is in a sling and the expression on his face looks very confused. Dad's been whispering his words all week. Ken sets his hand on Dad's shoulder. It's not your fault.

I pay attention a little bit, drifting in and out of the priest's remarks, then come back in when a river of legs and arms and faces, a chain of people, slowly starts circling the hole in the earth. They lean down and pinch specks of soil and grass, opening their fingers and dropping pebbles into the hole before walking away. Then my sister stands up, turns to face me, and I tense up with a feeling of being caught, like I'm in trouble, or have done something wrong. Bean's eyes are swollen, her face is ashen. She nods her head, motioning me to follow her lead. I understand after watching what she does that it is my turn to walk over and look at the casket for the very last time. I take one stride over to the hole in the ground, look down, and then I stop. In an instant, everything goes blank. I become frozen in time, strangled by a moment that will never quite make it into a memory.

But I do remember this: the mass is over, it is time to leave the funeral, but no one knows how. No one wants to be the one to take the lead. So everybody's eyes are concentrating on the grave, absorbed, staring hard, when in my periphery, I see Ken stand up. He rises slowly, steadily, with intent. And then, he starts buzzing. Buzzing like a hummingbird.

Shit, I think, *oh shit*, and Sabina grips my arm in terror. "What the hell is he doing?"

He's vibrating. The man is clearly vibrating. Purring,

practically, and the noise he's making is beginning to increase in volume.

Slow motion. I'm paralyzed. My lungs freeze. Like I'm smothered, like I'm trying to breathe through a flannel blanket. And then, fast motion. An assembly of heads, lost in thoughts, shoots up, baffled, and darts around like a collective arrow in the direction of the unexpected, odd sound. It's getting louder and louder; Ken's crescendo of buzzing. What is he doing? He's engulfed in it now, there's no stopping what has just started. This is my brother's funeral. What is this man doing?

Then Ken starts up with the words.

I look at Mom. She is staring at the grave; she's unreachable. I look at Dad. His eyes are closed and soft. Has he not heard the sound? Doesn't he realize that his friend has just completely snapped? My father's chin is pointing up in the direction of the sky and his mouth is just a little bit open. He looks peaceful, continuing to sit effortlessly still and his lips are parted in an O shape. I lean toward him.

"Dad?" I whisper.

Listening, I watch his lips and wait for a response until his mouth starts moving, slowly, just a little, like a dog in a dream, but he's not saying anything, and he's not answering me.

"Dad?" I ask again, keeping my eyes on him, on his mouth. Again, I see his lips shaping and fitting, and I start to see he's mouthing his lips over the words and sounds that are buzzing from Ken.

A song. Ken is singing, and Dad knows this song. By now, the volume of Ken's buzzing has grown strong enough that it's able to latch onto a key. It's a song, with a key, and Dad knows the words. *"Tuba mirum spargens sonum."*

The priest joins in.

"Per sepulcra regionum, Coget omnes ante thronum." An eerie chant in a minor key, a requiem now coming from deep inside Ken's stomach. A warbling of long, flat, melancholic pitches, his chant sounds ancient and sad, like rain. The priest can barely keep with Ken's depth, his grief, so he switches over to the harmony. It grows and grows so loud, covers all of us like a warm wind, and somehow, everyone understands what he is singing. Then, the song reaches its last, long note, which Ken holds up for us for a very long time. Then he stops, steps back into his seat, and folds his arms. He looks at the tomb and smiles, and then clicks together his front teeth two or three times as if nothing has just happened.

Down the way, the two lost geese have hoisted their bodies up into the air. They wave faster and harder in order to catch up to the rest of their platoon. Completely numb, mind reset and totally void of any understanding of anything, I watch the geese swoop over a caravan of mobile homes, minivans, and station wagons headed to Tallahassee, Florida, and Yuma, Arizona; the Texaco stations, the cloverleaf interchanges, the McDonald's, the Cinnabon stations, the Cracker Barrels. We call these people "snowbirds"—Midwesterners who pack up and head south before the cold winter months arrive. But unlike humans, the geese are unbound. They carry no emotional baggage with them, just the purposeful intensity that will get them to the kinder, warmer part of the hemisphere on time.

nine

"I want to know the sex of this baby."

Andrew and I are on our way to our twenty-week ultrasound appointment when I realize, rather strongly, that I need to know. It's more than impatience; it's a need. I need to see little baby hands and baby feet, to finally pick a name. I need for this pregnancy to start feeling real, to start feeling delightful. I want to feel what real moms, good moms, feel. Giddy, pretty, glowing, strong, attached.

We are on the 6 train, the metal meatloaf hauling itself through the undergrounds of Manhattan. The engineering and purpose of the New York subway system both fascinates and frightens me: earth blasted away by dynamite to make way for tubes and tracks; a mechanism that delivers nearly five million people a day—New Yorkers reading newspapers, New Yorkers begging for change, New Yorkers looking away and displaying themselves as preoccupied; foreigners, tourists, commuters, live mariachi bands, all shooting forty-five miles per hour through bedrock and soil (soil!) to get to their desired location.

I am lucky to get a seat on the train during this particular time of the day—morning rush hour. If you are disabled, you deserve a seat. If you are blind, geriatric, pregnant, or wounded, you have your grounds, but mostly people just look away. If you smell like old piss, then the plastic chairs around you grudgingly unload themselves. I put on my woe-and-weary Ellis Island face and stuck out my belly until someone finally scooched over. That's how I got my seat.

I want to know the sex of this baby, and we have some time before we reach Beth Israel, so I take the opportunity to convince Andrew to let go of the stupid element of surprise.

"No more surprises," I say.

Gripping a subway pole, Andrew crouches down until his face is level with mine. "Oh come on, Boo," he says. "Let's just wait to find out when you deliver." He taps my belly twice. "The surprise will be exciting." An optimist.

I reach out and slide my fingertips over Andrew's eyebrows. His face looks pretty. He always looks so pure, so charmed, unscathed. He has lived a charmed life, his face says. Long, giraffe eyelashes fluttering over ardent, brown eyes, the heat making his forehead sweat then shimmer. *I am Medium Boo. You are Papa Boo. Maybe is Miniature Boo. This leaves room for what? What will we call our baby? Baby Boo?* "Everything already is exciting," I say. "It is not humanly possible for me to be any more surprised."

"All right, all right," he says. "Let's make a bet. Boy or girl?"

I look around. Across from me is a woman, maybe twice my age. She's gnawing on an ear of corn. She reaches the end, then slides her mouth back to a new row like she's a typewriter in a cartoon. I watch as she takes one last chomp on the cob and then reaches into her left pocket and pulls out another ear. She puts this fresh one on her lap, dips her hand back into her pocket, pulls out a square of Saran Wrap, carefully unwraps it, sets the empty cob in the center of the plastic, wraps it up like a present, tucks it back into her pocket, then starts on the new cob of corn. Everyone is just trying to survive as best they can.

I slip out of my trance just as the train screeches to a halt and an invisible voice mumbles over the PA system: "Fourteenth-Street–Union Square." And we exit the tunnel with the rest of the swarm and reenter the swarm.

We arrive at Beth Israel Medical Center on First and 16th, just as the summer heat is beginning to liquefy the gum on the sidewalks. "It's locked," Andrew says, pulling on the handle of the door to the building. Our appointment is right now, and we've been shut out of the place where we need to be. "Looks like you need a card."

"Since when do you need a card to get into a fucking hospital?" I ask and let out an impressive sigh as a security guard from inside looks up and ignores us.

When I was researching radiology clinics that my Medicaid would cover, I read that a hundred years ago, Beth Israel had

dedicated itself to serving Jewish immigrants living in the tene-
ment slums of the Lower East Side. At the time, Manhattan
hospitals weren't treating patients who had been in the city for
less than a year, so a group of Orthodox Jews paid twenty-five
cents apiece and set up a medical facility to serve immigrants,
particularly newcomers. I didn't find this information just
interesting—I found it baffling. A hospital denying the sick
treatment? What was the purpose of that? In fact, since moving
from Maine, nearly everything I'd encountered in the city was
difficult for me to comprehend: the transportation systems, the
isolation, the gentrification, the garbage, and now, the health
care system. It was all so hairy, so ridiculous, so free fall.

Andrew keeps tugging on the door to the hospital, so I start
knocking on the glass windows. Just as I'm about to give up and
ask the universe what the hell is wrong with people, a woman
in scrubs approaches from the inside. She exits the building,
supplying Andrew with the opportunity to stick his foot in and
hold the door open. She pounds a pack of cigarettes against her
wrist, and I ask her which floor the radiology department is on.
Sixth. We get in the elevator and press the button. It's a Tuesday,
middle of the morning on July 31, 2008.

The waiting room is threadbare and grim: linty floors, lacka-
daisical service, lack of reading materials, and an empty water
cooler. Thirty minutes pass. This is nothing like my father's
office. He would never allow this to happen in his waiting room.
I try to counter my growing cynicism by reminding myself that
things used to be, or could be, worse. *Think: at least this is an
appointment made for happy reasons. Think: at least you've got*

Medicaid. Think: at least you're insured. We skim through old magazines. Forty minutes, forty-five minutes, then the double door leading to the exam rooms swings open and a large, pregnant woman and her male counterpart exit. I try not to spy, but the woman looks horrible. Weeping, pink faced, distraught. Andrew nudges me and we look at one another. "That sucks," I mouth, thinking *sick baby*. As they exit the waiting room, I try not to watch. *How bad could it be?* I wonder. *Stillborn?* I can't imagine what could be worse. Another five minutes makes our wait fifty minutes, fifty-five, sixty. Finally, over an hour later, my name is called and a young Latina technician leads Andrew and me into a small, dim room.

The exam room is shadowy and baby blue, smells cold and sterile. I crawl onto a paper-topped table, lean back, and stare at the pockmarked ceiling. Next, I feel Andrew's warm hand grab mine. I'm jumpy. The technician lifts my blouse and, abruptly, a cool gel is squirted onto my stomach, and I let out a nervous laugh. The next thing I know, the woman is rubbing a wand over my belly.

A few days ago, a stranger—a peddler selling origami key chains from a sidewalk table in Chinatown—stopped me on the street to congratulate me on my baby bump. I pulled together a gracious, close-mouthed smile as the peddler continued to predict the sex, quickly deciding on a male. She said she could tell by the curves of my face; its cashew shape and durable cheekbones supposedly gave it away. Although I hadn't felt any kicking yet or identified any of the wives' tale indications (green urine, a craving for heels of bread), I went ahead and agreed with her.

But deep, deep down, and although it didn't matter much either way, a barely audible voice somewhere in my mind was telling me the opposite: my baby was going to be a girl.

Perched in the left corner of the room, just where the ceiling meets the wall, a black-and-white screen displays what the scanner is picking up under my skin. The image is completely indecipherable. Sonar swirls of hurricanes on a weather map. A strange submarine radar. Andrew points to the round mass and shows me what he thinks is the head. *Is that what it is?* I wonder. *Not a cloud? The ghost of a raisin? An X-ray? Am I seeing the head? Hands? A spine? Are those feet? Funny, they're facing inward, like a loose-stringed marionette.*

The probing continues while the room remains hushed and blooms with awkwardness. I imagine the technician is bored with her job, and as usual, I take it personally. Beyond my feet and backed up against the wall is a young woman, a soft brunette in a white lab coat, observing. It is her job to watch and record; she is a medical resident. But she isn't taking notes anymore. She's pressed her clipboard against her chest and appears rather uncomfortable, almost as though she doesn't want to be here.

"Would you please explain to us what we're looking at?" Andrew asks, but our technician remains silent and continues to roll the wand over me, as if she's casting some kind of spell. "What do you see?" I ask, but to no avail. Abruptly, she stops probing. We ask her to go back and point things out to us, cute things. Cute baby things like little fingers. A button nose. A tiny penis, even. She doesn't respond. We ask her, then, to just please explain the images. She tightens her lip. We begin to panic. "Is it a boy or a girl?" we ask. "Just tell us." She says she cannot. Instead, our technician prints some pictures, dryly mumbles that the doctor will be coming in momentarily, then scurries away.

In the semi-darkness, I sit up on my elbows. "Do you think everything is okay?" I ask.

Squeezing my hand, Andrew tells me of course everything is okay, but his optimism is whisper thin. "You have Medicaid, Boo," he reminds me. "You know what kind of care that means."

After a long moment, Dr. Stein enters the room. "Our technician believes she may have found some abnormalities," she tells us, "so I'm going to go ahead and have a look." Her voice sounds less alarmed than it does unswerving, and at first I'm calmed by this. She's just correcting the technician's mistake, that's what she's doing. *Go ahead,* doctor. *Go ahead and have a look.* We watch her roll up her sleeves, wash her hands, sit down, adjust her chair, pick up the probe.

Dr. Stein loops the wand around my belly, pushing with just the right amount of pressure that feels not hard but not gentle, either. I've stopped watching the radar. Finally, she speaks to us. "Yes, I am definitely seeing some abnormalities here," Dr. Stein says, her eyes still watching the screen. "A constellation of birth defects."

When we purchased the pregnancy test at a Second Avenue Rite Aid store down the street from his apartment, to get a rise out of me, Andrew asked the checkout girl if she thought its results would be positive or negative. The clerk was uninterested, but as she shrugged him off Andrew kept pushing. "I hope it's positive," he told her. "But I hope it's not ugly."

"What are you talking about?" Andrew now asks as I roll back onto the table. "Exactly what are you seeing?" He's getting upset and I don't know where to look, so I press his hand over my face as Dr. Stein begins firing off a list of what she sees:

"Here is the irregular heart structure."

"There is almost zero brain development."

"Here is the spina bifida."

"There are the clubbed feet."

Dr. Stein flips off the screen and turns on the lights, and before leaving us alone, asks, "Mira, would you still like to know the sex of the baby?"

All is lost. All is not lost. All is lost. All is not lost.

This is what I repeat in my head as the nurse writes down *female* on a piece of paper for Andrew, who will show me when we get home. Right now, I don't want to know the sex; Andrew does.

All is not lost. This is what I repeat in my head as the genetic counselor, Dr. Iglesias, explains to us the scientific facts of what may have gone wrong during the fetus's development. *Lost. Not lost.* The mantra makes me feel hopeful yet realistic at the same time, but mostly it helps me feel as if I'm underwater, dulling things to the point that they're blurry, like when your head is submerged and you open your eyes. The poor baby. Never had a chance.

A few minutes ago, Dr. Iglesias refused to talk to us. He made some fuss about the number of allowable visits Medicaid will cover in a single day; we told him we didn't know anything about the rule, asked who cared, this is a baby we're talking about here, but he would barely budge until the resident who witnessed the ultrasound, our new guardian angel, stepped in and took care of things. Somehow she convinced him to set aside regulations and rules, so now we are in the library of a genetic counselor and it smells like lettuce and mayonnaise and the rest of the lunch he just ate.

Lost, not lost. Dr. Iglesias sketches the twenty-three chromosomes. They look like Cheetos. I clutch my handbag. Andrew will speak for us. I've asked him to. Next, Dr. Iglesias outlines some possible theories of what happened.

"It could have been chromosome number three, or seven, or twenty-one, or twenty-three," he states, then asks for our family medical histories, and our own medical histories. He hands us pens. We are confused, shaken, tired.

"If it doesn't die before you deliver it, the baby will have very serious problems," he tells us. It will likely not achieve consciousness, and certainly will not live without some kind of extraordinary intervention."

I want to ask him if the baby ever was alive, alive on her own, if she was real, if she had what we all call, now generically, "a soul." As if there were an answer. He says he will have to do further testing on an amniotic fluid sample to try to understand the genetic issues of why it didn't work. He uses the word "it."

Andrew excuses himself to call into work to let them know he'll be out for the rest of the day.

"Unviable outside the womb," is what Dr. Iglesias says as he explains the results of the ultrasound. "It is sick with zero chance of survival."

"But I am still pregnant," I tell him.

Our guardian resident leads us back into the exam room where there is some muffled talk about an amniocentesis, something about a very long needle going into my belly to sample fluids and baby tissue. I put myself in the hands of the staff and go on autopilot.

With my back on the examination table, I close my eyes. I see Michigan. I see Battle Creek, Leila Hospital, the facility where my father used to work before it closed down. The same hospital where I saw my brother for the very last time. The only hospital, really, where I've ever spent any time. When we were little, Dad used to drop Jules and Sabina and me off in the pimped-out doctors' lounge before he made his rounds and tended to patients. At Leila, we got to watch TV, which was special because we never got to watch TV at home. For us, the hospital was an escape, almost like a Narnia. We'd do all the things we didn't get to do at home: Julian would channel surf, Sabina would read *People* magazine, and I'd scavenge through the Folgers coffee stand, digging for packets of dry hot cocoa mix to pour down my throat. I wanted to eat the marshmallows. I wanted television and I wanted sugar. I was narrow-minded and indifferent, a combination worse than anything else in the world.

Now, flat on my back with my eyes pinned tight and a needle in my belly, I wonder just what my father was doing and encountering in the hospital exam rooms, just what was going on down the hallways outside the doctors' lounge while I gluttonously flipped through the television channels and pounded the sugar packets, thinking only of my desires. Am I still that narrow-minded girl?

What have I done wrong to bring forth this situation when all I've been trying to do is make things right? Is karma finally making its rounds, or is this really just what Dr. Iglesias called it: a random genetic fluke?

I squeeze Andrew's earlobe, which will be like a rosary bead to me for the next two weeks. "How are we going to tell everyone?" I ask. "What are we going to do?"

"I don't know," he finally admits.

Nearly five hours later, a cab finally takes us home from the hospital. Completely defeated, we phone home and, on speakerphone, deliver the terrible news and the even more terrible choice ahead of us: do nothing and continue anyway or terminate. Andrew cries hard, then explains the chromosome lesson and the details of the options.

My parents say they're sorry. They cry a little bit, too, then I grab the phone and blurt out the baffling bit that Dr. Stein told me—"If you decide to do this, the baby will not feel a thing." Then I ask my mother, "Why is it that we always begin to cherish things the minute they start to disappear?"

ten

Several years ago, I met this girl, Nicole Carpenter. Nicole used to go through the city of Battle Creek like a walking middle finger. She was seventeen years old, fought, smoked, dipped, drank, and skipped school. Junior year, she dropped out.

Nicole wore sandy blonde cornrows that dropped to her waist and wrapped around her like seaweed. She'd sway her head side to side and fling those braids behind her shoulders, rake back the strays with two acrylic nails, then light up a Newport 100. And Nicole was exceptionally petite—at about four foot nine, she could've passed for an eleven-year-old.

When she found out she was pregnant (at age sixteen), Nicole moved out of her parents' place, picked up a job at Arby's, and moved in with the guy she thought might be the father of her baby. ("I mean, shoot, he prolly is, that muthafucker. He the only one who didn't wear a jimmy cap.")

My dad was Nicole's doctor and had been since she was a little baby. He was in maybe his twenty-eighth year practicing as a family physician, performing everything from wart removal to severing umbilical cords, when Nicole resurfaced, dangling her legs over a paper-wrapped table and he walked into the exam room. That was the same year Dad stopped delivering babies for good, and Nicole was one of the last patients he worked with in the delivery room.

Dad claims he was forced to stop delivering babies because the cost of malpractice insurance had gotten so high. But my mother didn't believe him. Mom says she fast-forwarded the decision after he got paged in the middle of Midnight Mass for the tenth Christmas Eve in a row, which is the night before Dad's birthday, and she gave him a talking to. But I think that Nicole, specifically Nicole's pregnancy, had an effect on the verdict, too. The whole thing just seemed to deflate him.

Being a doctor in such a small town, my dad was a bit of a celebrity. Folks had named their dogs after him (different variations of Phil, Philip, and Ptacin). There wasn't a time he could zip in and out of Felpausch grocery without getting cornered by folks seeking minor medical attention, which could be particularly embarrassing when you were with him, and your hands were balancing items like Pepto-Bismol, toilet paper, tampons, or anything that revealed to the world that you, too, used the toilet. But my dad would take his time, put his hand on the shoulder of the ailing individual, lean in as if to whisper a secret, and say, "How can I help?" I guess that's how I learned about patience—by watching him exhibit this untamed (or untainted) compassion. Dad has a Paul Bunyon-sized heart; my friends used to claim he was the Jesus reincarnate, but Mom says he's just a big baby. For instance, late one night, back when he was a medical student at Georgetown, Dad got mugged while jogging through campus. He had no cash or money on him, or to his name, really, but invited the thief back to his "minimalist" apartment anyway, for some fruit and to write him a check. Dad said that if the guy was going to don a black mask and attempt a mugging, then he needed the hundred bucks more.

Growing up, my family dinner conversations revolved around Dad's work stories. With our chins resting on our hands and our elbows framing our dinner plates, we'd listen to him talk about our town, about our time and our people. I remember chewing on a square piece of pork tenderloin when he told us the tale about the obese man with maggots in the sores on his legs and feet, or the one about the surgeon who stitched up a guy after a vasectomy and forgot to remove the gauze.

One night—I was about eighteen years old at the time—when we were all home for a Thanksgiving dinner, just shooting the breeze around the table, Nicole's name came up. Mom said, "Phil, did you tell our girls about Nicole, your patient with dying baby?" She shook her head. "Such a tragedy."

Julian had been dead for a year, and Mom had recently retired. After Jules died, Mom kept working, maybe even went into overdrive, pouring all her emotions and anger and energy into her work. She worked herself to the bone, but at a certain point, she realized it was not good for her. Maybe it was good for her at first, but maybe it soon was good only for everyone else, and maybe that's why she kept doing it. Mom said that she was doing her part to help support the family, but night after night, she'd have to watch her customers put their keys in the ignitions of their cars and drive home after they'd consumed a bottle of wine or more over the dinner she'd cooked them. After a certain point, she just couldn't handle being so close to the drinking and driving. So, at the stroke of midnight on the very last day of 1999, my mother gathered her staff and her family around a large dining room table at RSVP and announced the news: she was putting her restaurant up for sale and was retiring.

"Who's Nicole?" I asked.

Dad put down his silverware and blew out a long trail of breath. "Oh, Nicole," he said without looking up. "She's one of my patients."

"And is driving your Daddy down the wall," Mom added.

"It's 'up the wall,'" Sabina chimed.

"Nicole's been coming to my office since she was a little baby," he said, "but I hadn't seen her in years until she came in for a prenatal exam."

Mom interjected, "She thinks she's Mary, Mother of God."

Dad sighed again. "Nicole's a bit dramatic."

He told us that Nicole's pregnancy was a rare and complicated one. That Nicole was born with something called Russell-Silver Syndrome, a rare chromosomal abnormality that causes someone to be very small and look much younger than they are. When she came into my dad's office for her first prenatal checkup, all fresh faced and pregnant, Dad sent her to a specialist for extra testing to see if Russell-Silver Syndrome would affect her fetus at all. Results proved that it would not, but something else blipped up in the tests. Nicole's baby had anencephaly, a totally unrelated birth defect.

Dad took the paper napkin off his lap, unfolded it, and laid it out over the kitchen table. "Anencephaly refers to the incomplete development of a fetus's brain and spinal cord and their protective coverings."

He pulled a pen out of his pocket, one with a built-in laser pointer and the word *Celebrex* written up the side, and began sketching onto the cleaner side of the napkin: a line, a loop, a crescent.

"It occurs when the neural tube, which is a precursor to the baby's central nervous system"—the pen doubled back to complete a tulip, a pea pod, a tunnel—"fails to close. The tube is supposed to fold and close during the third or fourth week of pregnancy. And when it doesn't, this means a failure of major parts of the brain, and a failure of the skull and scalp to form."

I leaned in for a closer look at Dad's drawing. It looked like a roller coaster. "No brain? No shit?" I asked, and Sabina kicked me from under the table.

"Infants born with anencephaly are usually blind, deaf, and unconscious."

"And what is fate to the babies?" Mom asked.

"If Nicole's baby is born, it will have already suffered serious brain damage . . . won't be able to eat, not even breathe for long."

"Do they suffer, Dad?" I asked.

He put down the pen and handed me the napkin. I folded it up four times and slid it under my plate. "It's not a painful condition," he said, "but it is inevitably fatal."

"Poor baby. Poor her soul. It is very sad," Mom said, then joined Sabina, who was clearing the table. Dad pushed out his chair, and as he began to stand up, I stopped him.

"Wait, what happened next? To the girl?" I asked.

"The specialist explained all this to Nicole and recommended that she terminate the pregnancy."

"Then what?"

"Dad works at a Catholic hospital, Mira. They don't do abortions," Sabina said. She had recently renounced her Catholicism, claiming the church was homophobic, sexist, and past its prime. I envied that she got to sleep in during church. Our family hadn't really ever talked about the topic of abortion. Maybe it's because it never really came up. Maybe it's because we didn't have much of an opinion about it—we were Catholic, but we were smart enough to know that everyone's situation was different. It wasn't wise to generalize or judge. But the general consensus was that abortions weren't good, and Dad didn't perform them. I always figured that I'd never have to make a decision like that, so I never really thought about it.

"Nicole basically freaked out and drove straight back to my office."

"Screaming and crying like child," Mom called from the sink.

"Yes, screaming and crying and causing this huge commotion in the waiting room, demanding to see me." He carried his plate to the sink. I followed him.

"I pulled her into an exam room and tried to calm her down. Go get your dishes, please, Mira," Dad said.

I went to the table and returned with my plate. "Then what? Then what did you say to her?"

"Well, we talked. I explained that it wasn't her fault, that she didn't cause this and couldn't have prevented it. I just looked at her and said, 'Nicole, there is just nothing you or I or anyone can do about this. There's no surgery to do in the womb, no medicine you can take.' I just told her, 'Nicole, your baby just ain't going to survive.'"

Dad dropped a big spoon into the coffee beans, leveled off a scoop of decaf, tipped it into the coffeemaker, and pressed START. He walked over to Mom, who was loading bowls into the dishwasher, put his hands on her shoulders, kissed her forehead, and gently pushed her out of the kitchen. He handed Sabina a towel, rolled up his sleeves, and plunged a big pot into the kitchen sink.

"I told Nicole that she could transfer medical facilities if she'd prefer to abort the fetus."

"So did she get, you know, what Beanie said?"

Sabina threw a towel at me and told me to make myself useful.

"She panicked and became frightened by the thought of an abortion," Dad said. He folded his arms and leaned back against the ivory refrigerator door, which was checkered with magnets of our old school photos and Mom's kitchen wisdom quotes. One magnet said: *If Momma ain't happy, ain't nobody happy.* One magnet had a cartoon of two *makizushi* rolls on it and read: *Wake up, little sushi.* One magnet framed an old family photo: the five of us wearing matching St. Philip Elementary School sweatshirts, rosy cheeks, huddled in a tripod. Julian was alive in that photo.

"I remember Nicole sitting on the exam table, weeping. She said to me, 'This was a spark that had no chance at life without my help, so if my child was meant to live for five minutes, it is going to live for five minutes.'"

There was a moment of silence, which was quickly interrupted by the buzzing and scraping sound of Mom sliding the electric broom across the tile floor. I was taken aback by Nicole's response. I found it gallant and noble. Suddenly, to me, she was brilliant and almost saintlike.

"I agreed to ride it out with her," Dad said in what sounded like a whisper, even over the vacuum.

"Tell the girls about the board, Phil," Mom said, plowing the vacuum past us.

"What board? What happened?"

"So we continued giving Nicole care—a lot of care—during her pregnancy. She was a bit . . . high maintenance. She'd come into the office several times unannounced, saying she felt movement, or that she was having a miscarriage. She called constantly. We were there for her around the clock. But at the same time, the hospital was struggling with the technicalities of the delivery. It was like this: the baby would die outside the womb, and in a purely medical sense, whether Nicole delivered at twelve weeks or forty weeks, the question was moot. But because of the Silver Syndrome, because Nicole was such a tiny person, she wouldn't be able to deliver a normal-sized baby because it wouldn't fit through the bones of her pelvis."

"So what could she do?"

"She would have to have a Cesarean delivery, and for a woman of her size, this was a dangerous procedure."

The vacuuming stopped.

"Dis was huge production. Nearly took over everyone's lives. Daddy and de bishop had meetings during de week, during de time we are supposed to have dance class," Mom said.

"We formed an ethics committee. There was the director of the hospital, a lawyer, the Reverend Al Schipper, the hospital chaplain, and other doctors to determine how early Nicole could be induced without it being considered a termination of a pregnancy. We finally decided on a time, up to the very minute, of what was considered 'natural.'"

"Yeah, God's way," Sabina sighed.

"So what happened?" I asked again.

"The baby inside Nicole grew. She said she felt it kicking."

"What did she do?"

"She dug in her heels and carried the baby through the pregnancy. She learned the sex of the baby. She bought maternity clothes and pink baby clothes. She named the baby. Even the nurses at the hospital knitted booties and made a baby quilt. She hired Reverend Schipper from the ethics committee to facilitate the funeral of the baby."

"And then?"

"And then we induced her when it was the right time."

"And then?"

"And then Nicole delivered her baby, vaginally."

"And then?"

"And then after five hours, the baby girl died in Nicole's arms."

"Poor her soul, indeed," I agreed.

A few weeks after I learned about her, I met Nicole. I'm not sure why I did it, but I wanted to meet this person, this girl, this woman. I just had to get her story. I thought what she had done was selfless, heroic and brave. Here was this girl, raised with little money, not very educated, who put her fears aside and gave her baby all she could. I was enchanted. I had just turned eighteen. The year had taken my brother away and left me with so much confusion and grief, I thought Nicole might be carrying the kind of hope or answer or relief that I was looking for. I called her, told her I'd like to meet her, and she agreed. So one Saturday, I found Nicole in a booth at Home Spun Family Restaurant. I sat down across from her and ordered a coffee while she smoked feverishly.

"You wanna see a picture of my little girl?"

She slid the photo across the table, a 4 x 6 glossy with edges that were beginning to coil and curl toward the center, like a dried leaf. I continued to look at Nicole, afraid of what I might see.

"That's her. My li'l girl, Elizabeth," Nicole said, and I looked down at the photo in front of me, which was upside down. Nicole leaned over and rotated it counterclockwise with her left hand, the hand holding a cigarette, to face me.

The baby in the photo was dead. She was tiny, had a pink cap over her head, and looked like an old man. Not much different than any newborn—closed eyes and a pink complexion—but the baby was dead and I could tell. Nicole pulled a frilly scrapbook out of her purse and narrated the details of a few more photos: baby Elizabeth in a long, white, lace dress; Nicole's parents embracing Nicole on the hospital bed; a cluster of smiling nurses; and a tiny white casket.

"You should be proud of yourself," I told her, but saying it didn't feel the way I thought it would.

She said she was. "I'm talkin' to my parents again, and I might go back to school," she said. "This was just a blessin' in disguise, I guess." And while she was talking and smoking, I was thinking to myself that she seemed a little too happy, a little too flippant. *You're smoking*, I thought.

"Do you want kids?" I asked her, and she said yeah, maybe. "If it happens, you know?" And then my hope started to sink and I started to feel foolish. You were pregnant and your baby died and you're smoking and you seem just fine.

"I'm prolly movin' back home, movin' back with my parents," she said and tapped the ash off her cigarette. She seemed proud, not traumatized. I didn't like it.

I've been told that sometimes when a person is exposed to trauma, that person's basic assumptions get dislodged and shaken up. For one instant, right after the shake, everything stands still, in midair. Life. Just. Stops. For just that one second, there is clarity. And when the pieces drop back into place, nothing feels quite right. You pick up your feet to trudge forward, but the ground has shifted. You can't get back into the invisible rhythm, that way you felt you'd been moving your whole life up until then. Walking forward now feels like walking sideways. It's only then when you realize that you were really just at the mercy of time. *Like sands through the hourglass.*

Biologically speaking, there's a certain branch of science (it's called phylogenetics, "tribe" + "relative to birth" in Greek) that studies this kind of thing at the molecular level: the cavity-filled, lasagna-looking brain. How well equipped one is to handle traumatic events depends on how much corticotrophin-releasing hormone one has lining the brain walls. Some studies have suggested the possibility of physical shrinkage in the hippocampus and amygdala when trauma persists. In other words, you see a dead body, your brain shrinks and you act funny.

Therapists call such responses "post-something trauma." It's listed in their thick, slick DSMs as a type of disorder that can occur after an exposure to a terrifying event, and there are all kinds of post-traumas: post-cult trauma (intense emotional problems that some members of cults and new religious movements experience upon disaffection and disaffiliation); post-betrayal trauma (institutions we depend on for survival violate us in some way . . . may increase the likelihood of psychogenic amnesia). For more post-traumas, see: post-penetrating trauma. See also: post-blunt force trauma. See also: psychological trauma. See also: Nicole.

We have trauma, and we have grief. People die, and we find it baffling. Painful. Inexplicable. Grief is baffling. There are theories on how we react to loss and death, how we cope, how we handle loss. Some believe the range of emotions mourners experience is predictable, that grief can be monitored, as if mourners are following a checklist. But sorrow is less of a checklist, more like water. It's fluid, it has no set shape, never disappears, never ends. It doesn't go away. It just changes. It changes us.

About a year after she lost her baby, Nicole came back to my dad's office to announce she had gotten pregnant again, and that she had given birth to a healthy baby. Mom thought it'd be nice to round up a roomful of baby goods—diapers, a stroller, a crib, and a bunch of barely used onesies from the Salvation Army—and throw Nicole a belated baby shower. She thought Nicole needed support—maybe she was projecting— but she wanted to make her feel good. Celebrate life. Be there for another woman. Mom invited some nurses, some of her own friends (a couple of doctors' wives who happened to be immigrants, too), and Al Schipper, who led her first baby's funeral, to celebrate Nicole's new life.

See, look, I thought, *there is a reason for everything. God knows what he's doing. He will always make you happy again.* Then the day of the party came. The guests arrived, ready to shower Nicole with their streamers and white-frosting baby cake. Ten minutes passed, then twenty, then Nicole never showed up. Dad tried to call her and got a droning signal at the other end of the line, a recorded robot voice saying the phone number was no longer in service and had been disconnected. He checked the hospital records, which revealed she had had a baby boy, and that's it.

With wet eyes, Mom donated all the baby goods back to the Salvation Army and took the stroller to Kids "R" Us, bringing me along for the ride. In the car, I tried to be the optimist and come up with excuses for Nicole's absence, but it didn't fly.

"Maybe her baby got sick," I said, but my mother ignored me and my sugarcoating. "I'm sure Nicole is being a good mommy, Mom. Really, she probably just had to work," I insisted, even though I knew that I was doing what my mother had done before, too: latch on to Nicole in a fitful search for faith and hope. My mother needed to know that, as confusing as everything was, this was all part of the plan. Jules was dead, and Mom needed comfort, and maybe by giving this girl comfort, she might have received a little comfort of her own, too.

"Give me break," Mom said. "That girl was hussy and we both know it. She probably dump her baby wit de parents and is out tail chasing dis minute."

"Mom, maybe she had amnesia," I said, and that's when I started doubting my sense of the truth.

eleven

I am in California and I have just ridden a gondola into the Ice Age.

I bought the expensive cable car ticket because I wanted to catch a glimpse of the two-million-year-old lake everyone has been talking about. The lift carried me up two thousand vertical feet, over gray-green conifers, over brush fields with crunchy, thirsty-looking plants and gravel cliffs with caramel-colored soil. Steadily, I got higher and higher until suddenly, and only for about five or six seconds, I got to see the lake.

Lake Tahoe was giant, and startling, and still. The huge, blue mass came out of nowhere; it was as if the trees had briefly parted to reveal a secret brontosaurus stealing a nap. But the car kept moving up and on until we reached the nosebleed section of the mountain. The gondola stopped. I got out. And here I am.

Below me is the Squaw Valley USA ski resort. I didn't come to Squaw Valley to ski. It's August, and there's no snow. The reason I am here on the West Coast—at the opposite end of the country from my home, and high up in the Sierras—is because I am participating in a summer writer's conference. A week ago, shortly after the damning ultrasound, I left Manhattan and Andrew and Maybe for a literary retreat. I'd been planning on it, regardless. Now, it's an escape. I have three days left before I am to leave and resume my life back on East 32nd Street, but for the remainder of today, I will be hiking around Squaw Valley's High Camp. In doing this, I plan on appreciating nature. And by appreciating nature, I hope to make my mind clear and stable and make sense out of things, reach some sort of conclusion, some final decision. Our instructors gave us the whole afternoon off.

Squaw Valley's red-white-and-blue-colored pamphlet tells me that Lake Tahoe is subterranean; she's almost five hundred meters deep. Her waters are so still and unmoving that people flock from all over the planet just to bear witness to her clarity. The lake's creation was incidental and completely natural: millions of years ago, rain, melting snow, and runoff filled the lower basin. After eruptions from a now-extinct volcano called Mount Pluto, a dam was formed on the north side, and scouring glaciers from the Ice Age shaped the rest of the lake.

As I skim through the glossy brochure's scientific explanations, I see the words on the page as metaphors for my current situation: *formed by a series of large faults, capable of large magnitude earthquakes, located within Desolation Wilderness, the youngest deformation belt.* I smack the pamphlet with the backside of my hand, folding it up three times before tossing it into a nearby garbage can. "Shut up," I tell it. Just shut up.

I am in California and I am the only thing keeping the life inside me alive. Without me, the baby is powerless.

Once, I called her a parasite. "This thing is a fucking parasite," is what I said. I was about three months pregnant. It was weeks before the ultrasound. I felt so sick. I was so angry. I had spent the entire afternoon sprawled out on the tiled bathroom floor of our apartment like a piece of roadkill, stationed alongside the toilet. The moisture from the toilet's cool porcelain base had apprehended tiny pubic hairs and lavender-colored lint. The floor stank like ten-day-old urine. And the fact that the urine probably wasn't even mine made me feel even worse, and irrelevant. Besides the point. A means to an end.

For hours my brain and stomach had been churning like I had just stepped off a Tilt-A-Whirl. I couldn't get a grip. I couldn't control my vomiting. All I could get myself to do was moan. I was all alone in the apartment, all by myself, but I could hear the sounds of thousands of lives right next to me, lives right on my periphery, not even fifteen feet away, kept separate only by a piece of drywall, or a glass window. Traces of people were everywhere—voices of strangers reverberating in the hallway, Segundo cleaning the alleyway with a leaf blower, UPS trucks, honks and sirens. Eventually, I fell asleep and awoke to the sound of Maybe barking as Andrew arrived home, turned his key, and walked into the apartment.

When he called out for me, I pressed my shoulder blades against the bathtub and pushed my swollen feet against the bathroom door. "Go away!" I shouted. From behind the hollow door, Andrew laughed, told me I was adorable, but I refused to let him in.

"Can I come hang out with you in there, Medium Boo, please?" Andrew's words sounded muffled, as if his lips were pressing upon the tiny gap where the stile met the frame.

"I just want to be alone," I told him, and pulled my knees into to my chest as much as I could and dropped my heavy head into the space between them. That's right around the time I called the baby a fucking parasite.

"You're so mad. Why are you always so mad?" Andrew heaved a sigh. "That baby loves you," he said. "And I love you."

"It's just sucking the life right out of me," I said, and I wasn't sure if I was kidding or not.

I had been trying very hard to make sense of the new kind of love Andrew was talking about. It was difficult for me to understand because I had never experienced anything quite like it. The new love was completely unfamiliar, almost foreign, but at the same time it felt proverbial and natural. Also, it was fucking frightening. It was frightening because it was the kind of love that required a colossal amount of responsibility and tenderness, buoyancy and endurance, bravery and confidence—traits I wasn't sure I possessed, or ever would. It was frightening because, from what I understood, in order for it all to be successful, I had to be strong; and I was having difficulty being strong because the new love that was growing inside of me was draining every bit of love juice that I had right out of me. I had control over nothing.

I picked up my head and grimaced at the bathroom door. "The baby is making me feel like shit," I complained. My brown hair was pinned underneath a red bandanna, and the top button and zipper of my pants were undone. I wasn't even wearing deodorant, not because I was careless but because I was worried that the chemicals in the gel would get into my bloodstream, and that I would pump the chemicals into the baby. I suspected that deodorant was toxic.

"You did this," I said. I wanted to say something that would make Andrew feel the way I did—afraid and angry and embarrassed and sad—but there was nothing. It was a greedy notion but I couldn't dismantle it. I knew Andrew hadn't planned for this to happen, either. Neither one of us had asked for it, but Andrew was trying his best to make this work. He was confident. He didn't care what people thought. He didn't need to placate anyone.

I wasn't happy. I hadn't wanted to be a mother just yet, but I did think that once the baby came, my love for it would trump every fear I'd had about being pregnant. Nothing I felt had been simple, black or white. I was lost. And even though I was as unpleasant as a bee sting, Andrew remained happy, and very excited about me, his new love. He was excited about the baby and the new reality of the three of us becoming one family. I couldn't understand why I wasn't flying through the air or singing with joy. I loved Andrew. I liked babies. So why wasn't I feeling optimistic? Why was it so hard for me to be happy?

Eventually, I let down my guard, told Andrew he could come in if he still felt like it, and in he stepped, smiling unwaveringly.

He sat down next to me on the tiles, reached out his hand, and told me everything was going to be okay. I remember how hesitant I was to accept it.

Now I'm in California, and still, my breath and my blood and my body's nutrients are sustaining the life inside me. Without me, this baby is helpless. Without me, Lilly will die. I am her lifeline. I am her barrier to her mortality. Once she leaves my body, the pregnancy will end. The baby will disappear. Or, as the doctors told us after the ultrasound, *it will die.* The medical specialists rapidly fired all of this information and more upon me, so I went ahead and left Manhattan and flew to California.

The specialists bombarded us with genetic details, too. Their facts were incessant. Words I couldn't pronounce. *Holoprosencephaly.* Images I cannot forget. *Clubbed feet. Deformed spine. Collapsed skull. Broken heart.*

"It is sick and cannot survive outside the womb," they said. Therefore, "sick" was the adjective we used to deliver the prognosis to our friends, colleagues, and everyone else, but we called our baby a "baby," not an "it."

But it's been impossible for me to retain any of the scientific data and medical minutia, so Andrew acts as our secretary, our project manager. He is our ambassador. He's taken the wheel. While I am away in California gathering my composure, my fiancé is at home in the eye of the hurricane, collecting the explanations and updates, then relaying the data to me, to my parents, to his parents. He is doing more for me than a man I haven't even known for eight months should ever be expected to do. Over the phone, Andrew updates me with new validating points (amniocentesis test results are showing more neural tube defects); he tells me about more of the things he's taken care of that I won't have to worry about when I arrive home (the rent is paid, the apartment is clean, and our roommate will be heading to Long Island to give us a few days of privacy); he shares with me more facts he's researched on chromosomal flukes and genetic inheritances (coincidence, it's nobody's fault). I accept all his words like a soldier, even though no matter how many sentences come out of the telephone's earpiece, I hear only one single, solitary truth about this warped, colossal calamity: that this baby just ain't going to be. That this sweet and scary, gigantic and tiny new kind of love growing inside me won't be developing much more. That the end of the road is right up ahead of us, or so it seems.

I am standing on a plateau. The air is thin and difficult to breathe. The trees stretch to infinity and the gravel path is as gray as amnesia. I imagine the environment up here probably doesn't change too much. Pebbles, moss, pines, sky. Timeless and homeless; I could be anywhere right now. Any country, any state. Stable. Set. Fixed. Secure. Ahead of me, an upward-climbing path splits in two different directions. Take a left and I'll go through a parched meadow spotted with delicate violets and tiny yellow flowers, and white people walking through them, white people clad in expensive outdoor performance gear. Take a right and who knows? A fat jack pine blocks my view to the remainder of the trail. So I go right. And as I turn the bend, a pair of familiar faces emerges, arriving in long, upward lunges.

"Howdy," the gentleman says, panting. The two hikers lean on luxurious chrome walking sticks and carry CamelBak water packs with clear straws that rest on their shoulders. If they get thirsty, all they have to do is turn their heads to the right, wrap their lips around a plastic nipple, and suck.

I say "hello" back as his counterpart, a woman, begins unzipping the knees of her pants, turning them into shorts. We both watch.

"I'll bet your baby is going to be a forest ranger," the man says.

I rub the torso of my cotton T-shirt in a circular motion and force my lips into a discomfited grin. "Yes, maybe so."

"Or a mountaineer!" the woman adds.

I recognize these two faces from the dining hall. The woman is a playwright. The man is a fiction writer. Neither of them knows that what they're saying couldn't be further from the truth.

"Perhaps. We'll see. Thanks," I tell them.

"You go, girl!" perks the fiction writer.

"Okay. Thanks," I say and continue on.

The road in front of me morphs into a dried-up channel coated in pebbles and pinecones that may make it tricky for me keep my balance on the way down, but I see there is a reward at the bottom of the descent: nothing. At the bottom there is a big, open, natural plaza of tall grass and glittering soil, and nothingness. Absolute nothingness. *Your baby is going to be a mountaineer!* I can finally be alone.

Because there is never any escape. In Manhattan, there are nearly 1.7 million people living on a little island of less than twenty-three square miles, which means there are nearly 74,000 residents per square mile, which means there is never any respite. In New York City, you get no rest, no sympathy, no relief. Thousands of bodies constantly envelop you, but you're always alone in your grief. In New York, you gotta keep up. If you fall, you'll get left behind. You slow down, you'll get run over, most likely by a yellow cab.

Here in Northern California, though, it appears to be just the opposite. Here in the sunny, yawning, open state of California, life seems to move at a much slower pace. People have the luxury of space and sun. You can see the sky and you realize what kind of weather is surrounding you. And in California, people ask and people listen. In California, you get asked your story and people are interested in it. This does make sense, I suppose. After all, we are at a writers' colony.

Even so, I don't want to tell these strangers my particular story. Before I arrived at Squaw Valley, I decided not to tell anyone there the truth of what's really going on inside of me, underneath the surface of things. Why should I volunteer that information? I can just imagine the exchange:

Stranger asks: *How many months along?*

I respond, candidly: *About five. But perhaps only six more days left.*

I will not tell any of my fellow writers about my misfortune. I won't be bringing this story into workshop class. If I did, they'd ask me where the story is going. I'd tell them that I don't know, and they'd explore the possibilities from a writer's point of view, turn it into some narrative. They'd have to examine the elements of the story. The components: *Daughter of respectable Catholic parents gets pregnant out of wedlock. Baby will not live. Here lies the conflict. So whom are we rooting for? The mother? Is she the protagonist? Is she a student, a young woman, a daughter, a mother—what is she? What about the baby? Sorry to be insensitive, but the baby doesn't really have a brain, much less a working heart. (And by the way, is the dilemma a moral one or a medical one?) So it's the pregnant woman. Is she a hero or a villain? Is she at fault? For the baby? For her brother? Where did she go wrong?*

But the baby will die, so continue anyway? Should doctors induce for a vaginal delivery? Will she miscarry? Should she terminate? Termination. Abortion: there's the hook. It's an ongoing debate. Hot-button issue. We'll have to decide on the point of view, and how to frame it. The author will have to choose her words carefully: baby or fetus? "Fetus" when referring to an unborn child in the post-embryonic state—it sounds neutral and scientific. The term "baby" implies that we are talking about . . . a baby. We also have to decide on what to call the termination of the pregnancy. Partial-birth abortion? Sounds ugly. Such a harsh word choice. It would really influence the tone of the narrative. Like "heart attack" or "female genital mutilation." Next: hero or villain? Then, pregnant out of wedlock. Selfishness—this could be her moral wrong. So how does she alleviate it? Should she be passive? Also: what ethical standards are we going by? How does she make her decision? By listening to her instincts. If her heart is pure, yes, she will know. If it isn't, we shall see.

No, thank you. I'm going to keep this one to myself.

❦ ❦ ❦

After the ultrasound, the doctors told me I have three choices:

1. Terminate the pregnancy next week.
2. Do nothing at all and possibly miscarry.
3. Induce early and deliver next month.

Not long after the ultrasound, the doctors and specialists stopped sounding as if they were talking about a baby, but rather about something made out of metal. Their words were technical and cold. I got defensive and argumentative. So when I have any questions, Andrew gets answers and relays the information as gently as he knows how.

"She can't breathe on her own," he'll say.

"How can we be sure?"

"Lilly has no brain development."

"What if the doctors just aren't trying hard enough?"

"They said she's not quite a stillborn, but there is a strong possibility she may die in your womb," he explains. "You can do what you want, but she could die inside you. Any day."

Andrew hasn't asserted his feelings about any of the decisions I've been presented with and I haven't asked for too many details about my options. I can only handle so many details, facts, suggestions, opinions, feelings. The more voices I hear, the harder it is to decide.

My mother suggested Option #3: Induce and Deliver. She said, that way, unlike with Option #1, I could be conscious. I would be awake, lucid; I could play a part in it, push, deliver. "You'd get a chance to see your baby, hold her and say goodbye." Mom said this might give me closure, and that closure is a very important element in the process of healing. But when I think about Option #3, I picture myself draped in a baby-blue paper gown, feet propped, wearing slippers and a hairnet, pushing, sweating, bleeding, delivering a lifeless, barely recognizable, red-hot creature, or a gray-blue mass, and it terrifies me. My mother hasn't speculated as to what I would be giving birth to. And after I gave birth, would Lilly be alive? Would she move? And for how long? Would she make sounds? Coo? Cry? When would doctors decide to take her away? When would I want to let them? Where would she go? Option #3 sounded like the worst choice. What my mother didn't bring up was whether or not at five months a delivery would be painful. Or how much I might rip or tear. If I delivered, would I still adhere to my mantra of a "natural" and drug-free childbirth? While inducing sounded the most natural, it was what I least wanted. Option #3 horrified me.

There is Option #1: Terminate. Also known as "dilation and extraction." Dilation of the cervix, extraction of the fetus. Dr. Stein has been nudging Andrew to nudge me to consider termination. She gives him the facts, which he shares with me. The D&E would take three days and would be painful. First step: dilate the cervix by inserting laminaria rods ("They're made out of seaweed," Andrew told me. "Can you believe it?"). Andrew mentioned forceps, and when he started to explain the extraction process, I made him stop. I didn't want to hear the specifics—*what is the point?* The details don't matter because the result is going to be the same. Dr. Stein checks in on Andrew every day with a sense of urgency. She needs a decision from us soon. The procedure can only be performed up to twenty weeks into a pregnancy; I only have a few days until that window closes.

I am currently exercising Option #2: Do nothing and wait.

I haven't made up my mind, but I am aware that once I arrive home from California, Andrew, my parents, and the doctors will expect me to have picked one of the three options and made a decision. I have promised myself that today, before I come down from this mountain, I will have brought down the gavel. *Focus.*

I clutch my abdomen. I just don't want to be selfish.

For nearly five months, Lilly and I have spent every second together, but I still haven't really felt her. There have been many times when I've held perfectly still at night, anticipating some kick or flutter, but she's never once kicked or fluttered. I've waited for her to give me a sign, for her to make this all seem real and recognizable, but I've never felt what I thought I should: a spark, another presence. There is my large belly, there is my nausea, but I don't feel *her*. I feel completely alone. Is it because I don't recognize her? Or is it because she's not really there? I've felt a million different things, but I can't tell which one is *her*.

I thought the ultrasound would make Lilly feel real, feel alive within me. I thought that once I saw her on the screen, the magic would envelop me. I would feel like a mother, not a child. I thought that once I saw the baby—not an invisible ball of emotions, but an actual baby—I would feel relief and love would take over. But the ultrasound was not what I had anticipated. Lilly remains a phantom. After the ultrasound, I began to feel that Lilly's fate was my fault. That my fears and anger from the unplanned pregnancy had damned her. Even though I believe in choice and reproductive freedom, even though I trust others to make decisions for themselves, when it comes to my own freedom to do what I feel is best for me, I'm not sure that I deserve to have such an easy way out. I don't believe in bad luck; I just think I've failed—as a young woman, as a daughter, at motherhood—and that I should be punished.

My pocket vibrates. I open my eyes, puzzled and squinting, and reach down for my phone. It's Andrew. He asks me how I am holding up, tells me he's okay, that Maybe is doing okay. His voice is bland and weak. He asks me how classes are, am I sleeping all right, eating okay, making friends; I lie and say that all is well.

"That's good," he says.

"My writing instructor is really fantastic."

"What else?" he asks.

"One of my new friends told me I am a hot pregnant lady," I tell him.

"That's nice," Andrew says. "Anything else?"

"She asked me if it's a boy or a girl. I told her that we've named her Lilly."

I try to keep the dialogue moving quickly, but our exchange becomes choppy, the pauses expand. The conversation hesitates, then halts, then Andrew brings up what I've been circumventing.

"Mira, did you decide?"

"Decide on what?"

"Boo, come on. Your decision. About Lilly?"

And abrasively, I say nothing back.

"Mira," Andrew says. "I just got off the phone with your dad."

The word "violent" has been fluttering in and out of the

conversations between Andrew, my parents, and me for the last three days since the options were presented. Dad told us that from what he understood, if I terminate the pregnancy, the procedure is a "violent" one. A late-term abortion means a violent surgery. What did this mean, "violent"? While it sounded the least natural, it was what I was leaning toward, but with such a word being used to describe the end of my pregnancy, I started to look at myself as a savage. I thought my parents would also start to look at me as a selfish brute and this made me defensive. Their opinion mattered too much. Their peace of mind was vital. They'd already lost a child. They lost a child in a moment that I may have been able to prevent.

Ever since Julian's funeral, I had calculated nearly all my bold moves in a way that would do the least damage, that would keep the most people safe. *Finally, no more news of death or dying.* In getting pregnant, I'd created more death. Just when they started getting excited about the baby, we learned that her life wasn't viable. I'd done it again. I was the worst. I tried not to get pregnant and I got pregnant. I tried to sustain life and I killed it. It's as if no matter how hard I tried to protect them, no matter what I did or didn't do, my actions kept harming my family. It was as if I was cursed: I couldn't *not* hurt them.

And now, no matter what, this baby is going to die. And I have to choose how. *A late-term abortion meant a violent surgery,* was what my father had said. And while my father meant this as a procedure that was the most violent on the patient, I kept thinking of it as an ethical issue. If I choose to terminate, would my parents view me as a selfish brute? A murderer? Their opinion weighs heavily on me. If I choose to terminate, I'll be what the pro-lifers hate. I'd choose what many call *partial-birth abortion*. Why? It's not that. It's not just three words. It's not "changed my mind." It's not "quick fix, please." Or "kill this baby." *Partial-birth abortion*. It doesn't just end there.

"Your dad called me after talking to Dr. Stein," Andrew says.

Frustrated and terrified, I start to cry, and listening to the ugly noise I'm making causes me to cry harder.

"Shhh, shhh, Boo, calm down," he says. "Look—"

"They think I don't care." Now I'm sobbing, taking long heaves of breath between my words. "You think that because I wasn't excited I don't care," I say, but when I say the words, something doesn't feel right.

"Stop."

"Jesus!" I cry. My mind is spinning like a car on ice. I have been looking everywhere for it, but the only answers are opinions. "I'm hanging up."

"Listen to me, Mira," Andrew says. "They talked to Dr. Stein. They think you should terminate."

"What?"

Andrew relays Dr. Stein's message: *Partial-birth abortion* is not an option. *Partial-birth abortion* is a political and inaccurate term not recognized as a medical term by the American Medical Association. Or the American College of Obstetricians and Gynecologists. It's inaccurate, a generalization, a terrible term. She says that my situation, right now, is my body's. That I have a choice in what I do with my body. That, as a doctor, she strongly recommends the healthiest option—dilation and extraction—and that

I couldn't have prevented any of this and that I haven't done anything wrong. She tells them that I need to understand this, and that this is a decision I need to make for myself based on what is best for me. And that the best decision, the healthiest choice, for me, in her opinion—as a health professional, as a woman, and as my doctor—is to end the pregnancy. That the only one who is going to survive this is me. Period. This doomed pregnancy is something that is fated, inevitable. Not a fate that I have any control over. Lilly is dead and she is not dead. She was never truly alive, but I am.

I lean back into a bed of twigs. There is nothing left in my mind. Beneath my eyelids, I see blue-black, and I can't think of a single thing. I will sit in this nothingness for as long as I can, and when the sun sets, I will make my way back to camp.

Under my eyes, I feel airy and weightless. I drift, doze. I fall into a trance—and suddenly, a blast of air and a firm pressure presses onto my face and my chest. The sense of a presence or the feeling that someone is watching me flashes me back into lucidity, and when I shoot up to see who is there, I'm still alone. There is nothing, other than the setting sun and a navy sky.

By the time I return to base camp after having just barely caught the last gondola down the slope, the dining hall is empty and the writers' colony appears completely cleared out. Only a handful of summer kitchen staff members remain, mopping the cafeteria floors and stacking chairs.

twelve

"They're going to be using seaweed," I whisper into the phone. One hand is holding the receiver and the other is cupping my mouth. It's four o'clock in the afternoon and our roommate still hasn't left for a friend's house on Long Island—hence, the hushed details of my personal life.

"*Seaweed?*" asks the voice on the other end of the line. "As in a weed from the sea?" It's Amanda, my best friend back home in Michigan.

"Yes," I say. "The surgeon is going to put seaweed in my vagina. To open up my cervix."

It's close to dinnertime and I'm still in my baggy, pink pajama bottoms and a grainy T-shirt that reads: *Strictly for my ninjas!*

Amanda gave it to me last November for my birthday and it's my favorite shirt.

"As in *kelp*?" Amanda says.

"That's what I've been told," I say. I'm paraphrasing to her the information about the procedure that my dad gave me earlier in the day, which wasn't much.

"That can't be right," she says. "It just sounds like some holistic new-agey voodoo shit. Are you sure you heard them right?"

My father had mentioned something about the seaweed before the doctors and nurses got around to it, but other than that fact, he didn't know much about the procedure I had picked—Dad had never performed it and he wouldn't perform it, and he'd never seen the surgery being done, either. The most he could give me were a few bits and pieces, remembrances of things he'd read in medical journals and textbooks.

Seaweed? Baffling. When I told Andrew about it, he jumped on the computer and began investigating.

"It's called a D and C," I tell Amanda. "What does D and C stand for, babe?" I ask Andrew.

Drone-like, Andrew is sitting across the room from me at our square, wooden table, researching the upcoming three-day-long procedure. My fiancé's big, brown eyes are hastily scanning the screen of my laptop.

"Dilation and curettage," Andrew says without looking up, and I repeat it to Amanda.

"Cutterage? Seaweed and *cutting*?" Amanda starts to whimper. "Oh my *God*. Just what are they going to be doing to you?"

"No, not cutterage. *Curettage.* As in *cure*," I say.

"I think Dr. Reich said you're too far along to get a D and C. I think the surgery is a D and *E*," Andrew replies without looking up. "Not C. And it stands for dilation and extraction."

"I mean D and E," I tell Amanda. "I think the surgery is a dilation and extraction. But please, don't worry. Please. It'll be fine. I promise, I'll be fine."

At least I'm pretty sure. To be honest, I don't really know what to expect when I show up at Beth Israel for my appointment tomorrow—day one of the three-day procedure. My surgeon didn't ever really get to that part, the part about what's going to happen the next day, the day after that, the day after that, and on and on from there. After I had made my decision to terminate the pregnancy and handed myself over to the medical specialists, the only thing I remember being told was where I had to be and when, when I could eat and drink and when I couldn't. The rest, I assumed, was going to be a surprise.

But right now, none of those things really matter to me. The particulars, the specifics. At the moment, I don't care. Right now, I can barely stand to think about anything beyond this moment.

I hang up the phone with my friend, promising to keep her posted, and waddle over to the table. I stand behind Andrew and run my fingers along the curves of his shoulders. They feel like billiard balls.

"It says here that the laminaria is really seaweed," Andrew says.

"Weird," I say, glancing over him at the image on the screen.

He continues. "Found in the North Atlantic and Pacific and in the warmer waters of the Mediterranean Sea."

I lean in.

"They're seaweed sticks. And they're some sort of algae, see?" Andrew moves his head to the side of the computer screen so I can get a closer look. The monitor reveals an illustration of a big, pea-green plant with flat, billowy blades.

"*Weird,*" I say again.

"I know, right? And here," he says, tapping on a thin paragraph on the screen, "here's you."

Andrew traces the words from left to right across the screen with his middle finger and reads them out loud: "*The name also refers to the function of these algae used to dilate the cervix when induction of pregnancy is necessary. It serves to absorb moisture and then expand, subsequently expanding the cervix.*"

As I listen to the description, my imagination kicks in. In my mind, I draw pictures and put together a scene: fleshy anemones, green leaves, and tadpoles, all shadowed by the undersides of lily pads.

He continues: "*The laminaria rods are inserted into the cervix, and over the course of several hours, they slowly absorb water and expand, dilating the cervix and eventually prompting labor.*"

A pond. A dark basement. An underwater forest, shrunken and quiet. Rolling mounds of brown sand folding over and over again, morphing into un-shapes.

Un-shapes. This is what I picture while Andrew describes what's coming to me. The rods, the cervix, dilation, and the labor? Not real. Whatever he is reading about is not me. When this is all supposedly happening, I'll be asleep. Anesthetized and numb, and it won't be real. And if I don't see it and never can recall it, it will never have really happened.

"*Some species are referred to by the common name 'Devil's apron,' due to their shape,*" Andrew says in a slow voice and I snap back.

"Stop that!"

"Stop what?"

"Just stop reading. Just stop reading about *this,*" I say bitterly.

I cross my arms and look through the barred window of our apartment. August in New York: clammy and oppressive. In the lot next to our building, the sun-drunk summer school kids are out for recess. Their arms and legs are wrapped around a primary-colored jungle gym, limbs stretched across poles and posts like little monkeys at the zoo. The playground attendant blows his whistle and the little monkeys unlatch, drop onto the rubber below them, then quickly scramble into a cockamamie row.

"When I blow my whistle," the attendant says sharply, "you are going to run."

The kids shift their weight.

"And when I blow my whistle again, you are going to stop."

The lineup wiggles.

"Are we clear on this?" the attendant shouts, his tone insufferably cold. "I said, *do I make myself clear?*"

"Just look up the procedure and tell me what it says," I tell Andrew, and he types into the search engine, hits the enter key.

"All right, here's one," he says. "But it's pretty blunt."

"It's fine. Just go," I say, still watching the playground.

"Okay: *The first step is to dilate the cervix, usually done a few hours before the surgery,"* he reads from the screen. *"The woman is usually put under general anesthesia before the procedure begins."*

The recess attendant blows the whistle and when its shrill sound pierces the air, the kids take off, scrambling around the pavement like electric sparks.

"The procedure involves the removal of uterine contents using a curette."

"What's a curette?" I ask and close the window so I can turn on the air conditioner, half of which is covered in pigeon shit.

"A curette is a surgical instrument designed for scraping biological tissue or debris in a biopsy, excision, or cleaning procedure. At the tip of the curette is a small scoop, hook, or gouge—"

"Did you say *gouge?*" I ask as our roommate walks into the kitchen and then immediately turns around and goes into her room, quietly shutting the door behind her. "Medicaid really covers this?"

"Do you want me to stop?" Andrew asks. "Or keep going?"

"Keep on going."

I look at the back of Andrew's skull. His dark hair is short and spikes straight up, and lately more and more gray hairs have begun to appear along the side of his head, lining his temples like a silver Greek laurel wreath. I stroke his crown with my fingers and exhale fully. *How did we arrive at this place?* I wonder. *How did I let myself end up here?*

Lately, a lot of questions have been brewing in my mind. Lots of strange questions and thoughts. *Am I really worthy of this decision? How do the doctors know the baby won't feel a thing?* And once I hear myself asking the questions, I quickly press my answers down; I dunk my reactions before I can become fully aware of what I have to say for myself.

But they don't all stay down, and they definitely don't disappear. They never do. The ones that I drown will ferment. And if they wiggle loose and bob back, I collect all the floating thoughts, questions, and ideas, make a pile of them, then cover it with a hefty wool blanket and walk away. But they're still there.

I look down at my stomach. *Who did this to you?* I ask it, and look back at Andrew's head. Did he? Is this his fault? Did you even want to have sex the night you ended up getting pregnant? Stop. You can't say that. You can't place the blame on someone else. That is malicious, selfish. *Stop.*

Then what about you? Are you sure this isn't your fault? You weren't really that happy about the pregnancy in the first place. What if you willed this to happen? What if you did this with your mind?

I can just see it: *Pregnant woman eliminates unborn child by telekinesis.* A baby killer.

Or maybe your body is broken. Maybe your organs don't work. Maybe you will never be given this chance again and never have children. Maybe this is punishment for something you did years ago. Maybe you are just a bad person. Maybe this is your entire fault. *Stop.*

"It says here that *the cervical canal is widened using a metal rod, and a curette is passed through the opening into the uterus cavity,*" Andrew says. "*The curette is used to gently scrape the lining of the uterus and remove the tissue in the uterus.*"

"Okay, okay, enough! I don't need to hear it," I say and sit down next to him. "Scoot over. I can do this myself," I say and start banging away at the computer, typing words into the keyboard and navigating to a new site.

. . . it has developed into a focal point of the abortion debate. In the United States, it was made illegal in most circumstances . . .

"Here," I say, aiming at the text, "read this line."

. . . was signed into law by President Bush on November 5, 2003 . . .

I feel my cheeks get hot and pale at the same time. "What the hell?" I ask no one in particular, and my eyes, welded to the screen, continue skimming the page.

. . . relying deferentially on Congress's findings that a partial-birth abortion is never needed to protect the health of a pregnant woman.

Exhausted, I get up and walk away from the computer and head to bed, taking off my clothes and leaving them on the floor, then climb into bed and pull the covers over my head, bracing myself for the next three days of the procedure I've decided to have.

Day One. Union Square. A dizzy, hot, hard day. A narrow clinic, everyone running behind schedule. A waiting room climbing with toddlers, women with round bellies and swollen ankles, women with flat stomachs and gray rings beneath their eyes, the entire room smelling like the chain-store coffee next door. Next, a small examining room with bright lights. A glass jar of Q-tips, tongue depressors, a box of tissues, and Latex gloves. A white sheet of paper rolled over a teal-blue examining table. The cold linoleum floor. A knock on the door and the remark of a medical resident ("Hey, I have that T-shirt, too!") after the doctor introduces us and informs me that the resident will be observing my case and the surgery.

I remember the sight of the dried laminaria rods, the *seaweed*, as the doctor laid them across the paper towel on a stainless-steel tray. To me, they looked like the rawhide bones I give my dog whenever I need to quiet her down. I remember leaning back, feet in stirrups, knees parted, wondering if the medical resident would ask herself how this girl could've let her pubic hair grow so out of control. And I remember thinking how this was a dumb thing to wonder, but still. She was my age. She might have thought it.

I remember the emptiness of not knowing, having no reference point and nothing to compare it to, to relate to—the vacant feeling of holding my knees in the air. I remember a nurse giving me a painkiller the size of an M&M, which was an insignificant amount. I remember Andrew asking if this would hurt me, and the tepid response of "She'll feel a little cramping, similar to menstrual cramps," which was an understatement.

I remember taking Andrew's hand once the surgeon said "Here we go," and how it felt after she slid in the thin, cool metal of the speculum; a black-magic periscope. And after, she began inserting each laminaria rod into my cervix, one by one. It felt like nothing I had ever experienced. It burned, cramped. The rigid sticks scraped my insides, felt like a switchblade, or the lip of a spade scraping off cartilage from my pelvis. Nails on a chalkboard.

Something pushed and pressed and it did not feel right, so I gripped Andrew's fingers tight as he rubbed the spot between my eyebrows with the thumb of his other hand. I couldn't register the sensation I was having or identify it as pain. All I could do was stare at his face.

"We have half of them in," the resident announced, and in between breaths, I asked Andrew to help me to breathe, to keep breathing. I had to discipline myself to respire. With each inhale, I commanded my lungs to draw in oxygen, then restrained myself to exhale slowly. In—*pull*. Out—*ahhh*. I remember how difficult it was to stay still on that table, to not get up and run away.

At the end of day one, I am somewhat able to walk. We go home, and Andrew's sister, Kerri, is on the couch, watching the Summer Olympics on the blurry television screen. Kerri is visiting us from Southern Illinois. She bought her ticket a month ago, planning on coming to visit us, get acquainted with her new sister-in-law and her future niece. I was planning on showing my future sister-in-law around the city, taking her to Chinatown to buy fake designer purses and eat expensive cupcakes from a famous bakery. Andrew told her about the situation. I wasn't around when they talked. She said she was coming anyway. I don't know why. I didn't question it, barely thought about it. I barely know her.

Kerri offers me orange juice and Andrew calls my dad on the phone, not to talk about their feelings but to talk about the facts. My mother gets on the phone and asks to talk to me.

A week ago, my mom suggested that she come to New York to be with me, but I told her it was okay, that I'd be okay. I didn't want to make it a bigger deal than it already was. Now, over the phone, she asks how I feel and I tell her it hurts really bad. I won't remember what she says back. My mother really wanted to be with me, but I told her I didn't need her. It was a mistake. I do. She has been trying to be strong for me and I've been trying to be strong for everyone else—especially them, especially Andrew.

Later that night, Andrew, Kerri, and I try to go to dinner at a new BBQ restaurant near our apartment, as if it's a prize. As if I've lost a tooth, or something like that. It is awkward and fake. I know they are trying to cheer me up, but I act like I don't need any cheering up. The joint is buzzing. The wood is shiny. The waitresses are wearing short shorts and lots of makeup and the dining room is loud, with electric dance music playing over speakers broadcasting sports games on flat-screen TVs. Our server has on perfume that smells like phony peaches and rubbing alcohol. When she flirts with our table, I order a pulled-pork sandwich and a root beer. People are drinking yellow pilsners and throwing their peanut shells onto the floor, and when I try to eat the cornbread and drink my pop with appreciation, I can't. I can barely sit on my bottom. The seaweed inside me is swelling and the M&Ms aren't helping to dull the pain. The laminaria sticks have been gathering moisture all afternoon and, bit by bit, they are expanding, pushing the walls of my cervix apart like jaws of life. And when my pulled-pork sandwich finally comes, all I can do is stare at it. The meat stares back up at me and it looks dead. Fleshy, flaccid, and dead, and it is going to make me throw up. All I want to do is go home, I need to go home, so Andrew puts the money down on the table, hoists me up over his shoulder, and carries me all the way home to 32nd Street, phones my father again, and asks him to call in a prescription for Vicodin.

Day Two. It's 6:45 in the morning and we're waiting in a dark space for the nurse, doctor, and medical resident to arrive. We're in the very same room at Beth Israel where, less than two weeks ago, the ultrasound was performed.

The room is quietly reverberating with invisible memories, like a theater after the show has ended, after the audience has gone home, the stage swept and the lights turned off. Andrew is wearing my panties on his head and is looking groggy. He appears to be conquered. Today is his thirty-second birthday, August 14. Soon, Andrew will have to split. After we leave this appointment, I will go back to our apartment and he will have to go back to work on 14th Street and sit in his cubicle. He'll send emails about building permits and make long-distance calls about backlogged orders from factories in China, and then around 3:30 in the afternoon, Andrew's coworkers will sneak up to his desk and surprise him with pastel-colored cupcakes. They'll clap and sing "Happy Birthday," and it'll make him feel just a little bit good.

But first, a knock on the door. Enter nurse, medical resident, and surgeon. I yank my underwear off Andrew's head and recline on the table. Legs spread, braced for the pain. After the doctor removes the first batch of seaweed sticks, she inserts the second batch, and my cervix is cracked open to a whole new level.

We begin: the powdered rubber gloves snapped on, the

speculum, the widening. Then the removal of yesterday's swollen laminaria rods. Each stick is clamped, pulled out slowly, then tossed into a garbage can. I wince, rub Andrew's ear. We're halfway there.

I squeeze his hand, trying hard to breathe, trying hard to focus on my breath, to focus on something. The pale-colored print on the wall. Two windows on my right. The shades drawn. Ivory-colored and dusty. I know that if I stare at an object long enough, time will go by faster. Or time will freeze, I can't remember. A black television set up in the corner. I hate this room.

This room and I are becoming well acquainted. We've been through some tough times together in the past few weeks. We've built some memories.

"Okay, Mira, we're going to begin inserting the last set. Are you ready?"

I hate this room.

The sticks go in, one by one, this time larger, jabbing, this time the pain just as bad, maybe even worse. I dig my nails into Andrew's wrist, and I draw blood. It's harder to breathe today than it was yesterday, but I try. I count each breath. And the next and the next, and then, they're in. The seaweed is set.

"It burns," I say, squeezing Andrew's fingers, and he tells me to think about Maybe. Think about her little tail wagging, he says.

I think about Maybe. The feeling of cuddling in bed with her. *Baby Maybe*. That's what I call her.

I remember two months ago, when we couldn't foresee things getting worse, how I caught the bedspread on fire. It was inadvertent. I had really just wanted to make something sweet, show

Andrew some affection, but instead I almost burned our lives down to a pile of charcoal and ash.

Right before the fire and right after, Andrew and I and Maybe climbed into bed and closed our eyes, the music started. *Billboard* hits from 1976. The Eagles. Through the wall, the lyrics of "Life in the Fast Lane" blasted out of Segundo's stereo and floated into our bedroom. Segundo had the song on repeat.

Andrew rolled his head across his pillow and smirked at me.

"Looks like someone is makin' sweet love to a hooker," he said.

I planted earplugs into my ears and tried to ignore the vibrations, but after the song's third or forth loop, I couldn't take it any more. I nudged Andrew with my elbow. "Can you please ask him to turn it down?" I begged.

Dutifully, Andrew pulled his blue jeans over his naked lower half and walked barefoot up the stairs, out into the hallway, and banged on Segundo's door, but to no avail. The track started up again, *He was a hard-headed man, he was brutally handsome.*

While Andrew proceeded to pound, I thought about how it'd be nice to thank him for taking such good care of me. I realized that ever since I got the results of the pregnancy test, I hadn't once initiated sex with Andrew, and I knew he was frustrated. Neither one of us would be falling asleep anytime soon, I thought, so why not thank him with a little affection?

I lit a match and touched the flame to the wicks of a couple of tea-light candles next to the bedpost. Then I pulled the dog into my lap, between my thighs, and waited. As the song hammered on, I rubbed the silky spot behind Maybe's black, velvet ears with the tip of my forefinger and thumb and watched my dog sleep.

I had always believed I made a far better owner to a dog than I ever would a mother to a child. To me, it seemed hardly believable that a person so maladroit and inelegant as myself would succeed in carrying, delivering, and rearing a thing so delicate, so vulnerable, and valuable as a human baby. The world had always been my china shop. But with my dog, I could do no wrong.

When I met Andrew, I met Maybe and became her Superwoman. She quickly became my furry little sidekick. She was like my child—she needed my care and protection. She was an orphan, she needed my love. And so the three of us—Andrew, Maybe, and I—became a perfect triangle. To me, it was as good as it could get. I didn't need a thing more. But then more came.

A baby? How could I handle anything other than a boyfriend and a canine? A baby? I already had a baby. Maybe was my baby. How was it possible for me to be responsible for and care for anyone beyond that?

Maybe had flipped onto her back and her mouth slid open a little ways. Her rubbery paws were resting on top of her pink belly, right above her ribs, and she was completely still. She almost looked dead. I watched the arc of her stomach until it rose up, just to make sure she was breathing and not dead—then suddenly, the knocking in the hallway stopped. About ten seconds later, the volume of the music lowered and then disappeared, and a few seconds after that, I smelled smoke. Then, out of the corner of my eye, I saw the golden flame flicker.

The blanket was on fire. I quickly scooped Maybe out from my lap, gently set her on the fourth or fifth step of the staircase, and shooed her up and away. *"Go!"* I told her, but she refused to leave me. The flame was starting to spread, so I grabbed a musty towel from the laundry heap beside our bed as the fire spread quickly to one pillow, then another. I threw the towel onto the blaze, smothering the blanket and pillows and extinguishing the fire before it spread even further and before Andrew came back downstairs and realized what I had done.

When he did come back, it was ridiculous to think I could possibly hide it. I had ruined the comforter. The room smelled terrible. I had wanted to make love, but instead I had caught the bed on fire. When Andrew reached the last step to our basement bedroom, here was the scene: me, naked and pregnant, basking under fluorescent lights, holding a scorched towel under one arm and a frightened puppy in the other, and spread out at my feet was our bed—as burnt as a marshmallow; the whole sorry scene set against the backdrop of a smoky, shrunken, now music-less, subterranean vault.

After the last laminaria rod is inserted, Andrew asks, "That wasn't so bad, right?" and I soften my grip. *It was so bad. You wouldn't know,* I think. *So shut up.* The nurse explains to him where I have to be tomorrow and at what time; when to stop eating, and when I can have my last glass of water (nine o'clock tonight). And then we are left alone.

I roll over onto my side and just stay there for a second. The sun is pulsating from behind the shades, and when I think about going back outside, my heart begins to harden. Then, using my arms, I push myself up like my yoga instructor always told us to do after corpse pose, one vertebra at a time up into the sitting position. Then I drop and dangle my legs down from the table and slide onto the floor.

I'm naked from my waist down except for my socks, and now my back is hunched over because I'm afraid to stand up all the way. I don't want to shift or jab anything around in there that's not supposed to be moved, and I'm afraid of what I might feel.

Andrew helps me put my underpants on, one foot through each loop at a time. As he pulls up my underwear, I hold onto his neck for balance and look into the garbage can. A bunch of yesterday's sticks have stuck to the top of the clear, plastic garbage bag. Swollen rods, red and slimy like a bouquet of metacarpals.

Day Three. It's the time of the day when the past and the future mingle, the morning of Day Three of the procedure, and this is what I think about as I roll out of bed: the mess I have made. I try to push the thought down, but I can't. After all I have done, how could anyone love me? The accidents, the calamities, the casualties. I am a human tornado. A natural disaster. Cursed. What if the flames from the fire had spread to the closet and the walls and the ceiling, eventually engulfing the whole building in flames? I could've burned down our apartment and ruined every single life in our building. How could I be deserving of trust? And to be honest, the moment I saw that the fire was catching, I didn't really care about the building burning down as much as I cared about saving Maybe. When the fire started, Andrew was in the hallway, close to the exit. He would've gotten out easily and I knew it. And I didn't care about whether or not I was in harm's way. All I cared about was my dog. My Maybe, my little Baby Maybe. She was completely vulnerable. All I cared about was keeping my Baby Maybe safe. Is this twisted and wrong? Do I even know how to love right?

It is the last day of the procedure. Nothing makes sense. I am numb. I throw on a summer dress, slip into flip-flops, and walk up the stairs. This morning, Kerri will be escorting me to the hospital where the surgery will be happening. Andrew is already at work. Maybe he is afraid to rock the boat, maybe he feels it is responsible, but Andrew doesn't want to take any more time off from his job. He has already gone over his limit in sick days and vacation days and has decided to work at his desk until the very last possible minute. Then he will leave and meet us at the entrance to Beth Israel.

"I'd like to walk the whole way there," I tell Kerri after she asks how we get to the hospital. I don't know why I choose this—maybe because I have to move. It hurts too much to sit still, but it hurts to do anything. I just want to get there on my own two feet; I need to feel each moment I get further from this one and closer to the last. Kerri and I pack our purses and set out for the twenty-minute walk down First Avenue to the hospital. The Vicodin isn't much help, so if I slow down, I will feel pain. If I am to stop moving, I may confront the reality of the situation—realize what is about to happen—and I may just lose my mind. We—my fiancé's sister and I—don't confront the situation; we don't talk. We walk. *Just move.*

Under the hard, hot sun, the cobbled sidewalk feels like jelly. We pass identical delis and bodegas vending bananas, apples, and cigarettes and newspapers from the US and the Middle East; we pass pharmacies with bedpans and sad wheelchairs in the display windows; we pass sleeping pubs that reek of dead beer. When we are about a block away from Beth Israel, I see Andrew leaning against the wall of the entryway to the hospital, left leg propped against a sallow pillar, face turned down, looking older and paler than he did that first night I met him, waiting for things to begin or end, I don't know.

The check-in room for surgery is full of the injured and their chaperones, bruised patients mummified in casts and bandages. Perfectly healthy children crawl over their mothers who couldn't find babysitters and the chorus of coughing, sneezing, and groaning accompanies the muffled noises of others shifting in their seats with ache and irritation. This room is bland and ugly, and smells of lozenges and bleach. A waiting room, room of waiting. Like purgatory.

The three of us—Andrew, Kerri, and I—survey the space for a place to sit. An old man with raisin skin nods off in a wheelchair next to three open chairs and we hustle over to them. I slowly lower myself down next to Kerri as Andrew walks over to the check-in desk. He has been irritable and angry all week, but when I see him flirting with the elderly receptionist, I take it as a good sign.

"I'd like to have the surgery performed on myself today, if you will," he tells her, and she snickers but still motions for me to come over instead and sign in. Then she hands me a white, plastic bracelet with my name and birthday on it and I go back to my seat.

The nurse from yesterday enters the room, walking toward me. She reaches out and gives me two small, white tablets and says, "You will need to slip these between your teeth and your gums." She folds my fingers over the chalky pills and squeezes my hand. "Do not chew or swallow them. And good luck."

"What is this for?" I ask Andrew, and I'm not sure if I want to know.

"I'm pretty sure they detach the fetus from the uterine wall," he says timidly and I open my mouth and set the pills in, right in the back between the gum of my cheeks and my incisors, and wait for them to dissolve.

Time passes. Andrew and Kerri skim through magazines. I reach over and pull one off the rack next to me. The magazine's publication date is more than three weeks old and it has been flipped through so many times that the edges to its pages are tattered and the staples holding it together are coming undone. I put the magazine in my lap and it makes me think of the magazines at my father's office, how several years ago Dad got rid of all the cheap literature, as he called it, and brought in healthier periodicals instead. *Discovery*, and *Highlights* for kids. *National Geographic* and *The Economist*—ones like that, ones that are good for you.

I open up the glossy to a two-page spread of a celebrity shopping at a grocery store. In the picture, the store is a regular one, and the woman is wearing enormous, dark sunglasses and glamorous clothing while she pushes the shopping cart down the aisle. At her side is a flock of toddlers. The cart is carelessly piled with plastic-wrapped food with primary-colored lettering, food heavy in corn syrup, salt, and starches. The celebrity has maybe five or six kids, and I suspect she adopted most of them to suit her own amusement, satisfy her own publicity cravings, or suppress some kind of guilty superstar feelings. Bake a humble pie. Above the photo, a caption declares, *They're Just Like Us!* and I roll my eyes. *Fuck you,* I tell it. *No. They're not.*

I remember the big fish aquarium in my dad's office. He still has it. I remember how when he worked late, Mom would pile the kids into her minivan and bring Dad a Tupperware container filled with food. Lukewarm pork chops and mashed potatoes. Leftover sausage and sauerkraut. When we arrived, Sabina, Jules, and I would run around the hallways, chirping and scavenging the exam rooms for colorful Band-Aids and "I Got a Shot!" stickers to stuff into our jeans pockets. And while Mom was watching Dad eat, I'd drag a vinyl-covered chair from the lobby over to the aquarium and stand on top with a container of fish food and drop pieces of dried shrimp into the water. I remember that I'd watch the food fall to the bottom and always wait for the hermit crab to eat it. I always thought he looked sad and lonely, and I think I felt bad for him because he was the only creature in the aquarium that wasn't a fish.

Sitting in the chair in the waiting room at Beth Israel, I start to sense that, over the years, my understanding of the world has changed. My place in it has changed, too. Since moving to New York, I have become a different person. Nothing is just that simple anymore, nothing is cut and dried. Sitting in the waiting room at Beth Israel, the only thing I understand about life is that life has become much more complex and convoluted and confusing. Life has grown more tentacles. Life needs more care. And I need more care. This is my life.

I think about Nicole Carpenter. What if I had done what she had, taken her route, because I thought that was right? What if I did what I thought was best, even if it didn't feel right? Even if I mimicked Nicole, even then, the decision still wouldn't be the same. That was hers. Not mine. She had the moments and experiences that came before her loss, and the moments and experiences before the baby, and the moments and experiences before those. I'm not her, just like she isn't me. Do I think she was crazy for fawning over a dead baby? No. Yes. Both. Do I think she was a better person for delivering? Yes. No. It doesn't matter. She had her reasons. After these years, I see that Nicole and I are the same woman and we are not.

Now, during this moment, sitting in this room, as I think about Nicole, I yawn and press my hand over my mouth and realize that what I do feel about everything else is this: indifference.

⚘ ⚘ ⚘

In the end, everything starts happening at once. I rub my stomach because it begins to cramp a little. Then a little more and a little more. Then it feels like I ate a whole lot of something, then drank coffee and smoked a hundred cigarettes, and now I feel like I have to go to the bathroom, like really bad, like now. Then the temperature drops. The waiting room gets cold and colder, and suddenly it's like I'm hanging from a hook in a meat freezer. The seat of my chair grows spikes and the floor turns to ice, then a dark figure steps out from behind a door and calls my name. I rise, and she escorts me through the set of swinging double doors and into a back corner room. The woman asks me to take off my jewelry and put it in a bag, and all I can give her is my engagement ring; it's all I have on. While she continues to request and record my information—my first name, my middle name, my mother's maiden name, my address, phone number, date of birth—and write it all down in boxes on a piece of paper, I start to shiver big shivers, uncontrollably. It's summertime in Manhattan and I'm colder than I've ever been in my whole life. And I'm from Michigan. My teeth are chattering hysterically and I try to stop them, to keep them steady as she asks who is my emergency contact.

"I'm so cold, please. I can't stop shaking," I tell her desperately.

"It's an effect of the medicine, dear," she says, "we're almost done in here," and continues to scribble down my information. "Who do I call?"

Next, a man leads me down a hallway lined with lockers. He hands me a plastic bag to put my clothing and my shoes in, and a cotton gown, slippers, and a hairnet to put on.

"Ouch," I say. "I feel sick. I feel terrible. I am so cold. Can I please see my husband?" I've been calling Andrew that—my husband. I suspect that if Andrew is my husband, he will be allowed to come back here and help me.

"Where is the bathroom? I have to use the bathroom," I plead, and he points, directing me down the hall. I rush in and close the door behind me, sit down on the toilet, and wait, but nothing comes out. I wait. The cramps are getting worse and worse. And I'm so cold, I can barely move. Nothing comes but the throbbing continues. Quickly, still sitting, I pull my sundress over my head and slip into the cotton gown and paper slippers.

I stand in the locker room hallway holding my stomach. It burns. It feels like my stomach is going to drop right out of me like a meteorite.

"Where do I go?" I ask the first staff person I see, and she loosely directs me to an open space further down. In it, a few chairs are lined up and facing a television. The synchronized swimming competition. I slide into a chair and try to breathe. Beijing, 2008. A 423-million-dollar stadium. Sitting next to me is a young man, roughly my age, maybe a year or two younger, with a gray cast on his leg. He shoots a difficult glance in my direction, then quickly looks away, and I can't take it. I get up and tell a woman behind a nearby desk that I can't take it. I need to see my fiancé. This hurts too much.

"Okay, dear. We have someone coming for you in just a minute. Just wait over there just a few more minutes," she says, motioning with her hand.

"I can't."

A set of wooden doors swings open and a glossy-faced man in blue scrubs enters pushing a wheelchair in front of him. The man tells me to climb in, and I do, then he veers me back through the set of double doors and through the waiting room.

"Andrew," I call as I'm steered past him and Kerri.

Andrew jolts up, rushes over. "What's going on here?" he asks, looking alarmed.

Next, the three of us get into an elevator. Inside, it is silent. My brain feels fuzzy and I'm shaking harder, great big chunks of shivers. A *ding* and the attendant rolls me out of the elevator and into the surgery prep room.

The prep room is a shiny, buzzing room full of patients and their escorts. Some people are in beds, some are waiting in chairs, and other than the curtain hanging around the beds, there is little privacy.

I'm struggling to get comfortable and take in air. I lean on my back, bend my knees, open and close my legs, fidget, roll, and moan. Through an opening in the curtain surrounding my bed, I see a young boy sitting next to his mother, looking back at me.

"I need medicine," I tell Andrew, quivering, and soon a nurse inserts an IV into my arm. Andrew holds my hand.

"What can I do for you?" he asks.

"Just stay here. Or get Dr. Reich. I need a painkiller. Get a doctor. No, stay here." I can't decide what I need. I can't think straight. I can't breathe. "Just stay here and help me find my breath," I say, and he does.

An hour passes. The pain in my belly increases. Andrew rubs my toes, my forehead, my fingers. I listen to the sound of his breath whistling through his nostrils. The sound of it is beautiful.

He is my guardian angel right now. His face is glowing. I absorb two, three, four IV bags of fluids and keep having to go to the bathroom. Andrew helps me out of the bed and escorts me through the crowded room and into the bathroom. There and back, there and back; he lifts my IV bag on the way to the toilet, and on the way back, he holds together the flaps of my hospital gown, covering my rear end.

When we ask how much longer, a nurse tells us that something has gone wrong in the surgery room. The patient who has gone before us is having complications; the surgeons are running fifty minutes behind. Soon it will be an hour and a half, two hours, two and a half hours more, and the burning in my pelvis is getting worse and worse.

"Screw it," I say, just before I flip over onto all fours. I need to make the painful throbbing become less, and Dr. Reich arrives. I'm relieved to see her. When she pulls open the drape, I'm on my hands and knees like a dog and I don't care. I moan a little bit.

"This is the position that got Mira here in the first place," Andrew jokes, and Danya rolls her eyes.

"Hello, my dear," my doctor says to me and begins drawing soft circles along my back with her nails. "How are you holding up?" Her touch is comforting.

"Just give me something to take away the pain," I mutter. "Let this be over, for God's sake."

When I'm finally given pain medication, the surgeons are ready for me. After the pain meds comes a sedative, something inserted into my IV that slows me down and spaces me out. The

juice makes me woozy, makes me lose my grip and my awareness, and the room spins.

Now two dark shadows appear at the front of my bed, wavy
cowboy silhouettes from a Wild West showdown. My bed sprouts
wheels, then wings, and Andrew flies with me and the two dark
cowboys as long as he can, all the way up until the last set of
doors. Then Andrew says he can't go any further, he's not allowed,
and I look up at his face. It looks like a painting, a painting that
is soaked in water. The lights behind him spin around Andrew's
face and now his eyes and nose and lips look funny, like a clown's,
and I start to giggle. I reach out and touch his face. He is a jellyfish. "You are silly, jellyfish," I tell him, and it is ever more funny
when Andrew's head shrinks as I fly away.

In the surgery room, the silhouettes maneuver and move
feverishly about. I look up from my bed and what I see is a
round sun, shining in my face. It is blinding until the moon
face of a woman eclipses the glare. The moon leans down,
asks me my birthday, and before I can answer her, everything
evaporates, then stops.

I am in our bedroom when I finally wake from the surgery. I
feel empty. The head of the electric fan surveys the surroundings
impassively, lulling everything within the room into a heavy,
hypnotic state. I look for Andrew. There he is, right next to me,
lying by my side.

"How did we get here?" I ask.

"You wanted to walk. So we walked until we were two blocks
away. Then we took a cab."

I have no response, nor do I struggle to comprehend. There is nothing. Just the hum of the fan, a sound shaped like a chanting monk, blowing on my face and pulling me deeper into the drug of sleep.

thirteen

When a child dies, there is an elemental shift in everyone. First, a monsoon of sympathy cards, warm, noodly foods, and flowers that bring the funeral parlor smell right into your home. A boy dies and, after the funeral, one bears witness to the miraculous generosity of a small town. There's not just an overload of Stargazer lilies and pastrami and Kaiser rolls; there's a surge of companionship. Constant companionship. One man down, one hundred step in. People reach out to you, step into your life, followed by more people—some family, many strangers. A boy dies and his family is given instant fame. They're the talk of the town. There are heartfelt condolences ("I'm sorry." "My deepest regrets." "I'm so sorry for your loss."), followed by the awkward response the bereaved can never figure out how to say ("It's okay" or "thanks"). A boy dies and a new dialect is employed—a robotic, cautious tongue—and all conversations are restricted to simple topics that are easy to understand. All things neutral. Topics that everyone can agree on, subjects that will ruffle no feathers or remind us that we cannot beat death. Lasagna. Fruit salad. They offend no one.

But all this fades. The cards stop arriving, the flowers wilt. People fall back into their regular routines. People move on. Who can blame them? Life must move on, just as the boy moved on. The company eventually retreats; some remain, but for the most part, after the drama evaporates, you're left alone to figure out what to do.

The dynamic of the family shifts, too. It contracts, expands, tightens, weakens. A week after Jules died, we took to our bases. Dad had sick patients that needed to be taken care of; Sabina drove back to college in Ann Arbor, two and a half hours away; and I was failing math and couldn't miss any more school. A week after the funeral, we all got back into the game. Life kept going, but we were just going through the motions. Mom said, "We have to be present."

Mom told me the restaurant was her salvation. When Jules died, her routine, one that was so deeply entrenched in her subconscious, vanished. She didn't have to take him to school anymore—just me. She didn't have to bug him to mow the lawn. She didn't have to buy him nicer shirts or pack him a lunch. She'd go into the kitchen and there would be no one sitting at the table eating Cheerios—just me. Everything was quieter, everything was a reminder of the emptiness. When Dad and I left for the day, Mom would be alone in the house. Her son was gone and there was nothing she could do about it, so Mom went back to the restaurant. The hardest part was always the beginning of the day.

I didn't know what to do with myself.

Mom told us to keep ourselves sane because that's what she tried to do. She was always pulled together. She got out of bed, ate, exercised, bathed, dressed, and went to work. She cooked. She worked long days and nights at RSVP, sometimes seven days a week, always appearing fresh and happy, no matter what was going on inside her heart and behind the bathroom doors. She cooked and cried at the restaurant, but by the time the guests arrived, she had pulled herself together, put on her red lipstick, and pushed open the doors from the kitchen to the dining room, smiling and greeting each person as they sat down to eat. Even if it was just a week after her son died. She pulled herself together, tightly, and she worked. She was always tired. We didn't talk much. I rarely saw her. It went on like this for a long time.

For a long time, she wouldn't go in or near his bedroom. The Jimi Hendrix poster to the left of his bed; the autographed Scottie Pippen basketball that Dad purchased at some charity auction; the photos of him and his neighborhood buddies swimming in the lake—it was all too much. Going into his room would turn him into a memory, not a person. Going into the room would turn the present into a past. He was a picky eater. He had a crush on a girl named Tina. He never needed braces for his teeth. He liked to be with his dad. He was good at math, and he was a good traveler. Once on a family trip to Poland,

Mom took him to visit his birthplace. We all arrived in the town where Jules was born and he got very quiet and afraid. He was worried we were there to drop him off, that we were getting rid of him or returning him. He actually thought we were going to leave him there.

"Drunk Kills Teen Everybody Liked." There was a thick stack of newspapers from the morning after, piled on top of a chair in his room. Lots of people from town saved it and for some reason gave their copies to us. "Julian Philip Ptacin, age 14." Not many people knew who he was, unless they knew my parents or played football for Pennfield High School or saw the yearbook photo of him in the *Battle Creek Enquirer* on the morning of Sunday, October 12, 1997.

But Jules was also the boy in the photo Mom held in her hands many mornings while sitting on her bed, crying and praying. I walked past this often. In the picture, he is standing next to his dog, Gonzo. They're approaching the edge of a forest, both in orange vests, preparing to hunt quail. Jules's smirk expresses ambivalent enthusiasm. They are going on an adventure, they are going to hunt down some birds, but he doesn't want to kill any of them, so he doesn't.

Jules was also the boy who would let his mother and sisters know that he loved them by sneaking up from behind and messing up their hair. Mom said he was an affectionate guy. She told me that anytime she drove him anywhere, he had to hold her hand if he was sitting in the passenger seat. She said Jules would take her hand willingly, as long as his friends weren't around, as long as nobody could see.

I didn't know what to do with myself.

Three months after I moved home, he died. I left the house, just for one night, and he died.

So I became docile. One child had died, so I needed to be the goodness of two. I became submissive. Obedient. When I had done things my way, I caused nothing but disaster. I didn't know what to do with myself.

I chose a college close to home. I'd visit every weekend. I'd make up for my past, my years of being a ridiculous child who thought she knew everything there was to know about life.

"Just try to keep yourself sane," is what Mom told us the very first morning we went to court. A couple months after he T-boned Dad and Jules with his car, James Gordon was summoned to court. We all were—Dad, Deborah, the policemen, hospital technicians that tested Gordon's blood samples, Bobby from the liquor store, and other eyewitnesses. None of us can remember how long the trial lasted—maybe ten days, maybe eight days—but it felt like eternity. It felt like purgatory, or hell with a business-casual dress code. It was horrible. We had to sit quietly and relive the night over and over and over as lawyers narrated different versions of how it all went down; day after day of contradictory accounts of what really happened the night Jules died. Each side battling to represent The Truth.

In court, Gordon showed no remorse. Mom said he looked arrogant, even, but all I could remember were the dirty looks his family gave ours every time we arrived at the courthouse, and the guilt I felt for being white. James Gordon was black. He had a couple of grown children who came to the trial, and they were black, too. Then there was Deborah and her family. Deb's family was white, but they were Gordon's family now. White versus black. I was worried the case was going to be perceived as a race issue. Gordon could've been polka-dotted and it wouldn't have mattered to me or anyone, but I was worried the difference in skin color would be used against us by Gordon's lawyers. It was.

After Jules died and before the trial began, Deborah and Gordon got married, maybe so she wouldn't have to testify against him, but it didn't do much good; the defense had no case. The only question in the trial in need of an answer was whether or not the following had happened: Gordon drank a lot of liquor, ran a stop sign, and crashed into another car. Black or white. There was no gray area. Either it happened or didn't. And it did happen.

Still, words scissored through the truth as Gordon's lawyers concocted reason after reason for why it all happened. Their theories were bizarre and insensitive: the police tampered with the evidence, the stop sign was hidden, the road was too slippery. They suggested my dad was a liar, mentioned something about it being a race issue, or that the hospital technicians altered Gordon's blood-alcohol test results because Dad was a doctor. When my father was on the witness stand, Gordon's lawyers toyed with him. They drilled him and impatiently waited for his response. Dad tried to answer as honestly as he could, tried to be transparent and to answer all their questions, but Gordon's lawyers made him cry. One defense lawyer sighed, rolled his eyes, and kept pushing, and we weren't allowed to do anything about it. We had to just sit there. They brought out photos of the accident scene. I remember the picture of the car. The car was black and shiny and smashed. It looked like an accordion.

We tried to be contained; we tried to be present and strong like Mom suggested we be, but a couple of times we couldn't hold it in. Once, when Sabina and I were returning from a lunch break, Gordon's lawyers jumped into our elevator just as the doors were shutting. One of the guys, the plump one, stuck his foot in the door and pried it open. They both slid in, smiling. Their suits were ugly. Once the elevator started to move, they tried to make small talk with Sabina and me, as if what had been happening inside the courtroom wasn't really real, like it was all business, or theater, or make-believe. I started to get really hot, but I kept to myself. Sabina didn't. "You are scum," she said to them. "You are scum of the earth." Another time, an early morning when we arrived at the courthouse, Mom lost control. She walked over to Gordon's lawyers and, in a steaming breath, asked them how they could do their work with a clear conscience.

They lost the case, and Gordon got eight to fifteen years (and was released after eleven). But it didn't matter. We were drained, now even more brittle with sadness. None of it could bring Jules back.

Months passed. I hung around. I was meek. We turned gray. We cried a lot. Mom cried a lot, too, but she didn't always let us see it. She worked a lot. She prayed. She'd go to church with her friend Claire, to a small cathedral called The Chapel of Perpetual Adoration. She read books about death and dying, books about people having paranormal experiences. She tried to find something that would give her hope. She hoped that maybe she'd have some kind of message or communication from Jules, like what the people in the books said they'd had. Sometimes, when she was alone, she would float into his bedroom, look at his pictures, touch his pillow.

Mom said this was around the time she learned how sweet people in small towns really are. For months, there would always be fresh flowers on Julian's grave. For months, people put things on his headstone: pretty stones, flowers, stuffed animals. They still do. Even though she had a hard time going to Pennfield football games because it was too painful not to see him there. Amanda and I would go with her, though, and she said she had to be sensitive to his classmates—they invited her to their school to visit. She also wanted to be considerate to his class, she wanted to help them grieve, let them know there was someone there with them.

Either before or after work, Mom would drive to the cemetery and just sit there, sit in the car just to be physically close to Jules. She said it gave her some idea that they were being together. It was something that reminded her of him. For a long time, that's how it was: Mom worked at the restaurant, Mom worked for peace, and Mom worked to preserve the memory of her son in her mind. For a long time, she worked tirelessly to conserve the image of him in her heart.

I stayed at home. I was quiet. I just watched. Mom said she had to be strong for the other people. She would take care of Dad, support him when he needed it. She became very involved in Mothers Against Drunk Driving (MADD). She met a lot of people, people who felt the same things she had felt: Sadness.

Anger. That knot of grief. When she wasn't working, she'd get in her van and drive two hours north for MADD meetings, then two hours back. On the drives up, she'd listen to NPR. On the drives home, she'd cry the whole time. She would come home so angry. She'd be tired and frustrated because she'd be talking about things that reminded her of Jules's death even more vividly. Soon, she became an advocate and spokesperson for MADD. She worked with the Michigan government to change the law, and she went to D.C. to speak to Congress. She stayed busy; she said it kept her sane. Tell yourself, *At least Julian's death can help someone else. It doesn't have to be in vain.* She told us that the people she worked with were nice people. She said some had lost their kids, too, or were injured by a drunk driver. They rallied together.

She and I grew apart.

In August, ten months after the accident, I left home. I was starting my freshman year at college in Kalamazoo, Michigan, the same college I was visiting the night Jules died. On a Saturday, Dad and Sabina helped me pack my belongings into the van and unpack them into a dorm room that smelled like wet carpet. Mom was working at the restaurant that night. School started, I got on with my life. I'd come home every weekend to visit, but I didn't get to see her that much.

The hardest part was—still is—the passage of time. My sister driving back to college. Me back in school. Grass growing over the fresh soil at the gravesite. Football season turning into basketball season. The passage of time meant that it would be one day more that Julian was gone, one day more difficult to remember things that were fresh in the mind. Soon, it would be six months, seven, eight, ten, fifty. When the one-year anniversary of his death approached, none of us knew what to do. I suggested we go for barbecue, wherever we were, regardless of whether we were vegetarians or not, in honor of Julian's favorite food.

Soon after, my parents started to develop their own traditions of remembering Julian. They began traveling with their friends during the week surrounding October 11th. Mom's friend Claire suggested it—that they take a road trip to someplace they'd never been to. That it'd be something happy happening around that time of year, something positive to look forward to, where they could talk about their kids, where they could talk about Julian. They dubbed themselves the FUN PIGs: Four Unusually Nice People In General. The first year, they went to Vermont to see the fall foliage. The year after, they went to Intercourse, Pennsylvania. They sent me postcards.

I did well in college. I worked hard. I made friends. I got along okay. I avoided taking risks. I didn't party. I played racquetball. I stopped playing the violin. I avoided participating in the arts; I dated a violinist and watched him play. I bought a ticket and sat in the audience instead. I visited home every weekend. I was restless. Afraid. Maybe a little bored. Soon, I graduated college, and moved to Maine, and then New York. I didn't know what to do.

A child dies and there is an elemental shift in everyone. But who is moved when that child was never born?

fourteen

September 13, 2008

It is raining hard outside. Andrew and I are standing before our mothers, and our mothers are facing us, dressed in gowns, perfumed and glowing, with their arms entwined. They are both short, and at this point, they are both crying. Andrew's mom wipes a tear off my mother's cheek with a tissue as mine addresses us: *"If I speak in tongues of men and of angels but have not love, I am just a noisy gong or a clanging cymbal."*

I steal a glance at Andrew. His posture is very upright and very proud. He is in a tuxedo and is listening to the words my mother is giving us. His brows are furrowed, as if he's concentrating very hard, trying to memorize everything. He looks like a real man, and together we look like a giant replica of two miniature figures that belong on top of a wedding cake in a bakery storefront window.

My mother continues. *"If I have prophecy and know all the mysteries and knowledge, if I have all the faith so as to remove the mountains but have not love, I am nothing."*

She has known all her life that this is the chapter she would be reading. Corinthians 13. *That,* she was prepared for. Last night, I helped my mother print two copies of the Bible verse (one extra script for backup) on two thick sheets from the box in the computer room. Fancy sheets, the leftover paper Mom used to print her restaurant's holiday menus on. The stock we chose is the kind she used for Valentine's Day dinners. It is salmon-colored, with cupids and roses and lacy hearts. Mom is gripping the pink paper now, and although her voice is steady, I can see the Corinthians trembling between her fingers. *"Love is patient,"* she continues. *"Love is kind. Love does not envy, it does not boast, it is not proud or rude."*

We are forming an arrow out of our bodies. On this side are my maids: my sister, Sabina; my best friend, Amanda; cousin Maya; and Andrew's sister, Kerri. My maids are in bright red satin gowns and each woman cups a yellow sunflower with her hands. On that side are Andrew's men: four square-shouldered boys from Murphysboro, Illinois. The boys of his youth. Country boys. Andrew's men are in black tuxedos and all hold their fisted hands in front of their crotches, like they're shielding them from something. Then there is Andrew and me. We almost make the tip of the arrow—we just need to move a few steps closer together—but it's not quite time.

I'm wearing scarlet lipstick and have a plastic, white orchid in my hair. I wear a long, light gown. A versatile dress; a white maternity wedding gown, versatile in the sense that I can still look just fine in it even though I'm not pregnant. I'm not pregnant anymore, even though I just was. It feels like it was yesterday; it feels like it never happened; it feels like it did happen, years ago, all at once. I still fill the dress nicely, but I am anxious to move in it. I'm trying to look good, just get through this and steer away any attention from the tragedy, keep things moving forward, be celebratory. I'm trying to listen to my mother's reading, but I need to come up with an alternative route to the unity candle, some way I can get over to that table without showing my backside—what if I've started to bleed again? I'm not wearing a pad. This silk is thin. There's no way to know if it's going to start again. And watch the breasts, careful with the breasts. Any sudden squeeze may bring about leakage or lactation. This dress is white. *Damn it.* I let out a breath of tension and look over again at Andrew. He's still concentrating on my mother's words and I remind myself to try and follow his example.

"Love is not self-seeking and does not delight in evil," she reads, *"but rejoices with the truth. Love always protects, always trusts, always hopes, always perseveres."*

A finger-thin branch flings itself into the glass window behind our mothers. Outside, pruned green bushes tremble in the wind. The storm has gotten so torrential that we can't even see St. Mary's Lake. The sky is dumping water like the whole state is on fire. Andrew and I had hoped to have our wedding outside. We had planned on declaring our love for one another in front of our families and the pine trees and the grass (*God is nature*, Andrew and I both agreed), but an hour or so before the ceremony, a tornado hit our town. This is not normal. It is September 13, 2008, in Battle Creek, Michigan.

"Love never fails."

I hear sirens in the distance. It is possible that our matrimonial ceremony may be moved downstairs, into the cellar, but we feel safe enough where we stand, so we keep on going. There is a Victorian-looking couch facing the altar, where Andrew's mother now sits, sniffling, and in one of the few armchairs to the side is my father. There are more people standing at the altar than there are in the crowd. When the storm hit and we moved inside, we only needed about five chairs. We are sheltered within these walls, among this flowery wallpaper, these portrait oil paintings and watercolors, these aged, oval mirrors and lightly tarnished brass knickknacks. We are getting married in the living room of Greencrest Manor, the bed-and-breakfast down the street from my childhood home. It is a fun house of antiques and old memories.

"As for prophecies, they will pass away; as for tongues, they will cease; as for knowledge, it will pass away."

I want them to think I'm good, that I'm not crazy or a bad person. This is the first time I have met Andrew's best men and I am worried they might think that this was all a part of my plan. That I had motives and had a crafted plan. That I was a crazy woman from the Internet who would do whatever it took to find a husband and be a bride. I want them to trust me. I'm doing my best.

My mom has reminded me that men need sex—this is how they heal. But I may not be capable. Her advice makes me angry, and I don't understand why she'd say this. Is she worried that is the only way I can keep Andrew from leaving me? Surely she doesn't think that is what my role is in this marriage. And Andrew must understand why, and despite it being a tradition, I don't want to have sex tonight, even if it is our wedding night. Surely I shouldn't have to defend myself. Right now I am getting married and I want to explode, but I'm really making an effort to keep myself together, and I am not wearing a maxi pad and I might still be bleeding.

I wonder, do I come across as bizarre? As a wacko? I realize I have been very quiet these past few days; I've had trouble with the small talk and getting into the festivities this weekend. I want everyone to know that we are partners and that I really do love this man; it's just that I am currently in a bit of a state of shock. It has only been a month since the baby.

"When I was a child, I spoke like a child, thought like a child, reasoned like a child. When I became a man, I gave up childish ways."

Last night, Andrew and I slept in separate places. Separate homes, separate rooms, separate beds. Separate for the last time. We wanted to participate in at least one customary tradition—it's supposed to bring good luck. We wanted to do something normal. We want things to be normal. Last night, after Andrew kissed me goodbye and was carried off into his final hours as a bachelor, I stayed home and stood around the kitchen, waiting for the appropriate time to excuse myself, say goodnight, and retreat to my bedroom. All I wanted to do was be alone. I didn't want to sip champagne. We had no ceremony. There was no spa day, no manicures, nothing traditional. I hadn't had the energy to put one together, but maybe people expected me to. No one else organized anything. There was nothing old or borrowed or blue.

The boys grabbed Andrew for a rowdy night out, which my family suggested he needed. Before they left, I pulled Andrew aside, and asked him to be considerate of me, of us, and of what just happened, and to be sober for our wedding tomorrow. I added a request that he please not patronize a strip joint, and away they went. The house got silent, people puttered around wordlessly, so I just threw on my sweatpants and retreated to the vault of my bedroom, a world frozen in time. I had nothing left to give, nothing to say. I just needed peace and quiet and a night of familiarity and solitude before I delved into a new existence.

Within the walls of my bedroom, I thought about what was about to happen, or what just had, but I didn't realize anything, just that I was exhausted, sore, and needed to sleep. But I wasn't alone—I shared my bed with the dog. Gonzo, the furry relic of my youth, the living artifact that always made me feel like I was still just a little girl no matter how old I was, and that nothing had really changed. Gonzo snored all night.

"Repeat after me," Reverend Schipper says. "I, Andrew, take you, Mira."

Andrew tries, but he cannot. There is a rock in his throat, a twisted lump of vocal cords. My man cannot stop choking up.

He wipes his eye with his thumb, smiling and crying at the same time, and witnessing this makes me believe he really means what he is trying to say. "I promise to be true to you in good times and in bad," is about as far as Andrew can get until he tears up again. Finally, he reaches the finish line—until "death do us part"—and it is my turn.

I've heard my lines before. I recognize them from films, novels, real weddings. And now I am the one delivering them. It feels funny but okay. Okay, Reverend Schipper, I will repeat after you. I look into Andrew's eyes and give it a try, but I cannot. My lips and my mouth have taken over. They expand so wide and I start to giggle. I try again, ". . . to be my husband . . ." and I have to stop and laugh. I try, but it's the same airy, embarrassed laugh that came out when Andrew proposed. I can't repeat more than a few of the preacher's words before my body takes over. I really do mean this, but there is something so ticklish about the script. ". . . in sickness and in health . . ." The words are so short and what is happening right now is just so . . . immense. ". . . 'til death do us part," I finally promise, and "I do." And then, just like that, we are married, in what feels like less than an instant.

After the wedding, we will drive to the hospital to pay Andrew's father a visit—he was taken there last night for stomach pains. He had to miss the wedding. It's still drizzling and storm sirens are still howling far off in the distance somewhere in Battle Creek. Intestines, my dad explained. He had severely obstructed bowels. And as my father, my new husband, and I walk down the hallways of Battle Creek Community Hospital, we realize that the reason all the patients are out of their beds, slumped in wheelchairs, and lining the halls isn't because we are catwalking down the corridors in our wedding garb, but because all the patients were evacuated out of their rooms during the storm. Hand in hand, Andrew and I follow my father down the hallway, looking for one particular patient, and judging by the faces of all the others we pass, I imagine Andrew and I look like two trick-or-treaters looking for doorbells and my father, our chaperone.

After the hospital, we will drive to my home, where Mom has organized our wedding reception dinner. She has made fruity tortes and parfaits. Chocolate cake. Lobster. My parents will be glowing; there will be lots of champagne and toasts. Kerri will deliver her father's speech and blessings for him, and it will make us think about the institution we just entered. And about the tumultuous journey we took just to get here. And how everything is somewhat normal now. Established, safe, peaceful. I think about the vows we just made, and the way Andrew cried all the way through them. Something about his tears and our promises made me feel like a child and an adult all at once. Something about being married—it was so adult-like, so grown-up, so swift. Something about it all left me with a feeling that I just cannot name. So I don't try.

fifteen

I know some things. I know you set the backyard on fire. It was autumn. You were six years old. The oak leaves were dry and crispy. You and your pal Don Johnson, that blond-haired, blue-eyed kid from St. Philip Elementary School who threw up every time he got excited, were playing in the backyard. I'm assuming you guys found the matches in the pile on Dad's workbench.

"Mom, the backyard is on fire." She said that's how you told them, Mom and her best friend, Claire.

Suspenders hold up your blue jeans. Velcro shoes. You never actually fessed up to whose idea it had been, who had lit the first match, maybe the only match, but the fact is someone had lit the backyard on fire, and Mom and Claire had to subdue the flames until the fire squad arrived. Back and forth they ran from the shores of St. Mary's Lake to the kindergarten blaze, dumping two gallons of water at a time. You must've loved those fire trucks.

Mom says that people always remember things the way they want to remember them instead of the way it was, because it was never just one way. That memory isn't what happened; it's what happens over time. She says she was never really mad at you. That she was laughing while the yard was burning. She said it was because of your delivery—your Abe Lincoln honesty had been so blunt. That, and the fact that Don Johnson was barfing the whole time.

My memories of you are a special kind of truth. Your laugh, the things that made you bite your fingernails, what it felt like to be around you—a feeling I can only achieve when I am asleep and you appear in my dream. It's the only time I can really sense your essence.

She said you gave someone the gift of sight. The night of the accident, a nurse came to her, less than an hour after you died, and said something like this: "Your son, Julian, was a young, healthy man. Would you like to donate any of his organs?"

On your last human day, I was leaving the house and you said to me, "See ya, scrub." Then you threw a sock at my face. Then you died. To me, it's just so crazy that one day I see you and the next day your eyes are in somebody else's body. You throw a sock and then you're gone. You become a memory, a ghost, just like that. For me, the idea is still taking some getting used to.

You died and we were taken to a different place. We didn't choose to be the survivors, but we chose to survive. After you died, Mom said we must be responsible for ourselves, that we must be strong. After you died, Dad told me this: "Individually, we will have trouble. But when we come together, we are strong. We press on."

After you died, I didn't become the homecoming queen. I didn't want anything to do with it in the first place. There was the homecoming game. I didn't want to go and stand in the middle of a football field with hundreds of people watching me wait to see if I was a winner. Dad had his arm in a sling and Mom wore her ankle-length fox-fur coat and they escorted me down the bleachers and out onto the field and I knew what everyone was thinking: *There goes that naughty girl whose brother was just killed.* And when the announcer called our names on the loudspeaker—"Mira Ptacin with her parents, Dr. Philip and Maria Ptacin"—it was Mom who led Dad and me onto the football field. As we were walking, people behind us were clapping, and before we even reached the field, Mom stopped, dropped our arms, turned around to face the crowd, and waved both hands at them triumphantly. We weren't even halfway there, but she just turned and started waving. Her entire body. She looked so strong, the way she addressed the faces in the bleachers with her entire body. It was as if she was conducting whatever love they had inside of them. As if she was thanking the world for its love, thanking the world for us, and for her own life, even though she had just lost her only son. The way Mom looked in that moment, it was as if she were looking at God and saying thank you for my beautiful life.

Mom told me that I prepared her for losing you. That when

I ran away, it was worse, it was a crueler experience than losing you because she had no control over losing you. When you died, Mom and Dad were already very strong. She said the most difficult thing was choosing your coffin. Just a couple of hours after you died, they had to be logical, make "arrangements," think about things like the budget, and stationery, and coffins. They picked a plain, wooden one. Mom made sure it was a wooden coffin, because that's how her parents did it. The natural way to go into the earth. And she said she couldn't donate anything but your corneas, because the car accident was under a criminal investigation.

Here's a memory: I am seventeen years old and inside your closet. It is late morning, a few days after your funeral. I've shut the door. Your shirtsleeves rustle my shoulders like the leaves of hanging ferns. I am looking down at your big shoes, smelling your clothing, the darkness, and I am vaguely aware of the noises going on outside of your bedroom. There are dozens upon dozens of people in our house. As I step out of your closet, metal hangers clang. I walk out of your bedroom, past Gonzo who is still waiting for you, and as I step out of your room, I see Mom and Dad sitting Indian-style on the carpeted hallway, holding one another. They are rocking and weeping. Their shoulders shake up and down. Dad's ribs are broken and his arm is in a sling. I see the years falling away from them. If they were to speak, their voices would be those of children.

All that week, I take long drags off Parliaments and Amanda forces me to eat. After the boys take the shoe box of *Playboys*, we find a homemade escape ladder hidden under your bed and a notebook of poems, tucked deep back in your T-shirt drawer. A book of poems, written by you.

What the Yellow Had to Say
By Julian Ptacin

I am the joy of a flower
the singing of birds.
I am a promise
The happiness that fills your body
I am the delight of friendship
The feeling of being with someone.
I am the light shining through your window
Making you warm
The sight of someone you love
I am the peacekeeper,
The never-ending joy.

We never knew about this, that you were a secret poet. I am starting to see that, often, you kept your thoughts hidden from the rest of the world, too. Those parts deep within us that are so difficult to share. Tender things, like regrets and beliefs that, when exposed, make us even more vulnerable. The stories we write, the notebooks we hide, never knowing if they will be read with someone else's eyes.

sixteen

It's mid-October and my girlfriend has harvested her eggs. She's done it: sold her eggs. I'm on foot now, headed to pick her up from the procedure. The fertility clinic is on the Upper East Side and shaped like a Lego. I arrive and walk to the check-in desk, where a receptionist is chatting with a coworker. She ignores me, but her perfume permeates the air between us with a scent of baby powder and Grammy's medicine cabinet.

"I'm here to pick up my friend," I say to the receptionist at the desk. I'm standing in front of her in my hoodie sweatshirt, gripping a bag of Dunkin' Donuts breakfast. Pretty gross. I smell like an everything bagel and I look like the Unabomber, or a gym shoe. *I am a worn-out gym shoe and you are a business-casual pump.* I wait for her to look up, but she's not seeing me. It is as if she is deliberately ignoring me. As if I'm an untouchable. *It will be called The Battle of the Shoes.*

"Her name is Grace," I say, and she directs me to sit down. I unwrap my bagel and wait.

A nurse sauntering down the hall whisper-yells, *"Hey! Hey you!"* to get my attention, and when I look up she mouths, *"You can't eat in here,"* lifts her hands up to mouth level, then chomps down on an imaginary hamburger. My stomach growls. I wait.

I wait and wonder if my mother would be proud or pissed at me for assisting Grace with her egg harvest. As a kid, I spent a bit of time with former meth addicts and recovering alcoholics that Mom had hired from the local mission to rake leaves in our backyard or powerwash the siding on the house. Mom called the ensemble "Mission Possible." She fed them egg salad and tuna sandwiches, and invited them to Christmas Eve dinner. My mom always admired troublemakers and underdogs. She rooted for those who paved their *own* path, especially if their path was paved with the intention of escaping injustice or any type of shit show. I just don't know if my mom would consider Grace's method of paying off her student loans a survival technique or soul selling. But it doesn't matter. Grace is doing what she thinks she needs to do. Whether or not I believe in it, she needs a friend.

Just as I pull out my phone to check the time, a nurse walks through a set of swinging doors with Grace treading softly behind her. Grace's face is overcast. She looks like shit. We hug, board the elevator, I hail us a cab, we get in and give the driver the best route to her apartment deep in Brooklyn.

"Are you in pain?" I ask her.

"I dunno. Just crampy," she says, and it won't occur to me for many months that this is not a typical thing for a young woman to do on a Friday afternoon in October in America. Or is it?

We merge onto the smooth ribbon of the FDR, whirl a bend, then our cab whips over the Brooklyn Bridge like a roller coaster cart when Grace slides an envelope from her bag: $8,000 and she's not telling her parents. She's created a separate bank account for it and the ones that will follow. I ask her if she's okay, mentally. She says yeah, sort of. Make sure you take the weekend off, relax. She says she just plans on watching old movies and not doing homework. I tell her it's pretty fucked up that we have to pay an arm and a leg for higher education, and we both note the awkwardness of the phrase.

Locked within the bars of P.S. 116's concrete playground, a recess supervisor wishes he were a drill sergeant, and the children, it seems, are too scared to play. It seems as if that playground is never unpopulated. Like right now, it's about 7 P.M. and dark out, and there are a bunch of kids still on the monkey bars. I'm watching them from one of the windows of our apartment. Andrew usually doesn't get home until after eight. This allows me just enough time to take Maybe to Madison Square Park. We walk six blocks there; we play games like catch or "chase me," and then walk six blocks back home. This is followed by a bath to rinse off all the dust she collects at the dog run. Afterward, Maybe is pretty spent, so I can work for a bit in quiet while the room is asleep and purring. Tonight I seem to have things under control.

Earlier today, before picking up Grace, I drank wine out of a urine cup. It was just a few sips. We were leaving Phillips Family Practice, about to leave the examination room, when Andrew busted out a half-full bottle of wine and suggested we polish it off, that we have a toast. We weren't celebrating the abortion; we were celebrating the end of our trips to Phillips Family Practice. We were not celebrating the end of the pregnancy, the end of the procedures, or the prodding of my uterus. We were celebrating our marriage. "To a new life," Andrew said.

I didn't expect the toast. Dr. Reich finished the checkup, explained how long the common physical aftereffects of this trauma to the uterus and the body might last, how much longer it would be until my breasts stopped lactating completely, how I should be wearing frozen cabbage in my bra and why, how much longer before my regular menstrual cycle would start back up again, and told me that it'd be totally fine for me to have sex with Andrew again—not that I'd be eager to acknowledge that I was a sexual being anytime soon. In fact, that's what Danya said. "How the hell you'd want to think about sex, I'm not sure. But whenever you're ready, now ya know." She congratulated us on our one-month wedding anniversary. She said she hoped everything would be normal for us, that we would have a normal, uneventful next few years, and wished us good luck.

That's when, all of a sudden, Andrew slipped a bottle of red wine out from his messenger bag. He took three (unused) plastic urine sample cups, poured a few sips into each one, and the three of us shared a toast. To our new marriage. To the new life we were starting together. Then, Andrew suggested we toast again, this time to the baby. "To a little girl who never had a chance," Andrew said, and I tightened up. I don't know why, but it didn't feel right. Almost like he was making a joke of it. Like he was teasing Lilly. "To Lilly, that she may rest in peace," I saluted, but that didn't feel right or real, either. It didn't feel like any kind of closure, if that's what we were going for. *Our daughter.* I hadn't even begun to wrap my head around that word, or anything that had just happened, for that matter. I just didn't know what to think, other than I never wanted to go back to Phillips Family Practice ever again. All I wanted to do was step out and leave my grief and sadness in the examination room where it had started. But stepping out of Phillips Family Practice, I still felt as afraid and as vulnerable as I had when I stepped in six months ago.

Then, I went to go get Grace.

I'm trying to be a good woman. I'm trying to be a good wife. I owe Andrew a good wife—he's done his best. I want to be normal and productive and useful; I want to catch up with everyone else. I'm trying to be pragmatic and organized and in control of all my things. Sometimes I change the date on my homework so my professors don't think I procrastinate. Sometimes, if all the plates are spinning, I have time to write. I do this at the table where we eat our meals, right above our bedroom. There are two windows next to the table. They are very large, but give us very little natural light. We only get the reflected light and shadows from the elementary school next door. Outside, below the window, I see Segundo. He has strapped a leaf blower to his back and is stirring up the leaves, napkins, wrappers, and dust from the alley between our building and P.S. 116.

Yesterday, Segundo turned on the heat in the building. We have no way of controlling the temperature. I open the window. Dirt and dust sneak through the window, spread and settle on pots, pans, my shoes, the furniture.

I open my computer, I try to clear my mind and write, but I'm thinking about Grace and feel I should check in on her. She's been home for a few hours. She's probably sleeping it off. I'd rather not call. I'd rather email; for some reason I think it's safer. I don't want to bombard her. Maybe she's not ready to open herself up yet. Maybe she doesn't need my support right now. But I'm feeling bad about things. I feel sorry for her. I'm worried about her. Does she have anyone to help her? Is there something I could be doing for her right now? I'm thinking of the future here, wondering what the likelihood is that an event like hers today could transmit trauma further down the road. I'm wondering if this is okay. Should I be providing her more comfort, more than her bed and DVDs are right now? When she left the fertility clinic this afternoon and the cab whisked her away to Brooklyn, when it flew over the Manhattan bridge, darting in between other drivers and zipping past face after face after face, and finally screeched to a halt and deposited her on the sidewalk in her gentrifying Brooklyn neighborhood, was she too raw?

I hear the front door click and Maybe hops to her feet, runs to the door barking and wagging her tail. It's only 7:20.

"What are you doing home so early?" I ask, and Andrew looks at me with an expression reflecting the implication of what I just said, and I'm sorry.

"Maybe is practicing her *h* sounds," I explain. I'm trying to create conversation. Something neutral. Andrew breathes out through his nose, "Hmmh," not looking up from the carrot-covered cutting board as he chops veggies for our dinner. He's a little afraid of me. He said this. That I'm like a ticking time bomb. I explode when he tries to touch me.

There's a saying in Savannah that goes like this: "Naked is when you have no clothes on. Neked is when you have no clothes on and you're up to no good." Maybe and I are over on the couch. Her collar is off, all chewed up, and she's totally neked. *Hhhehh, hhhehh,* she whisper-barks, then clamps her rice-teeth down into the skin of my knuckles. We are pack animals. *Hhhehh, hhhehh.* I echo her tease and a shudder of recognition passes through us. It's times like these when we realize each other. We are wild domestics. Me: woman. Maybe: canine. I imagine that this new home of hers is a giant board game. I imagine that to a spirited pup like Maybe, growing up in a metal crate on a dirt floor was no good. I imagine that sprouting into a burrito-sized dog at the no-kill shelter in Anna, Illinois, wasn't the best coming-of-age. I imagine if she could've talked to me then, *smooshed* would've been her first word. Within the walls of our apartment, the dog and I play games like "chase me" and "put 'er dere, put 'er dere."

Chutes and Ladders. Life-size Candy Land. A labyrinthine puzzle to be taken apart. It must be irresistible to you, this apartment of ours. You do, after all, have Jack Russell in your blood. You spend your lonesome dog days chewing and prodding about. I know, because I've seen you. On my lonesome dog days, I watch you bury rawhide treat-treats in the nooks and the mouse holes. On my lonesome dog days, this home has the charm and dimensions of a bomb shelter. Oh my dog, has it ever occurred to you that, as a four-legged creature, you are forever in the push-up position? I read somewhere that a young girl rescued a dog and taught it to walk on its hind legs, like a person. A year later, it learned how to smoke. Don't evolve any more, Maybe. Nowadays, I consider it to be dangerous. They say dogs are direct descendants of wolves, obedient to their instincts— eating, sleeping, following the pack. I have never seen you get angry. So on second thought, perhaps your first word wouldn't be *smooshed*. Perhaps it would be *How do you say . . . no hard feelings?*

Pack mentality. Obedient to instincts. The rawhides you've buried about like Easter eggs are starting to attract ants. Even though you believe they're covered by the invisible soil you shoveled with your snout, I still land directly onto a dried pig ear jerky when I drop my head onto the pillow at night.

The floor to the left of our bed mumbles from the movement of a giant, steel centipede: beneath us, the Long Island Railroad is taking commuters to their jobs. Slowly, the few cars on the street will be replaced by traffic. Two more hours until parents drop off their children at the playground of P.S. 116; for two more hours I can sleep. Above us, the radiator hisses. We've opened all the windows in the apartment and have a fan on in our bedroom, blowing onto our bed. It will be left on every night until spring comes, when Segundo turns off the heat and our bedroom cools down. In the winter, the snow turns our street into a wilderness. In a couple of months or less, flakes will fall from the sky and cover up all the dirty bits and pieces that make up our block and, for a couple of hours, everything will be illuminated and beautiful. Then, all the snow will turn brown and slushy and it won't be easy to go on bike rides. Two more months until December, two more hours of sleep.

I flip my pillow over to feel the cool side of it on my cheek. Andrew's back is turned to me; it's ivory and soft and smooth and smells like dried sweat, like sweet corn. Six and a half hours ago, we did it. We had sex—a small victory. I'm still afraid to do it, to activate the thing that got me here in the first place. I don't want to get pregnant. I'm waiting for my trust to come back. I'm waiting to regain my ability to control things. Like my body. And I'm still a little afraid that I'm damaged, that my insides might fall out. Six hours ago, I let go of my fears as much as I could, tried to ignore my made-up fears. Next time, maybe I'll say something. I'll tell Andrew that I'm not ready. Because I love him, and we're supposed to communicate. This is what married couples are supposed to do. Everyone says, "Marriage takes work." I am working on this—communicating, talking about it, pushing past my comfort zone. Less afraid my body. I see its flaws. I want to find it as perfect as my husband does. It's still so unfamiliar to me, and twenty pounds heavier. The weight from the pregnancy, and the ice cream. It's like a reminder of what never came, and I want it to go away. Nothing fits except the maternity clothing. Andrew finds it amazing. I want to love my body again. Hold my head high, shoulders back, move my arms around, take long strides, smile. I want to wear colorful clothing, accessorize, and I want to wear a tiny bikini when we take a vacation in February and visit the beaches of Puerto Rico for Valentine's Day. I love how the women there flaunt their curves. They're proud of their bodies. They show it. They own it.

I can get used to the dog being in the room—Maybe just chews on a bone, probably thinking she should be doing something productive. She's part terrier. But I get distracted by thoughts of Segundo. I wonder if Segundo knows when we do it. I wonder if Segundo isn't just listening in on our carnal grunts; maybe he is much more clever than we suspect. Maybe he has drilled a hole into the bedroom wall by our closet. Maybe he peeks in on us. A spectator of our sex life. Or perhaps Segundo has been a witness to even more than just our sex life. Maybe he has followed the entire story that followed the sex, the story of what has happened inside our bedroom, our kitchen, the walls of our apartment, from the very beginning of us up until now.

Maybe I should find out. Tear down the barriers. Maybe I should get to know the man, or at least visit him every once in a while like Andrew does. The next occasion: Christmas. When Christmastime arrives, I will join my husband when he delivers Segundo's gift—an expensive bottle of Caribbean rum. Maybe I'll go downstairs with Andrew and finally see Segundo's apartment, finally get a look at what's going on in there. "Welcome, my dear neighbors, please come in," he'll say, holding the door open in a red flannel and Carhartt jeans as Andrew and I walk past him and enter his domain. Segundo will lead us down a narrow set of stairs and into his home.

It is warm. The walls are plastered with photographs, old black and sepia ones of his ancestors in oval-shaped, bronze frames. There's a crackling record of holiday music played on an acoustic guitar. "A toast to new friends!" Segundo proposes, and the three of us take a shot. He explains who is in the photographs on his wall: this is Adriana, this is Alfonso, this is Alberto. He tells us the story of how his grandfather sold two hogs to pay for Adriana's wedding ring. We laugh. Then the story of his wife's death of cancer, of his children who live in Seattle, and of a child in Queens, and one in Sheboygan, Wisconsin. The story of the little glass bells he collects. The soggy, ash-blue tattoo from his stint in the navy. The Basic cigarettes. The tiny TV set. His penchant for Mel Gibson movies. The bag of Mesquite BBQ potato chips. The ginger ale on top of the fridge. The Dirt Devil in the corner of the apartment, with no other place to be stored. Now Segundo's workbench. Now his tools. Now I laugh tears when, after more two more shots of expensive Christmas rum, Andrew and Segundo start wrestling in the living room. We laugh as Segundo demonstrates how to perform a Hair Pin Hangman. The boys wrestle. I laugh. We take another shot. I laugh as Andrew demonstrates a Running Powerslam on Segundo. We drink, they wrestle, laugh. But after Segundo pulls a Diving Double Axe Handle on Andrew, their bodies tumble and fall, taking down with them a tiny glass snow globe off Segundo's coffee table. The globe breaks into many pieces, and we must all slow down.

seventeen

As I help Mom pull on her jacket, my eyes fix on the scar on her left upper arm. The marking of it—a soft halo shape—reminds me of a summer night a few years ago when the two of us went skinny-dipping in a Minnesota lake (Boundary Waters, way up by the Canadian border). As we waded into the water and the black waves cupped our naked bodies, Mom turned to me and said, "There are enough stars in the sky for everyone."

When she was a little girl, Mom got three shots in her upper triceps—vaccines for typhoid and hepatitis in her right arm, then the smallpox vaccine in her left. It never occurred to me that the soft rings on her skin were flaws; to me the scars looked like dandelion seeds or quarter-sized snowflakes, and noticing again their strange beauty made me aware of the sense I've always had of my mom's magnificence, which I used to mistake for magic.

Today, we are in Michigan, on the first Saturday of November—early, golden brown and reddish days draped in a mild breeze that reminds us of last year's snow, or of the approaching winter. It is November 1st, and tonight we'll be celebrating our own holiday. My family calls it, "Thanks, But No Thanksgiving." We recently established the tradition after Mom proposed we celebrate Thanksgiving a couple weeks before the official Thursday it falls on. She said that this way, her daughters (and now son-in-law) could evade expensive airline tickets and she could avoid the crowded grocery stores. She said the tradition of having Thanksgiving on one specific Thursday was pointless and obsolete and we all agreed—we've had enough with waiting in lines for overpriced flights—so here we are.

I zip up my fleece and slide my hands into Dad's wool gloves; I left mine in New York because I wanted to pack light, but instead I packed stupid. I also grab his Russian fur trooper hat out of the hall closet just as Mom steps out of our house for the walk around St. Mary's Lake. Our intention isn't to circle the whole thing—it's about a four-mile loop, but our blood and our conversations don't start flowing until we're approaching mile two, so we might as well do the whole circle rather than turn back the way we came.

Nobody has ever told me which Saint Mary the lake is named after, but I like to think it was Mary Magdalene, the adulteress saved by Jesus from death by stoning. I root for the underdog.

And thanks to *The Da Vinci Code* and people who only go to church for Easter Sunday or Christmas Eve or funeral masses, rumor has it that Mary Magdalene was also Jesus' secret wife and they had a baby named Sarah. (*Sarah?*) Also, the lake is man-made.

When my parents moved to this neighborhood over twenty-two years ago, there were fewer houses on St. Mary's than there were boats. We could swim across the water without having to worry about getting diced by an engine fueled by gasoline and a six-pack of Sam Adams. Nowadays, the chorus of red-winged blackbirds and cawing gulls has been replaced by the buzz of Jet Skis and speedboats. Nowadays, McMansions sprout out from the unkempt gardens behind old pea-green fishermen cabins, making the perimeter of St. Mary's Lake look like an over-dentated mouth. Overpopulation at its finest.

"Doggies stay at home," Mom says as we walk into the garage and past the dogs' triangle-topped doghouses.

This year, Gonzo will turn seventeen, and even though that's quite old for a dog—almost 119 years old, when converted to human years—the old buddy still behaves like a puppy. Except for today. Today, for some reason, Gonzo has barely gotten out of his doghouse, which isn't normal. I suspect he's got an upset tummy from the sweet potato peelings and apple shavings Mom had (intentionally) been dropping on the floor as she was cooking up tonight's Thanksgiving feast. Mom still cooks all the time, but only at home. And now when she cooks at home, it's for her and her family. Sweet potatoes, apples skins, cucumbers, even the sudsy puddles from the open dishwasher . . . that dog will eat *anything*. Keeps his coat shiny, Mom insists, and his unrestrained appetite is what probably has kept the big guy alive this long. By now, she swears, Gonzo is a certified sous chef.

"Not even The Professor?"

"Not even Gonzo," Mom says. "Just you and me," and she flips the switch on the wall that activates the invisible fence.

"You guys still use that stupid thing?" I ask.

A few years ago, the neighbors down Sylvan Drive convinced my parents to put up an invisible electric fence around our yard to keep Yolanda and Gonzo out of theirs. Before that, our dogs had mastered the art of breaking and entering. They'd dig holes under our front gate like convicts escaping, then caper about the neighborhood, smash into screened porches, and leap through open windows, eventually making their way into our neighbors' kitchens to steal rhubarb pies cooling on countertops, or whatever else they could get their paws on. (Once, after catching him in the act, we learned that Gonzo had even figured out how to nudge open the revolving cabinets with his snout.) After a satisfying romp around the neighborhood, the dogs would return to our house at the dead end of the street bearing trophies, such as empty pizza boxes or spice jars or bags of Wonder Bread. One time, and Lord knows where and how he found it, Gonzo brought home a deer hoof. But after the dogs crashed a wedding reception at Greencrest Manor for the fourth or fifth time, Tom and Kathy VanDaff left a message on our answering machine telling my folks that if our dogs sabotaged one more of their buffet tables, they would call the pound and not let us know. I thought what the dogs did was hilarious, but Mom said they would lose them their clients. That's right around the time the fence went up.

Mom thought the idea of electrocuting Gonzo was cruel, so after the fence was installed, Dad strapped on one of the shock collars around his neck and patrolled the perimeter of our yard to assure her that the electric shock couldn't be *that* bad. From the kitchen window, we all watched as Dad tiptoed around the grass, listening for beeps and buzzes. Eventually, he walked right through the front gate with the band still around his bare neck just to prove to his wife that the jolt was puny and bearable and humane, even though later Dad confided in me that the shock hurt like a sonofabitch.

"Ready, Mom?" I ask and she presses her lips together and inhales the cold air. She dyed her hair for our visit—this time it's vampire black with two hot-pink brush strokes along her temples—and she's wearing serious red lipstick, a bold shade of scarlet. *Always wear lipstick.* That's one of Mom's mantras—always wear lipstick, even if you're only going for a hike. She always looked good.

"I'm always ready. How far should we go?" she asks.

I suggested a family walk around St. Mary's Lake but Mom said it would be just the two of us. We step out of the garage, down the driveway, through our front gate, and stroll along the edge of a crusty, beige-colored lawn. Our neighbor's lot. The Crandalls. Duane and Stella Crandall are both dead. Duane passed when I was eleven, and Stella died just a few years ago after smoking for nearly forty-five. Now their house belongs to their daughter, Duana, Stella and Duane's only child. The Crandalls' yard looks just as drab and lifeless as Stella's rock garden.

I can barely remember Duane, neither his face nor his funeral, only that several uniformed men shot a cannon at his memorial service and that he was soft-spoken, was always wearing denim overalls and always fixing something, but I remember Stella. As a child, I loathed Stella, and could never figure out what my mother saw in her. Why was she was so nice to her? At Stella's funeral, our neighbors all made speeches about how nice she was, how she was the bedrock of our neighborhood and all that hogwash, but all I could think about was how each year Stella was the first to set up her garage sale and how much of a grouch she was, always yelling at us kids for stealing the spiky chestnuts out of her backyard for our chestnut wars, which Stella hated. She smoked Merit 100's on a bench in her rock garden, and read romance novels—paperbacks with pictures of burly men on mountain peaks and big-breasted women clinging to their ankles. And whenever Mom couldn't find a babysitter, she'd send Jules and Sabina and me to the Crandalls', where we'd get stuck clipping newspaper coupons and watching soap operas with Stella until Mom telephoned and we were released back home, reeking like ashtrays.

"Were you aware Stella was a poet?" Mom asks.

"No way. That old grump?"

"Really, Mira. After Stella died, her daughter found hundreds of her poems," she says. "Stella was a clandestine poet. A secret artist."

I had only been in the Crandalls' house once since Stella

passed and Duana moved in. It was the very first day of the year, New Year's morning. The night before, just before the clock struck midnight, I had been outside taking out the compost when I found a cat in the middle of our yard, dead as a rock. Mom knew exactly whose cat it was: Duana's, a tabby that she had recently rescued and adopted. The next morning, the first day of January, she sent Dad to go deliver the news. Before he left the house, Dad knocked on my bedroom door, woke me up by saying, "Mira, would you like to learn how to tell someone something they loved very much is very much dead?"

On the way to the Crandalls', Dad compared his technique of breaking the news to the act of ripping off a Band-Aid. "You just gotta do it. None of that, 'I've got some good news and I've got some bad news' bologna," he said. "You just gotta be quick, and to the point." It was good advice. And so we trudged over to the Crandalls' property, up their stone sidewalk, and pressed the doorbell. And before she could even say "Happy New Year" from behind the screen door, Dad just came out and said it: "Duana, your cat is dead."

We buried the cat right afterward, right behind Mom's compost pile and beneath the three pine trees where we buried all our pets that had passed. The ground was frozen, but we went for it anyway, with two spade shovels and lingering guilt. About four feet later, we set the stiff cat in a black garbage bag, covered the hole, put a recognizable rock on top of it, and when we were all finished, I asked my dad if maybe we should say something. "I guess maybe we should," he answered, and after meditating on it for several seconds, my father said, "Cat? We respect you."

We pass the Crandalls' driveway, and with great effort I conjure up some words to represent the feelings I am itching to share, knowing that they will come out jumbled and all wrong, then gracelessly release them:

"Mom? How does one feel better? I mean, what was it like for you after Jules died? How long did you feel bad? When did you start to feel better, or heal, or move on but not forget, you know?"

Mom points to a rectangle of dry, patchy grass behind the Crandalls' house. "It's such a shame," she says, raising her eyebrows. "It's such a shame no one takes care of Stella's garden anymore."

I continue clumsily, "I mean, it's just that I am always so frustrated and angry and gloomy, like I just left a funeral or a wake, and I'm always so irritated and livid and tense, it's getting worse," I ramble. "How do I feel better? I just can't feel better."

She wrinkles her nose. My insides instantly stiffen from the extra feeling that I have said too much too fast. Mom stares hard, her eyes fixed on something I can't see, and, in words as thin as a pastry shell, she says, "Do you know what precious treasure I kept after Jules die?"

"No," I say, this time delicately.

"His big shoe," she sighs. "In back of my closet, I keep Julian's big gym shoe he wore on de day when he died," she tells me, then walks forward.

Ghosts of our past have been taking up residence in every yard we pass. The Ferraris' house, the Smiths' house, the Kunitzers', the Millers'. Carol Miller was still breeding the Samoyeds, the white, puffy dogs that pull sleds in places like Siberia. We walk in tense silence.

"After Jules die," she finally says, "I'd cry and pray. Pray that Jules was safe, that somehow he'd give me a signal in some way that he is okay. I prayed to God but never got angry at God." She explains that she never believed God was this guy who had this idea that Julian would be killed, like a manager who meddles in our lives. "After Jules died, I still believed that God existed. My faith was that everything that is beautiful is the work of God. That there is no chaos in the world unless there is man-made chaos; that often, people just mess this world up a lot." She tells me that we are here to make our own decisions, we have free will. That she prayed to God for faith and peace, and with prayer, she found peace. "The peace was probably self-induced," she says. "But still, I have faith."

As we walk, Mom tells me that a while after that, she saw Jules. She dreamt that she woke up and saw Julian alive. He was sitting at a picnic table somewhere in some kind of park or garden, some kind of place with bright greens and blues, a place that looked like paradise. Mom and Jules sat across from each other, holding hands. They just sat there, looking at one another and smiling. Then Jules said, plain and simple, *Mom, I have died. I am in a great place. Don't cry. I am happy.*

"That is when I started to think about him differently. I let go and gave in to the truth." She allowed it to exist, both within her and separate from her. She stopped fighting. That's about the time she started to heal.

As we advance past Carol's tall, brown fence, we smell dog

poop. For as long as I can recall, that stink has always seemed to magically rise up from behind the dogs' breeding cages, over the shrubs, and into the street, never to leave the area. And I have never heard Carol's dogs *not* barking. As kids, whenever my sister and I tried to sneak out on weeknights, howls would crescendo once we approached the Miller's house, and we had to either make a run for it or turn back home as fast as we could before we got caught with our pants down and were grounded for weeks. We pass the Lindows, the Burkes, and the Waters homes. Behind a stack of bricks at the front of his gate, I see Mr. Waters shining his red convertible with a waxed rag. Even though Mom and I have always had our own interpretations of each neighborhood landmark, our sentiments about Mr. Waters have always been the same.

"His place looks like a Chinese restaurant," I say.

"I concur. I don't understand why he builds that huge brick wall next to his driveway."

"It's to keep you pesky immigrants out, Mom."

The two of them never got along, and I can testify it's because Mom is a foreigner. Mr. Waters never welcomed her into the neighborhood; he did the opposite, treated her as if she weren't a real person just because she wasn't a "real" American. So many times, so many people figured my mother was stupid just because she talked a little different or arranged words in her own kind of way. Sometimes people would speak louder and slower, even yell as if my mom were hard of hearing, or dumb.

"He hates Polish people," Mom says.

"But he likes to *Polish* his sports cars," I tease.

In Chicago, after she'd first met Dad, and for a long time after they got married, she felt like an outsider in her new family. She thought that Dad's sisters, Mary Madeline, Mary Virginia, and Mary Joan hated her. She said Dad's mother was cold to her; and she thought his parents only reluctantly came to her wedding, which she paid for with all the savings she had been storing since she immigrated to Chicago. She thought it was all because they wanted Dad to marry an American woman, not a Polish woman. I think it's because she never held back from speaking her mind, no matter the time or place or language. But we all have our own interpretations.

"What was it like with your mom, Mom?" I ask and then remember: questions like this are never simple ones that elicit direct answers from her. Questions about Mom's childhood always stir up a hearty stew of memories, painful ones, recollections of things that drove her out of Poland. And no matter what, no matter where she has moved, Mom has never been able to get away from what she ran from. And no matter what questions I ask, I will never be able to totally understand. Her relationship with her past has always been a push-pull, love-hate kind of relationship, and it will probably be like that for the rest of her life. My fingers start to cramp, so I move to Mom's right side and take her other hand.

"My mother taught me what is essential: You take good care of yourself. You take good care of you husband. You take good care of you family, and you know how to cook," she says as she accepts my hand.

I think hard about Andrew, my brand-new husband who is back in the kitchen of my childhood home, preparing a pomegranate and kale salad for tonight's feast. I think about what Andrew was doing before that—earlier in the day, when I caught a glimpse of him from the living room window. Andrew had taken Gonzo outside with him to do some yard work. While the big dog dragged small sticks, Andrew voluntarily reengineered Dad's woodpile, clearing rotted logs and restructuring the stack of firewood next to Jules's dogwood memory tree.

While Andrew was outside at the woodpile, I was in the kitchen stuffing Cornish hens and listening to Mom talk on the phone with her brother Matteo. She was speaking quickly, and in Polish. I barely paid attention—the only words I caught were *dobry*, *żądza*, and diarrhea, but I could tell they were arguing.

Mom was taking care of Uncle Matteo yet again, and I couldn't understand why. In Poland, after their parents' death, Mom got stuck taking care of her brothers because the only things that seemed to matter to them at the time were tall women, downhill skiing, and sports cars. But then she left Poland, and she thought she'd said goodbye to all, that but she hadn't. Everything just seemed to follow her, or maybe she just felt sorry and let it back in, again and again.

Over the years, he was up and down all the time. Divorced twice. He was behind on mortgage payments and refused to sell his Jaguar to pay for his three children's tuitions. At first, Mom said he was like a badly behaved child that needed to be disciplined. Then Mom said he was sick. And apparently, Uncle

Matteo got sicker and sicker until, one day, Mom said he was a manic-depressive person who needed help badly, and for some reason, she couldn't let her brother fall. What he needed was his family, and their love. And so my mother and his ex-wife Mary, and their children Mark and Maya stepped up, and put him on the road to recovery. The family regrouped and reunited. Love is patient. Love is kind.

Life ain't fair, I think to myself. Never has been, and never will be. Those three words became the mantra Mom and Dad poured into our heads since before we could even stand on our own fat baby legs. Life wasn't fair. It was a good thing to be reminded of, and it was even better to be warned, so you could be ready for whatever hit you when you least expected it. *Life ain't fair.* I had got it back then, but back then I didn't realize that my parents weren't always referring to me and my problems when they said it.

"Besides," Mom chimes, "I never got a chance to get to know my mother once I became a grown woman. After I became a woman, she died."

"Mom?" I want to ask her what she thinks of her daughter. If she is mad at me, if she has forgiven me, and I'm afraid of her reaction. But I need to know. "What would you have done if you were me?" I ask. "I mean, with the pregnancy? In the end?"

"I'm not a believer in abortion," she says, and I tense up. "In July, when you called and told me what doctors found, my first thought was for you to wait and see. I thought, *Miracles can happen.*"

"What was I supposed to do?" I feel defensive, and she picks up on it.

"Wait, Mira. Listen. When doctors told us there was no hope, and it made sense your baby wouldn't live . . . well . . ."

I hold my breath. I want an answer because I didn't know what the right thing to do was at the time. I still don't. But deep inside me, I wanted to feel forgiveness. I felt ignorant. I was worried that I hadn't changed much since I was seventeen. My selfish behavior before Jules died, the loss of my baby, I was afraid that, deep down, my mom held these things against me. I was worried that I kept doing things over and over again that made her resent me. That I was a bad person and couldn't help it. I wanted her to love me, no matter what. I wanted to be accepted and understood, not to stand out.

"What would you have done?" I ask and hold my breath while my heart beats in a state of suspended animation for what feels like eternity.

"I think that if I were in de same story," she says gently, "I presume I would have done de same."

The same thing?

"You are strong," she tells me, and the affirmation makes me swell. I feel light, as if an invisible burden has been lifted.

I want to talk more about it. I ask her more questions, and she does the same with me. She explains her views: If there was no chance at life, if the fetus couldn't survive, she wouldn't have delivered either because of the trauma and pain of the delivery.

"Exactly," I say.

She says she wouldn't be able to cope. If there is no hope, there is no point.

"Yes," I say.

"I see 'Right to Life' in Catholic Church," she says, "but there are other parts church is forgetting: death penalty, immigration, eldery care, poverty. So many people without medicine, without health care, without love. So many 'rights to life' the church does nothing about."

We start down the hill, past the Hamiltons, past the Redmans, past the Benkes. We turn the bend around Jukas's house. Two thick, stone pillars frame his driveway, standing alone and unconnected to any kind of fence or gate. I look down the asphalt path for Jukas's car.

Jukas graduated from college the same year that I did, but I left for Maine and he stayed with his parents, camped out in their shag-carpet basement, and mixed drugs, which he always pushed onto all the other kids around the lake. Once, when I was home for Christmas, Jukas gave me and Joey Kunitzer a bag of dried herbs called Salvia divinorum. I had no idea what it was. "Merry Christmas," he said and explained that he boiled the herbs down to make their medicinal qualities more concentrated and potent, and that if we smoked it we'd go straight through a rabbit hole. I told Joey Kunitzer that I wouldn't be touching any shit called saliva and Joey told me that it wasn't saliva, but *Salvia*, and it was legal. "It's called 'the sage of the seers,'" Joey said. "And it'll make you shit stars." So we took the Salvia down to the shores of St. Mary's Lake and sat on a giant rock. We looked for satellites and watched Gonzo walk on the ice while we puffed and passed the herb back and forth, and waited for it to kick in. Then I started to get really warm, then really hot. Next, my face melted and I touched a constellation, and then it was all over.

"Everything looks different in life at the moment when you're dealing with things than it does when you're looking back on them," she says.

My mother tells me about a woman who was pregnant with twins. One twin died while in utero and the mother carried it until she went into labor with the other one. She never miscarried. She never aborted. She carried the dead baby around with her so that the other one would survive. "She was special," Mom says.

"And what about Nicole?" I ask.

"Who?"

"Nicole Carpenter."

"What about Nicole?"

"What do you think about what she did?"

"She was a kooky girl, naïve, hard to deal with. But it was beautiful that she could do that. I'm not sure I could have done that."

"Why do you think she chose to deliver?" She says that she doesn't know. That maybe it was something Nicole wanted to do for herself. She also had lots of support from the nurses and delivery staff. Maybe it gave her some validity. Maybe that was the only way she could get attention from other people. And love.

The sky drops a shade darker, and about ten thousand birds bark and dart over our heads. Crows. Sparrows. Finches. Nuthatches. The flock whizzes over to the long, black silhouette of a pine tree forest, and from behind the trees, I hear the shrill cry of birds I am afraid of: blue jays. Those evil little bastards, probably out murdering their own kind.

"It smells familiar here," Mom says and I study the scent.

"It smells like the first grade," I say. A red-breasted robin, pecking at the roadside weeds beside us in a staccato fashion, stops her movement and looks up at us. Mom walks past the bird, unaware of its presence, but I look down at it. For a moment the robin seems to look at me in a secret way, connecting her dewy eyes with mine as if to say: *you know me*.

"When did you finally realize it, Mom?" I say abruptly, surprising myself.

"Realize what?"

"What had happened. Like, when did it finally become true to you that Julian was gone? That he had died?" After I ask, the question feels raw and rude, the way it does when you ask a grown woman her age, even though I know it isn't.

"I lived in a dream," she says. "Up until his funeral, I assumed I was only dreaming."

Since the surprise pregnancy and its terrible, abrupt ending, everything in my world has felt like a hallucination or a dream. I have somehow put myself in a trance, and I want to realize that I'm not a bad person for not being able to bring myself into a sharper, pointier reality. Anytime I do start to feel something *real*, something instantly happens inside of me, like in my stomach or my brain, that makes me feel enormously tired and sleepy before I can realize what I've just begun to start feeling.

"Up until Julian's funeral, I was on autopilot," Mom says.

"What happened at the funeral that made you realize, or see the truth of the whole thing?" I ask.

"Two days after Julian died, we arrived at St. Philip Church for his funeral. Church was completely full. People spilled into streets and police blocked all the roads. I saw so many faces, so many people who came from all different walks of life, came just to say goodbye to this young boy they had never even met. And when I walk into the church," she says, sounding far away, "and I walk down the red church carpet to the alter . . . this was when I realize, *It is my last walk with my son.* This is when it all became real for me."

"Do you ever feel alone in your feelings?"

"What kind of feelings, Mirunia?" she says.

"Like the kind of feelings you get when you're pushed out onto a dance floor but the rhythm hasn't hit your bones yet."

She turns back and looks at me, confused.

"Like the suspicion that there is something wrong with you but no one else can see it," I say.

"Mirunia," she says, squeezing my hand. "It takes time."

I look over my shoulder, checking to see if there are any strangers nearby who might overhear. A country cat is stretched out under a white birch tree. Next to her are ten or eleven squares of yellow hay and a big FOR SALE sign. It comes from the same family Dad used to buy barrels of hay from to cushion the trees at the bottom of our hill during winter sledding season.

"Mira, do you know how many couples in Battle Creek alone have lost children?"

"I'm not talking about the baby right now, Mom," I say defensively.

"Why not? Then what are you talking about?"

"I'm talking about segregation. Feeling completely isolated," I say. "Even when you're with your husband, your partner."

Mom told me that while Andrew and I had been flying through the air from LaGuardia to Kalamazoo, Dad had been shaving his head. She said he wanted his hair to be just like Andrew's because he thought Andrew's buzz cut (really, Andrew) was the bee's knees. Dad told us that he had a surprise waiting for us when we arrived in Michigan, and when we walked through the front door, I saw my father as I had never seen him before: nearly bald. Dad looked just like Andrew, and Andrew looked just like my father. They both smiled luminously at each other, like two rascals.

"Mira," my mother says. "My darling, precious girl. Sometimes we presume things in our heads, and sometimes our presumption is totally different from what is more true." I feel myself stiffening as she continues.

"For instance, after Jules died, it felt like Daddy was a man becoming a child. A child who needed to be hugged and held and embraced."

I let go of her hand. "What are you talking about?"

"Let me ask you this," she says. "Do you know how men cope?"

"Sex."

"Sex. Sometimes, sex would help Daddy to cope."

"Ew, Mom. Come on."

"Oh, no Mira, you come on. We get married and we make love. No bigger intimacy than making love," she says, and I can feel myself tightening.

"Fine," I sigh. "Sorry. Go ahead."

"With sex, men feel close, emotionally. After Julian die, and Daddy wanted it, I thought, *How could he do that?* As a woman, I could not make love."

"Mom . . ."

"Oh Mira," she says, rolling her eyes. "I am afraid you know exactly zero about marriage and men, and this worries me. Mirunia, just listen to me. Andrew is not a woman."

"No shit," I mutter.

"He is man and he will respond differently. Dat is interesting about women and men and sex and grief; we all respond differently. When we naked, our insecurities are exposed. And for men, making love to a woman they love is like having a blanket of security. Dis is how men cope."

"But what if *I* don't want to have sex?" I argue. I am beginning to sense that I have been exhausting myself by trying to cover my tracks, trying to right my "wrongs" just sitting with what has just happened. I have been busying myself, trying to comfort Andrew, to comfort anyone, so they would feel better. Why have I been doing this? "Maybe I'm not ready." I've been boosting everyone else forward, and I don't even know what I want. "Maybe *I* don't want to be naked and exposed."

The road bends and we turn onto our street.

"Mira," she says. "I know you feel most vulnerable this way, too."

"No. Actually, I do not," I say, feeling both embarrassed and angry at the same time.

"Maybe you are afraid of getting pregnant," she says. "You are afraid because you believe there is something wrong with you," she says. "You will feel better when you have another baby. You can prepare yourself for project number two."

"That's not what I want."

"Losing a baby is very traumatic, but you will sanctify your body again. Subconsciously will feel better about your body, connect body with soul."

"Mom, please."

"You are just afraid, Mirunia. And there is nothing wrong with dat," she says. "You just need to let yourself be love."

We reach East Sylvan Drive, our street, and head up the hill to our home on the dead end. I look to the right, past the Ferraris' house and down the hill. Through the poplar trees, I can see a flock of geese landing on the glassy surface of the lake. Their little rubber feet skim the water and it looks as if they're water-skiing, which, in fact, they are. About thirteen summers ago, Dad taught us all how to water-ski, all except for Mom, who refused to try it. "You are not going to make me do something I do not want to do, Phil," she had scolded, so my mother became the spotter on the back of the boat, keeping an eye out in case any of her children were to take a dive. To be honest, I hated waterskiing too, and never really wanted to do it because it made my thighs sore and gave me the biggest wedgie imaginable every time I lost my balance and hit the water going thirty miles per hour. I only did it because I thought I was supposed to. It was supposed to be fun. I did it, each time waiting for it to start feeling fun, even though, each time, it never did.

Before Jules died, we used to spend all our summer days down by the lake, together but separate: Sabina would spread her beach towel on the dock and work on her tan while Mom practiced water aerobics, shrieking every few minutes when a fish bit her nipple. Dad napped on the hammock with his mouth wide open, snoring like a motorboat while Jules swam underwater with his eyes open, looking for shells, interesting-looking rocks, and soggy, used-up firework wrappers. I'd sit in the sand and watch Gonzo as he'd wade through the water, staring at minnows and bluegills while they circled his giant black paws. His tail would wag rapidly while the rest of his body stood perfectly still, and when the moment was right, Gonzo would plunge into the water after the fish, then immediately look up at my family to see if anyone had been watching him. "Good boy, Gonzo!" we'd cheer, and he'd wag his tail faster, pleased and congratulated.

"Look," Mom says, slows her pace to a halt, then turns to me. "Dere are many people who have lost dere kids in Battle Creek. So many of them have divorced. Loss, especially in a tragic accident, causes divorce. When Jules die, I just cry for years. I cry by myself a lot, and dis is fine. Both Daddy and I were at a loss, and we both kind of cried different times, but we *talked*, and now we are much closer because of it," she says. "You have to talk. You and Andrew. You must talk to one another."

After a long pause, she continues, "Mira, just guess how many couples?"

I think for a moment, and give no answer.

"So many," she says, and after hearing her words, it feels like I should either clap or collapse. "You never get over it, you just learn how to live with it. I don't have too much time left, so now I'd really like to live in the moment. With Jules, he is always with me. He is gone, but he's in my heart. I miss him, I'm sad because you don't have your brother, I don't have my son. But, he was one hell of a kid."

We hold hands and walk a little ways in silence until we finally reach the Crandalls' house again. I ask for one last story.

"Before we go in, Mom, will you tell me once more about how you met Dad?"

I know her account by heart, and I want to hear it again. Maybe I want to put it up next to how Andrew and I met. Maybe I want her to see how I am seeing things: that she and I are very much alike, but not everything is the same. Not everything that is true for her is true for me. Her marriage and mine are completely and utterly different events: my parents met at Presbyterian/St. Luke's hospital, in Chicago. Mom had just mastered English and gotten hired into a research lab in the pulmonology department where Dad was interning as a medical student. She worked in the lab where he was making his rounds. Dad was curly-haired and wet-eared. Mom was bashful and gorgeous, and she ignored him completely.

"And I was dating Herman Rabinovitch at the time," she says. "I did like you daddy, though. But you daddy was so shy." It was a long courtship. Dad finished school and went back to

Georgetown, Herman ended up cheating on my mother, and a year later my parents fortuitously bought tickets for seats in the same row at the same theater on the same night—*Brecht on Brecht*—and that's when they reconnected. I've heard the story a million times, but this time it sounds less romantic.

"First you dated, then you got married, then you lost your *Catholic virginity*," I tease, "then you got pregnant, gave birth to Sabina, moved to Battle Creek, and then you had me! And the rest is history."

"Well, not exactly. But something like that," she replies with hesitation, which is surprising because this has always been that same exact plot.

"What do you mean? The story goes you guys found each other, got married, you got pregnant with Beanie on your wedding night, and then moved to Michigan."

"Yes, that is true."

"Then what is missing?"

"I wasn't a virgin."

"No, Mom, you lost your virginity to Dad, right? On your wedding night, right? That's what you told me. That's what you've always said."

Mom's wedding night isn't something I've imagined in vivid detail, but I've always figured she was chaste and pure and proper. Ever since I had my first training bra, Mom drilled it into my head that sex is a beautiful thing—*once you are married*—and I've been harboring guilt ever since I was sixteen and lost my innocence to Seth during a *Nightmare on Elm Street* marathon. (It was okay.)

"No," she says under her breath. "It was to Herman."

"What?"

"But I was a twenty-eight-year-old virgin!"

"Mom! *Herman?*"

"But it was *terrible*."

"Mom!" I yip. "Mom. All this time . . . really?"

"Shhh! Don't tell your Daddy!" she whispers as we arrive back at our garage and go into the house.

In the evening, we will have our Thanks, But No Thanksgiving dinner. Mom will have roasted thirteen Cornish hens and mashed up sweet potatoes smothered in bourbon. She'll dish up perfect, homemade borscht, kale, and pomegranate salad, butternut squash and creamed-spinach gratin, and we'll give thanks. Between the salmon spread and pierogies, I'll be thinking about Herman Rabinovitch and Mom's minor moral blemish. I'll start to feel a little better, and a little lighter. Hopeful, with a flicker of confidence. Brave. Then around midnight, Mom will ditch the pumpkin pie and serve tiramisu and pear tart instead, but I won't get to try any of it because around midnight will be the time I arrive at the hospital in Kalamazoo.

But before that, while we are eating our dinner, Gonzo will be drooling and aimlessly nosing around the kitchen. He will start moaning. Then he will get worse. Dad is the sober one, so he will drive Gonzo, Andrew, and me to an emergency vet hospital in Kalamazoo while Mom tells our guests not to worry as she plates their desserts. Dad will carry the dog into the examining room, and after looking at some X-rays, it won't take long for the vet to come to a conclusion. He'll look into my dad's eyes, not mine, and tell us that Gonzo's stomach has flipped, that surgery for this type of thing on this old a dog would be dangerous and expensive. The vet will speak carefully and say that the dog may not even survive, and if he does, he'll probably spend the rest of his days in pain and misery. "Fuck him and his diagnosis," I'll say to the vet, looking at Andrew, but Andrew will know what I really mean. What I really mean is that saying goodbye isn't something I want to do, or even know how to do. What I mean is Gonzo is the last bit of Julian I think I have left, the last tangible bit of my youth, and that I am loath to let someone take something like that, something I love very much, away from me, too. But what I won't realize just yet is that it will be the end of a story, a story that I have to let end in order for the next one to begin.

"Call Mom," will be all I can spit out when Dad asks for my final verdict. "Just call Mom and ask her what she thinks we should do." And after Mom and Dad talk about what we all know is right, the three of us—my father, my new husband, and I—will stand in a circle around the old dog and weep while we give him our last goodbye.

eighteen

The next Saturday, my professor holds class at his home in Brooklyn to discuss a book we've all been assigned to read—a memoir about misguided love, forbidden relationships, confessions. Basically, it's a book about incest.

The library of my teacher's house smells like coriander and the inside of a piano. My classmates and I all nod in agreement that it is a strange book, and as we sit stiffly, facing one another in a circle on our professor's couch and chairs, everyone is thinking about how the book has left us feeling uncomfortable, but nobody will just come out and say it.

"The purpose of this assignment," our professor finally says, "was to show you how not to write." During class I learn that the psychology of the author's story is the same as what happened in the story, so this makes her story one-dimensional. He tells us that the book is not playful, and that art must be playful. I take lots of notes and ask lots of questions because I want to understand how to find what's taking place underneath the surface of things and uproot it in my writing.

Today is my birthday. November 8, 2008. Sometime around six-thirty on this cold, gray morning, I turned twenty-nine. I was the first person to arrive at my professor's house, and when I did, he gave me a beautiful cake, a hug, and told me I should throw away what I'm writing about (the Happy Spa) and write about "the uterus and the American dream" instead. After class ends, my professor, my classmates, and I all eat the cake. Andrew shows up, eats a piece of cake, too, then a handful of us walk to a nearby bar on Smith Street. The bar has a red, tin ceiling, a bartender who wears a bowtie and a white apron, and a jukebox that plays Motown songs and rockabilly oldies, ones by Smokey Robinson and Roy Orbison. One of my classmates has two cocktails, then tells me I'm such a smarty, a teacher's pet.

"Look," I tell him, "I'm almost thirty years old, I took out two huge loans for higher education, and I am not going to just sit on my thumbs and wait for something good to happen to me." What my classmate doesn't know is that sometimes I sing the alphabet to know which letter comes before the other.

None of them ever says anything about the baby. They've never asked how I might be feeling. They saw me when I was pregnant, they knew and had congratulated me, but they haven't said anything since then. Do they think the baby just disappeared? What wouldn't they ask?

"I already have an agent for my book," my classmate replies.

"Well, guess what? It's my birthday," I tell him, "and I don't have time for your shit."

I see Grace sitting at a table next to the jukebox, so I go sit down across from her. Her face looks like a porcelain doll's. Her arms are stretched out in front of her with both hands in half-fingered wool gloves, wrapped around her beer. When I ask her how things are going, she tells me not good.

"I've been drinking a lot lately," she says, and I ask her if it has anything to do with that thingy from a couple of weeks ago. I know it is. It's gotta be. She doesn't have anyone else. She's all by herself here.

Grace doesn't look up but answers, "Well yeah, sort of, I guess. I kind of lied to them," she says.

She says she heard that sometimes people react to anesthesia in bad ways, so right as she was going under, Grace thought about it and got scared, and in her dreamlike state she blurted out, "I'm on antidepressants and I've done acid before!" because she thought she might die during the harvest, and didn't want anything to fuck anything up.

"Those sons of bitches," says Grace. "They told me I deceived them. They said that I was a liar and was only doing it for the money."

I get up and put three dollars in the jukebox. E9 "Function at the Junction," F8 "Tears of a Clown," B5 "Superstition."

Poor Grace. I can't say I never considered donating my eggs, but she actually did it. She doesn't realize how fragile she is, or at least didn't back then and now she's feeling like shit and nobody else cares. They don't know, but still, would it matter? No one talks about these things. No one asks about our vaginas. My classmates know about me but they don't ask me what happened. How I'm feeling. What I'm thinking. I don't want Grace to feel loneliness like this. Isolation. Segregation. She's got no one. We are women. We should be comrades. It will make us stronger. Louder. As powerless as I feel, I'm hoping that I have something to give to Grace. If anything, at least I can offer my presence as support. Poor girl, the poor soul had no idea what she was getting into, I think, and sit back down across from Grace.

"They said that to you? They called you that?"

"Yeah. A liar. A liar who did it for money."

"Well, did you?"

"No shit I did it for money!" Grace says. "Can you show me one fool who wouldn't?"

"Screw 'em," I tell her. "You don't need them and their caviar collecting anyway."

Grace lets out a sigh and says, "Yeah, well, they said I can never do it again. I don't know how I'm going to pay my loans now. I'm not sure what I'm gonna do."

"Who cares? It's stupid. You don't need to. You're working hard, you're a good writer, you're young, and you're good enough, Gracie Grace. You're good enough and you're gonna be fine," I say as my song comes on the jukebox. "You'll see. You'll survive just fine."

nineteen

"These cactus are so phallic."

This is what I say to Andrew in the early moments of what will spread into an entire February day spent wringing the narrow backroads of Puerto Rico. We're just coming out of Arecibo after visiting the world's largest telescope, rounding another bend in the road, when a knotty constellation of Prickly Pear bursts from a cliff of burgundy, dry soil.

So phallic.

The moment I say it is the moment I realize that what I've said will have the opposite effect of my intention. It sounds dogmatic, not silly, but considering what erupted last night, and what's to come, how could it not?

"I know the rules," I continue while Andrew says nothing. "I know it's cacti, it's just that cactus sounds much better."

Looking out the window, I can't help but think that everything I'm seeing just seems too charged with meaning, too cliché: the unripe banana trees and farmers in aged, red pickup trucks. The lipsticked ladies in apple-bottom, muffin-top jeans appreciated by the blond-haired, blue-eyed surfers. Their bumper stickers. The low, womanly hills along which we coast. It's all just too textbook, too . . . perfect. Even the stray dogs look as if they've been cast for their role; their nipples hang down, grazing the bridges on which they stand guard.

And then, the Organ Pipe.

The Wooly Nipple.

The *Cephalocereus millspaughhi,* more commonly known to the islanders as the Dildo Cactus.

Phallic. No shit it's phallic, I think, *and providing the perfect varnish of irony to our current state of affairs.*

We are rubes in this mysterious land of marriage. Last night, Andrew and I sat on the back deck of an Aguadilla fish joint, one with an old jukebox covered and tucked behind the booth of a live DJ playing Western pop music CDs. We ate off Styrofoam plates with disposable forks that made me think of rusty garbage barges that float under the sky, homeless and aimlessly drifting like sad, blind manatees.

"Let's pretend we're on our honeymoon," Andrew said.

We've already been married five months.

"Let's have a bunch of honeymoons," I said as the waitress

brought me a cocktail. It was indigo and expensive tasting, like Savannah saltwater taffy. "Tell me about the telescope we're visiting tomorrow."

Andrew propped his feet up against the railing of the deck and leaned back in his chair. "What do you want to know?"

I was excited about the giant telescope. How it would help us see the stars and the planets and all the other things we don't think about during the daytime or forget to look for at night. "Tell me about how it all works," I said.

The telescope was what Andrew called a marvel of modern engineering. He has studied structural engineering, so for him, it's an architectural wonder. People just come and look at it.

"Will we be able to see into other galaxies?" I asked.

"Not really. Those study energy at different wavelengths," he said.

I felt my face contorting. I could sense that my husband was on the verge of speaking a language entirely different from mine.

Andrew lifted his arm and directed my gaze to the restaurant's open kitchen. "See those lamps? When the bulb glows, you see light energy."

Inside the small kitchen, three cooks in dirty, white aprons were throwing various breaded things into a vat of boiling oil. It looked fun. I bit down hard in a dogged effort to round up all my concentration, furrowed my brow, and braced myself. "Okay?"

"What you *feel* is infrared," Andrew said. "Thing is, when you have something like a light bulb or a galaxy, you can see the glow in the visible light spectrum. But there is energy you can't see with your eyes." He took a sip of beer. "Our eyes only see a narrow slice of things."

A long arm deposited a red-and-white-checkered basket onto the table in front of us, and I popped a hush puppy into my mouth, then wiped the tips of my fingers onto my shorts.

"How do you remember all this, man?" I said.

"How do you remember anything?"

"I don't," I mumbled.

Andrew started tracing the rise and fall of an imaginary line onto the palette of the charcoal sky above us. "You remember the spectrum of visible light, right? The colors of the rainbow?"

"Please excuse my dear Aunt Sally?"

"Um, no."

"Wait, wait. Don't tell me. Red, orange, yellow, green, blue, indigo, violet . . . Roy G. Biv!"

"Right. Your eyes can see part of the rainbow's spectrum, which is related to its wavelength."

He was beginning to lose me again. Why was information like this so hard for me to retain? Even if I did remember everything Andrew was telling me, it'd be more like I was reciting the rules of some club I'd just joined. *But what are the underlying causes of Roy G. Biv?* I wondered. In a story, it was always love. Lack of love, secret love, tainted love, unrequited love, lust. But with physics and math, each explanation and answer always seemed to leave me more puzzled than the question.

We finished our drinks and ordered another round of the same. "Hold on," I said. "Why is it long or short?"

A Maraschino cherry sank to the bottom of my cup and lay

trapped underneath a pile of ice cubes. I swirled them around with a tiny pirate sword, hoping to spear the cherry out.

"Energy," Andrew said. "It's all just energy." He let out a sigh, thinking we were done.

But I was starting to become pleased with myself, or maybe just drunk, which made me feel a small, self-congratulatory flush of pride. I felt like I had all the answers to my questions.

"Energy is coffee," I declared.

"There you go. Visible light is coffee on a day-to-day level."

My thoughts drifted to how I could never get through math in school, and how I'd always felt guilty for that.

"Andrew, this is all just memorization, rules. Systems. Policies. This is exactly why I couldn't get through this shit in school. Because we are supposed to memorize these things, and the things that go before them, and the things that go before them. But it always just makes me ask the question, 'But why?'"

"Then don't try to memorize it," he said. "*Visualize* it."

"Oh Jeez," I slurred and took another mouthful of my cocktail.

"Think of oil," Andrew said. "Oil has heat when you burn it. And what do you have without heat and light?" he asked.

"Michigan?"

And with nothing more interesting to say, I looked back behind me and surveyed the restaurant. Everyone was dressed up. Women carried boxes of Whitman's and had balloons tied to their wrists. I'd forgotten it was Valentine's Day. "This place looks like the Ball Joint," I told Andrew and nodded to the waitress to bring another Blue Lagoon or whatever the drink had been carelessly named. "Did you ever go to the Ball Joint? That big sports bar in my hometown?"

"When would I have gone there?" he answered.

And then, something.

Ever since the sudden end of my pregnancy, I couldn't have a drop of alcohol without changing into an entirely different person. A few swallows, and I'd simultaneously become relaxed and outraged.

When would I have gone there? This question gnawed at me because I had recently found out that, in the late hours of his bachelor party, the groomsmen had taken Andrew to Hots, the one and only strip club in my hometown of Battle Creek, Michigan. It's open 24-7, and in the morning, they serve Breast-fast.

An aggressive pang hit me in the middle of my forehead as I slowly turned back to Andrew, who had ordered himself another beer and was looking quite content.

"Not even for your bachelor party?" That instant, with a sudden twinge, we both knew where we'd be going next.

"I just don't see anything wrong with going for a bachelor party," Andrew said.

"Give me a break," I said and crossed my arms. "You went, after I asked you not to go."

"Come on," he pleaded. "The boys took me there. I had no choice."

"For Christ's sake, Andrew! It wasn't a normal wedding! We. Did. Not. Have. A. Normal. Wedding." I cried, slid off my ring, and threw it at him.

The waitress winced at us from behind the kitchen. "Happy

Valentine's Day," Andrew said and sighed tragically as she brought us a menu.

"Look," he said. "I don't remember anything other than Gabe falling in love with one of the strippers. And if you really want to know, since I was the groom, I got dragged onto the stage and whipped, but I just sat there."

"I asked you not to go, and you said you wouldn't. It was disrespectful."

"Look," he said.

"No, you look. Do you know where I was when you were getting spanked on a stage?"

"At a male strip club?"

We were getting nowhere fast.

"No," I said, and stood up. "I was at home." Then I twisted the knife. "And I was still bleeding!"

"Please," Andrew said. "Maybe you just weren't quite ready to be married."

With that, Valentine's Day quickly drowned under a tidal wave of misunderstanding.

"So what'd you think about Arecibo?" I ask Andrew as our car passes another village nestled in the flora. "Did the telescope blow your mind?"

"It was okay. It's just cool that we have these big machines that can look deep into the universe."

I thought Arecibo was okay, too. I ate some astronaut ice cream from the gift shop and learned that a James Bond movie was filmed inside the telescope, but mostly I enjoyed watching my husband's face when we walked onto the ramp and saw the telescope. He looked like a little boy.

"I'd put it in the same category as going to see the Golden Gate Bridge," Andrew says. "I really wanted to climb around it, but they don't let you."

"It looked like an egg. And it seemed like it was being cradled and protected by all the pastures and hills surrounding it," I add, twisting the wedding band around my finger.

"You know," says Andrew, "all the energy from space travels at the speed of light, so it takes a few minutes for the sun to reach us." He scratches his ear. "So in a sense, what we see today might have happened years ago. In a sense, we're looking at the past."

At the end of last night's dinner, Andrew and I sat in our car in the restaurant parking lot with the engine turned off. We could hear the muted laughter of people walking behind us and into the restaurant. We didn't talk. We didn't try. We just sat and just let everything be. After a brief foray into silence and introspection, we looked at things from a different perspective—from a distance, and together, as a team—finally agreeing that the strip club was not the issue.

The issue was that we were moving on. We were experiencing life from different perspectives, just as we always had, but I suspected we'd continue to see things differently, much differently. I didn't want to grow apart. I didn't want to be alone. I was afraid. Ever since losing the baby, everything that was once common and normal about life was bizarre and hard for me to overlook. I wanted Andrew to see things the same way as I did because I wanted proof that I wasn't crazy, but it was clear to me that the common ground between us was being overshadowed by the differences, and this made me angry. I was a changed person. I was terrified of myself, this new self. And despite it being terrifying, at the end of last night, I realized that I would never see things the exact same way as my husband, or that I never had. I knew that we would never fully lose the baby we never had.

"I need you to see it," I said. "Just try to see how I might feel." But I knew he couldn't, and he never would, so I leaned over and pulled my wedding ring out of Andrew's blue jeans pocket, where he'd safely placed it after I'd thrown it at him, and set it on his knee. Eventually, the atmosphere between us thawed. He asked me to be his wife again, put the wedding ring back on my finger, and kissed it.

"So do they just sit and wait? I mean, at Arecibo, do they ever find what they're looking for?" I ask as our car pulls onto a freshly paved road.

"I mean, they don't see images, because if you look at something burning across different wavelengths, you can pretty much register everything from uranium to gold to nitrogen to helium," Andrew says.

"So aren't the stars just exploding gases?" I say, petting his head.

"They're nuclear explosions," he answers.

"Like the sun?"

"Like the sun."

"Like Uranus?" I kid.

"Exactly."

epilogue

After Puerto Rico, we return to New York and try to settle back into things. Andrew goes back to work. I achieve my master's degree. I continue working like a maniac on my thesis, but feel guilty about Maybe being bored while I work. Andrew and I talk about adopting another dog; I want to save another animal. I find a rescue from the South, a Bluetick coonhound–Shar-Pei mutt with a giant head and incredibly long tail that was fostered in a men's prison in Kentucky and has been in need of a loving home for some time, according to his online profile. His profile also says he likes to collect things and put them into organized little piles. Once I show Andrew the dog's photos, he falls in love. We adopt the mutt and name him Huckleberry. Maybe is pissed.

We gently kick out our roommate in the hope of living as real newlyweds. We invent routines. We have dinner parties. We go to the movies. Shouldn't I be joyous? Shouldn't I be relieved? No. I am tired. I am tired. I am tired.

Life is moving on. I try to move on, too, but I can't. It's been months since I lost Lilly, and still, I feel like my body is filled with cement, yet fragile and faulty. *Lilly is gone and it's not my fault.* I've accepted this fact, but my heart is still electric and popping with rage.

I venture out of my apartment cocoon and force myself to be around friends, a few of the girls from grad school, because they are women and young and ambitious and fun. They are also artists, and from Sarah Lawrence, too, so I figure they're feminists, at least mildly at their core; I figure they would understand my pain, hold a fist to the air in my honor. I am invited to a get-well gathering for a classmate who has broken a bone in her foot and just had surgery to fix it. We bring her flowers and casseroles and balloons; she tells us how hard it has been for her, what a traumatic experience it has been, and everyone coos like hens. None of these faces were ever in my hospital room, ever in my apartment like this. Still, I do it, too. I coo.

When it is over, I walk home, wondering, *Why her foot but not my baby?* I am thinking about it with a red-hot wretchedness and, as I turn the corner to our street, a giant man walks directly into my body and keeps walking. "Get the fuck out of my way!" he shouts.

Soon, too exhausted by feigning contentment, I cut off my relationships. I embrace solitude. My Manhattan apartment becomes a bomb shelter where, for weeks, I spend my time zoned out on a couch with a tub of peanut butter ice cream, flipping through TV channels. I don't read, I don't write, I don't exercise, and I can't fit anything on my body. I have the old maternity clothes, too big in the waist, too much a reminder of the loss. Nothing is fitting me. This enrages me. I become paralyzed. So I sit and I wait: wait for Andrew to come home from work, wait for the day to end, wait to feel better again. But the longer I avoid examining my grief, the stronger it becomes.

When Andrew kisses me or touches my shoulder, I tense up or squirm away. My body feels foreign, dried up and stale. But Andrew is calm. Andrew is peaceful. "Fuck you and your Zen bullshit," I tell him from the bathtub. "Why don't you cry? Do you not have feelings?" I shout that my vagina is a rotted tree stump.

I don't tell him this, but I hate him sometimes. Sometimes all it takes is his smile. Sometimes it is his snoring. But sometimes the hardness in my heart melts and I break down and apologize for my vehemence and seclusion. I do feel bad. Revealing my own tenderness feels like defeat, but the balm of compliance soothes my pain. It's a track on repeat. I ask Andrew for forgiveness. Then I beg him to give me a solution, an answer, to fix it for me. They call it grief but it feels like insanity. "Make it go away," I plead, but he can't. No one can.

It's inevitable that it would come to this—that we'd start in the same place but finish differently. We always finish differently. This is how it always begins: sex. At night, there is this person next to me in bed and I am distracted from my sorrow.

Then I start to feel something different, something more, something that is louder: his desire. His wants and needs. It's an inaudible scream. It starts in bed, with Andrew touching me lightly. I fold up and turn over. Then he sighs heavily and that's when my anger is triggered. He tells me he's a man, that he can't help it, that he needs it. That he has strong physical needs. "It's just like hunger," he says, but I can't speed myself up. It is quite the predicament.

It has been six months since we lost Lilly and I am just finally realizing what has happened, but everyone else has already moved on and this is how it always ends: I throw my rings at Andrew; he says, "I can't give you what you need"; and I start dramatically packing my suitcase, always freezing once I reach the door.

We try to keep going. My parents offer to pay for marriage counseling, so we go see a therapist. The first one cries when we tell her our "what happened" summary, so we try another therapist. Then three more. Each time, we have to tell them our story and it becomes an elevator pitch—the past becomes frozen in choice fragments—and each time, we get nowhere other than distorted. We stop marriage counseling and I start going alone.

Her name is Camilla, a cognitive therapist, and a lesbian. She is tough on me. At first, our appointments are once a week, but soon she recommends I visit her biweekly. Camilla has me talk, stop, answer her question. They're not pretty questions. They're unsympathetic and feel a bit torturous; I wonder if she is actually bullying me, like a cat with a gimpy mouse.

"What do you mean you were afraid of the abortion? Describe what you were afraid to see, describe it in detail."

I do my best. I include sensory detail, something my classmates would recommend in my writing workshop critiques when they had nothing more insightful to offer. Show don't tell.

I give her my secrets. I share my mother's advice: keep your husband fed and well-sexed and freedom comes with that. We talk about the dreams I have at night. We talk about the girl with the broken foot. I tell her what my professor declared one night after a couple of cocktails at a book release party when I showed him a photo of our new dog, Huckleberry. ("So the dog is the replacement for the baby you lost.")

Camilla scolds me. "How are you not breaking this chair right now? Why aren't you screaming and yelling at these people?" But I can't come up with words to describe the feelings of cement feet and paralysis of the mouth.

"I was just raised to be polite," I tell her, my tone rising at the end as if I'm asking a question.

I continue to see Camilla for months, earnestly working hard to create a solution to my emotional recovery, but as the months pass, the more I sense no end in sight. Nothing changes. I am fucked, and eventually, Camilla tells me there is nothing more that she thinks she can do for me. She diagnoses me as Clinically Depressed with Post-Traumatic Stress Disorder. She says she tried, she hoped I could get through it without medication, but my condition is not improving. With her pen, she scribbles down the name of an (expensive) Upper West Side psychiatrist onto a piece of paper, then wishes me luck.

I am clinically depressed. On my walk home, I see the words in my head. By accepting her diagnosis, I feel like something has finished or started, I don't know. I feel grouped, like a member of a category or a team, I don't know. But now I can give my fever dream a name; what feels like a witch's curse is actually medical, legitimate.

"PTSD." By whispering the letters out into the air, I am determined to open the festering cage of my heart. I will awaken whatever is dormant and still clean inside of me. "I have PTSD, I have PTSD," I repeat rapidly and urgently, excited and eager to accept the diagnosis. I explain my diagnosis to Andrew the best way I can. "I'm not making myself be like this. I have PTSD."

But medication? I don't want to take a pill unless it's fun. I'm already a wife; now I am a New Yorker who takes a pill for my brain every morning? The idea seems too 1991, too power suit with shoulder pads, too cliché. I want to feel alive again; eager and adventuresome, like the girl I was at age five, twelve, twenty-five. I simply want to end my suffering. What if they don't work? What if the pills aren't making me genuinely happy but only diluting my grief? I am reluctant but I am desperate. I am desperate. I am desperate.

A day or two before my intake appointment with the psychiatrist on the Upper West Side, I receive a call from a close friend. He has been calling twice a week after the loss of Lilly to check in on me. When I tell him that I've found a solution to my misery and explain where I'll be going and what I'll be getting and taking, he scoffs.

"Pills? Come on, Mira. You moving to Prozac Nation now?"

"I need to," I tell him. "My serotonin levels are all jacked up. It's *clinical*."

"You fool," he says. "You ain't no *Girl, Interrupted*. Why don't you just go for a jog instead?"

And then, in that instant, everything changes.

In the beginning, I can't run for the life of me. Not even a mile. I start off strong, following Andrew's pace. I feel the burn, get a side stitch, and slow down. I power walk, embarrassed, then quit. I fault Andrew for going too fast, for going too slow, for breathing too loud, for not paying attention to my pace, and for all crimes against humanity. I quit and I tell him to go ahead without me before he kisses my forehead and jogs ahead. At first, his fitness makes me feel weak, and I am ashamed of my weakness.

Andrew doesn't give up on me that easily, and he doesn't let me give up, either. Each run is as unpleasant as the one before it and feels unsuccessful, but we go again. And again. And again. Soon, we compromise and find a rhythm—he moves a little slower, I push a little harder. After a little while, I get up to three miles, then four, then five. Gradually, I stop focusing on Andrew and start paying attention to my own body, listening to my own body: my breath, my toes, my hips. I eat to fuel myself, not because I have to, not because it's dinnertime. I set goals. I stop looking at my body and start looking at myself in the mirror naked. I walk around naked (in our apartment). I sleep naked. I run, and when I run, I pay attention to what I think is pain. I examine it rather than avoid it, and try to embrace it. It is not pain. It is just a feeling.

I am in control of my distance. I want to see what my body is capable of, so I aim for six. I run on the streets of Manhattan.

When I am running, I do not think. My mind becomes still, present, and I feel formless. I can feel my essence. It feels brave. Feisty, even.

One day, I call my father.

"I have a proposition," I declare. "Let's run. Twenty-six point two miles. In your hometown."

"Oh my gosh, Mir, I don't know about this. Really?"

"The Chicago Marathon. This October. Ten/ten/ten." The race would be held on the eve of the thirteenth anniversary of Julian's death.

Stimulated and bewildered, we break it down: We are not serious runners; we are not trying to win anything. We know that winning the marathon is impossible. But still, we can run. We know how difficult the twenty-six point two miles will be. We know how easy it might be to quit. We will get tired, our toenails will fall off, our bodies will cramp and tighten. The running won't feel very good. In fact, it will hurt and will continue to get worse. Our bodies don't want us to do this. We will run and our brains will tell us to stop. So our minds will have to be strong. When we feel pain, we will have to keep going. We can't be afraid. We have to examine it. Push through it. We will learn to make good with our grief. We will run.

My mother is not thrilled by the idea. She tells me, "He is getting old. He already works too hard." But she doesn't let him know this. She knows he has to do this. We begin the training across country and run in the evenings. During the day, while my father is at work, my mother complains to me, and when my father comes home from work, she is sweet to him. She vents about the challenge of finding enough protein-rich recipes for a vegetarian, but when my dad returns from his runs, she's smiling and stirring a bowl of vegetarian chili. She makes a batch of trail mix, the American snack.

My father and I train like prison pen pals. We share a progress chart and track our miles together while our spouses rub our feet and feed us.

Soon, Andrew, Maybe, Huckleberry, and I move to Brooklyn. We leave Manhattan to be closer to nature, or as close as one can be in New York, and find a spot near Prospect Park. I run every day. Rain or shine, I spend hours at night running the park's loop, passing Park Slope moms with SUV strollers, dog walkers with a spiderweb of mutts, hot dog vendors behind steaming tin boxes, Rastafarians in primary colors, curved cyclists zipping like sleek fish. I see other runners, too, and recognize the faces of the serious ones, the ones who are there every night, too, with the promises they've made to themselves, people with their own reasons and sorrows and goals. Their pain is painted on their face, the urgency of their hope is revealed in their gait.

Andrew designates himself my "coach" and most of the time he jogs alongside me, carrying my water bottle, reminding me to hydrate and refuel properly. I tell him he sounds like Richard Pryor when he's imitating how white people talk. "Reeefyeeewl properly, m'kay?" and he tells me to eat the sports goop, but I can't; it makes me gag and reminds me of semen. At the end of every run, we do a "go big and go home" and sprint the last one hundred yards of the track. Every single time, Andrew leaves me in his dust. But by now I know I'll never be as fast as him, and I know that's okay. That I'm not chasing him; he is just showing me where I'll be soon enough. When our runs are almost over and I'm convinced that I'm exhausted but I can still see the end of the road in the distance, I pretend it is the actual marathon, that I am running next to my father, and I imagine Sabina and Andrew and Mom and Jules and his black dog standing at the finish line, waiting for us, cheering for us. Then I feel a surge. I kick my feet and sprint toward them with something I didn't know I had left.

I am running ten miles, then twelve, fifteen. Now eighteen miles, and then I outrun Andrew. He rides his bike. I run twenty miles.

A few weeks before the marathon, I receive a letter in the mail from my father:

I have been running since med school, so since 1971, but not far and not often. When we all moved to Battle Creek is when I really started to run more regularly, three to four times a week—but only three to four miles at a time. And I have been a faithful runner in different countries (vacations) and all different times of the year. But I have never really studied running, never stretched, always had cheap shoes, just ran. I had thought about running the marathon occasionally but it always just seemed to be "way out there," over my head. I figured it would take too much time and dedication to prepare for a marathon.

*Then, all of a sudden, I hit age 60 and figured that it was
too late to even think about running a marathon. I was afraid
that I would hurt myself, my knees. When you suggested that
we run a marathon together . . . BOOM! I jumped at the
chance. Suddenly, it seemed possible. We could do it together.
I had new courage and motivation. I would never have done
this alone. Period.*

It is time for us to pick a name. We call our team "Good
Grief" and decide to wear yellow jerseys. October rolls around.
We all fly to Chicago and meet at the airport. On the eve of
the race, my father and I drive downtown to the expo center,
where we pick up our runner's numbers. The expo has the
energy of the first day of school, free samples of caffeinated
gels and cold compresses and nutrition bars and posters. I
spot a line of people waiting to have their photo taken with a
man I don't recognize. A stranger tells us that the guy is Dean
Karnazes, the "fittest man in the world." The guy ran fifty
marathons in fifty states in fifty days. Dad looks at Dean and
says that when a man gets to be that strong, he stops getting
his periods. We take a picture with a giant shoe instead.

In the evening, I go for one last jog. The purpose of this
run is to loosen up my muscles and get my blood flowing just
a little bit before the big race. Even though it's the last run, I
don't feel like doing it. Even though this is only a three-mile
run and even though I know I won't break a sweat, I don't
feel like doing it. This run is number 150 out of 150. Miles
471, 472, and 473 out of the 473 miles I've set for myself.

With this run, I will have reached the end of my training. So I run.

At 5 A.M. the next morning, the alarm rings and we walk to the elevated train that will take us to the windy city where we'll join the rest of the thirty-five thousand runners and something bigger than ourselves.

When we arrive, the sun has just risen and a cool breeze spreads the scent of Lake Michigan around Grant Park. We squeeze our way into the starting corral within the ten-minute-mile pace group. We all stand and we wait. We stretch our bodies. We hop up and down. Some people chat giddily, others stare straight ahead, unflinching. Some runners wear crimson, some green, white, navy. Some are fresh. Attractive, old, exotic, ugly, pigtailed, bland, talented, tender. Some are gazelles and some are aardvarks. There are fairies and caped superheroes, even an Eiffel Tower. We all come from different places, different countries, different families, but I begin to recognize the thing that we all have in common: we are tackling something tremendous.

There is "The Star-Spangled Banner." There is a gunshot. The wheelchairs take off. Then the elites. We are buzzing but we wait. Slowly, the landscape of human bodies ahead of us starts bouncing. The feet in front of ours start to shuffle and move, so we start shuffling and moving, and suddenly we are underneath a giant digital clock and passing the official start line. Dad looks at me, we clap hands, and we begin.

The first pain comes quickly. Not even at mile two. It's my breast. It's from Dad—we are running side by side and he is swinging his arms as he runs, unaware that he is repetitively hitting me in the chest. We keep running. I look at my father. He is looking ahead, smiling.

Mom, Sabina, and Andrew have stationed themselves along the sidelines with the thousands of spectators, but my mother has figured out a way to be seen. Top-to-bottom lavender. We call it the Elvis jumpsuit and she's gotten it right, because we spot them at mile eight, then again at mile twelve: the lavender Elvis jumpsuit. They push us through mile twelve and will be waiting for us at mile twenty-two with the rest of the family: my sister, Sabina; my mother's brother Matteo and my aunt Mary; my father's sister and brothers—all cheering and hugging alongside my mother, who is jumping and waving. We will see all of them together. We are all in this together.

We run through Boystown, a neighborhood draped with rainbows. A plywood stage topped with go-go dancers singing "It's Raining Men." We run. A Chinese gong band, a high school marching band, cheerleaders in uniform, a tattooed man wearing a snake, elderly people, salsa dancers. We pass pharmacies and churches, pet shops and hospitals, guitar stores and chain cafes. We reach West Melrose Street and Dad nudges me.

"Look, Mir," he gasps. "Your Mom and I used to live there." He points to the left and I try to see which building it was, but we can't stop moving. "Our first apartment. That's where it all began."

My sister was conceived on Melrose Street. I was conceived in Michigan, apparently after my parents returned from a dance hall on a Saturday night. When I was in elementary school, before I even knew what conception was, my dad taught a sex-ed course to the high schoolers at St. Phil. He explained the mechanics of the penis, the complexity of the vagina, how conception really works. He talked about family planning and contraceptives. How condoms prevent the spread of disease. How to be safe and healthy. Since he was volunteering, he couldn't get fired, but apparently after he mentioned the benefits of birth control, Dad was never asked to teach there again.

When we were little, my parents were very involved in our schools. They often came to share what they knew so well: their expertise. When I was in kindergarten, my mother used to come to my class dressed as Albert Einstein. She'd wear a white explosion of a wig, don a perfectly ironed lab coat, and perform science experiments. She blew the world's largest bubbles, made a tornado in a two-liter bottle, baked an apple pie with no apples and no oven—and it was delicious. I remember one experiment where my mother mixed together cornstarch and water to create a substance that was both stiff and molten: when you held it, it melted and dripped from your cupped hands. When you pressed and squeezed and tapped it, the liquid got as hard as clay.

Right now, that's what I feel like. With each slap on the asphalt, my wet body tenses up like a cold rubber band. I want to stop and walk, walk it off just for a minute, but I can't. I don't have a good enough excuse to give Dad, or myself, because there isn't one. The pain isn't pain; it's only annoying.

Around mile eighteen, the abundance of spectators thins out. The leftovers look lost, or apathetic, flaccidly clapping along the sidelines, bored. I glare at them, directing my frustration into their eyeballs, but Dad waves, practically cheering for them, trying to wake them up, trying to make a connection. Some are smoking. We run on.

By mile nineteen, what was left of the crowd has dissolved. The course is flat and unenthusiastic and framed by abandoned warehouses that look like dead crab shells, gray and empty. I ask my dad how his knee is doing—his problem knee, the one that swells often—but he just smiles and looks ahead of him. I know he is hurting. Our hair is soaked and our skin is crusted with the salt from our own bodies. The air is dry and nearly eighty-five degrees, and a ghostly army of legs hovers over the pavement ahead of us. At least five more miles left. When I think about this, it feels like it will take an eternity and seems like an impossibility. With each stomp of my feet on the hot asphalt, a fiery bolt cracks through my body. I feel it underneath my skin, my muscles, all the way to my bones—starting with my ankles, then my shins, then my pelvis, all the way up to my neck. I can't talk. I don't want to smile. I need to stop. I hate this. I have broken a bone in my foot. My arms are falling off. I've pooped my pants. My hair is falling out. I'm bleeding. I'm dying. And just as I am about to quit, to tell Dad that this is fucking bullshit and I need to stop, he raises his hands and shouts.

"I love this sun! I love this heat!" His hands are cupped and pointing toward the sky. "I'm so happy to be getting my vitamin D fix!"

I stare at the ground. The pavement is littered with empty, green paper cups, making it slippery but reminding me that there are people ahead, people who are finishing. I shuffle along. I try to close my eyes, but someone jumps in front of me. A lavender jumpsuit. Short and skippy, there she is. Little Warsaw, my mother. She runs toward us, holding her fists in the air and rolling them, bouncing and yipping, practically popping, and for the first time, Dad stops. He bends down and kisses his wife. I tap my mother's behind and keep shuffling, knowing if I stop, I won't be able to start again; I have to keep moving. I see my sister. Next to Sabina is my Uncle Matteo, then his ex-wife Mary, then Dad's sisters, Aunt Mary Madeleine and Aunt Mary Joan, their husbands and their children. There is Dad's brother Brogan and his wife Ann, and all my cousins and everyone I didn't know would be here, smiling and clapping and laughing and crying and telling us to keep going, keep going, you're doing it, you're doing it. And then Andrew runs into the street, kisses me, and peels off. I can't keep up with my father.

Good grief. The words are so short and simple, but the road to get here was not. Sorrow. Grief. The stages aren't a checklist. There is no deadline. Grief is unpredictable. Messy. Imagine: You are in the driver's seat. You are with your child. You are asking about homework or talking about the dog and suddenly your entire life gets flipped upside down. There is a crash, broken glass, and then your son expires right in your arms. You are carrying your child and then he dies. How do you go on after that? You become weighed down by sorrow. By denial, anger, bargaining, depression. When does acceptance come? You want your grief to be temporary, predictable. You want to see the stages of grief and identify with them, check them off, but grief never ends. Maybe you expect a time limit where you can put it behind you and go on with your life, but how can you? You just do. Because the grief narrative never ends; it has become woven in, part of the braid of your life. After that last green bean casserole, the world moves on, but you cannot, and that is not wrong. To continue to grieve does not mean you're doing something incorrectly. The question isn't: When will I stop grieving? The question is: How do you keep on living? And I believe the answer is: You accept your sadness. You sink into it. Dad says you do this: You put one foot in front of the other and you go on. You run. You live.

After the race, Andrew and I will fly back to New York, and shortly after, we will rent a Uhaul, pack up our belongings and our dogs, and we will leave. We will drive and we will keep driving. We will pass interstate rest stops, pine trees, moose-crossing signs. We'll pass steeples and public suppers. We will cross Commercial Street and drive our car onto the Casco Bay Lines ferry and motor across Portland Harbor until we reach our little sanctuary on Peaks Island, Maine. Population: 800. I will feel a flutter in my stomach, and know that it is the kicking of a baby, whom I will deliver a few months later. A baby boy. Theo Julian. Ten pounds, twenty-two inches. My joy.

But right now, it is just us. Team Good Grief. My father and me and the home stretch. The twenty-fifth mile.

The sidewalks are again full of people. Hundreds of them, but they're silent. They're not shrieking and whooping. They aren't disinterested or unimpressed, either. They're just observing.

Standing there, silently looking at these running people, these lunatics, thousands of them who, for some reason, decided to go out and do this. Why would they punish themselves like that? Put their bodies through some kind of torture—why? Thousands of them, just running, and now these maniacs are floating by and approaching their end.

For several strides I watch the faces of the spectators watching us. Their eyes all have the same ambivalent expression. Worn yet hopeful, humbled and petrified, as if a tidal wave were approaching. Looking forward, I see what they see: that moment right before the runners turn the corner and disappear. It's as if we are witnessing the moment right before a person lets go, dies, enters heaven. We run that way, too.

Ahead of us, a right turn and then a sign. Zero point two miles to go. A steep peak over a bridge and, at the top, a sharp left. That's when we see it: the finish. The end of the line. On their own, our legs pick up speed and my father grabs my hand.

"This is it," he says, and we take off.

To me, it is a shock and a lift. I become numb. My thoughts are made clear, not like I'm a human being. Like I'm a spirit, and I just go. I run.

acknowledgments

First and foremost, I thank my parents, Philip and Maria Ptacin. You nourished my strengths, set me straight, and continue to demonstrate how simple it is to honor the world, to find beauty in all moments and people in life.

All my gratitude goes my champions at Soho Press: Bronwen Hruska, Abby Koski, Meredith Barnes, Rudy Martinez, Rachel Kowal, Janine Agro, Amara Hoshijo, Jon Fine, and especially to my editor, Mark Doten, whose insight, empathy, and confidence not only gave life to *Poor Your Soul,* but made it better.

Oh, what's that? Hello there, Celia Blue Johnson. Without you, my manuscript would still be collecting dust, I'd still be questioning my ability and worth as a writer, and this reader wouldn't be reading this book. My forever thanks.

There were a handful of optimistic midwives during the earliest stages of *Poor Your Soul* whose encouragement I haven't forgotten: Amanda Angelo, Jason Roberts, Suzanne Hoover, Vijay Seshadri, Lisa Grubka, Cheryl Pientka, Lisa Bankoff, Kendra Harpster, Ellen O'Connell, Allison Devers, Michelle Koufopoulus, Penina Roth, Victoria Comella, Tom Englehardt, Michael Ptacin, Kassi Underwood, Dr. Laura Mazikowski, Elissa Bassist, Jason Diamond, Molly Rose Quinn, Liza Monroy, Kate Hurley, Olga and Jenn, Chelsea and Rebecca, and Cathrin Wirtz. To Roxane Gay and Allison Wright for pushing me to aim higher, even when it hurt. A huge hug to my giant family at the Salt Institute for Documentary Studies, especially Donna Galluzzo. Donna: thank you for the tough love, endless faith, and for advising me on how to create a healthy and honorable foundation of what I now see was the beginning of my adult life. And a quick kiss to superwoman Kelli Schuit and dear Velvet Young taking loving care of Theo (and the pups) so that I could finish this book.

Thank you peanut butter chocolate ice cream.

Thank you to the Writers' Room and to the Squaw Valley Community of Writers, where this manuscript took shape and continued to grow. To all my dear friends at Guernica Magazine and The Rumpus: I'm grateful for your continuous encouragement and support, in so many ways.

To my aunts Claire Ott, Mary Piergies and Mary Joan Ptacin for always insisting for years that I was a writer, and that was a good thing. To my magnificent sister Sabina Ptacin-Hitchen (and Alex and George-Michael) for not letting me make excuses, and for making me go on that first date with Andrew. And the Jackson family, for accepting me immediately and loving me continuously.

I am most thankful to and for my own little family, starting with Huckleberry and Maybe, two jolly spirits who kept me company, kept me sane, and got me out of the house when I couldn't leave my desk (or sometimes my bed). My son Theo: You are my joy and greatest purpose. By making me a mother, you brought forth the strongest and purest part of me I never knew existed. And finally, my unending gratitude and respect goes to the best man I will ever meet, know, and love: my honorable and brilliant husband Andrew. You're beautiful. I would never have come out of the dark and gone this far without you by my side. I thank you.